"In his deeply researched *Thoughtful Christianity*, Matthew Shrader casts new light on the career of Alvah Hovey, an often neglected but influential theologian in Northern Baptist history. But the author does more than that. Shrader makes the compelling case that students of American religion need to rethink a number of their common assumptions about the nature of the Evangelical faith in the last half of the nineteenth century. Shrader's volume, then, is itself a 'thoughtful' piece of historical scholarship."

—JOHN WOODBRIDGE
Research Professor of Church History and Christian Thought,
Trinity Evangelical Divinity School

"The usual story that is remembered of the Northern Baptists in the nineteenth century is one of collapse under the juggernaut of higher criticism and schism as faithful Christians hived off into Fundamentalist communities. As Prof. Shrader's new monograph on the Northern Baptist scholar Alvah Hovey shows, however, this is not the only story from this era. Hovey upheld classical orthodoxy and wielded an enormous influence among his fellow Baptists—a thousand or so students sat under his tutelage and his teaching bore fruit. A welcome study on a key figure in a denominational group, the Baptists of the nineteenth century, who have not been given their due in the world of historical reflection."

—MICHAEL A. G. HAYKIN
Chair and Professor of Church History and Director of The Andrew Fuller Center for
Baptist Studies, The Southern Baptist Theological Seminary

"Alvah Hovey (1820–1903) is the most important Baptist in America about whom few nonspecialists have heard—and this is the first scholarly book about his massive scholarly footprint in Baptist life and American Christianity in general. Many thanks to Matthew Shrader for this first-rate scholarly monograph, and to Michael Haykin and friends for this crucial series of books. They are finally shining a light on an enormous but all-too-often neglected denomination in modern religious history."

—DOUGLAS A. SWEENEY
Dean and Professor of Divinity, Beeson Divinity School, Samford University

"A fine study into the thought of a theological stalwart. Hovey was the most significant American Baptist theologian of the nineteenth century because of his influence for thirty years as president of Newton Theological Institution, America's oldest Baptist seminary, and because of his voluminous literary output. Yet he has been that century's most under-studied Baptist champion largely because the ground shifted underneath him from the old orthodoxy to 'the new theology.' An important contribution!"

—JEFF STRAUB
Independent Scholar

Thoughtful Christianity

Monographs in Baptist History

VOLUME 19

SERIES EDITOR
Michael A. G. Haykin, The Southern Baptist Theological Seminary

EDITORIAL BOARD
Matthew Barrett, Midwestern Baptist Theological Seminary
Peter Beck, Charleston Southern University
Anthony L. Chute, California Baptist University
Jason G. Duesing, Midwest Baptist Theological Seminary
Nathan A. Finn, North Greenville University
Crawford Gribben, Queen's University, Belfast
Gordon L. Heath, McMaster Divinity College
Barry Howson, Heritage Theological Seminary
Jason K. Lee, Cedarville University
Thomas J. Nettles, The Southern Baptist Theological Seminary, retired
James A. Patterson, Union University
James M. Renihan, Institute of Reformed Baptist Studies
Jeffrey P. Straub, Independent Scholar
Brian R. Talbot, Broughty Ferry Baptist Church, Scotland
Malcolm B. Yarnell III, Southwestern Baptist Theological Seminary

Ours is a day in which not only the gaze of western culture but also increasingly that of Evangelicals is riveted to the present. The past seems to be nowhere in view and hence it is disparagingly dismissed as being of little value for our rapidly changing world. Such historical amnesia is fatal for any culture, but particularly so for Christian communities whose identity is profoundly bound up with their history. The goal of this new series of monographs, Studies in Baptist History, seeks to provide one of these Christian communities, that of evangelical Baptists, with reasons and resources for remembering the past. The editors are deeply convinced that Baptist history contains rich resources of theological reflection, praxis and spirituality that can help Baptists, as well as other Christians, live more Christianly in the present. The monographs in this series will therefore aim at illuminating various aspects of the Baptist tradition and in the process provide Baptists with a usable past.

Thoughtful Christianity

Alvah Hovey and the Problem of Authority within the Context of Nineteenth-Century Northern Baptists

Matthew C. Shrader

FOREWORD BY
Douglas A. Sweeney

☙PICKWICK *Publications* · Eugene, Oregon

THOUGHTFUL CHRISTIANITY
Alvah Hovey and the Problem of Authority within the Context of Nineteenth-Century Northern Baptists

Monographs in Baptist History 19

Copyright © 2021 Matthew C. Shrader. All rights reserved. Except for brief quotations in critical publications or reviews, no part of this book may be reproduced in any manner without prior written permission from the publisher. Write: Permissions, Wipf and Stock Publishers, 199 W. 8th Ave., Suite 3, Eugene, OR 97401.

Pickwick Publications
An Imprint of Wipf and Stock Publishers
199 W. 8th Ave., Suite 3
Eugene, OR 97401

www.wipfandstock.com

PAPERBACK ISBN: 978-1-7252-8922-2
HARDCOVER ISBN: 978-1-7252-8923-9
EBOOK ISBN: 978-1-7252-8924-6

Cataloguing-in-Publication data:

Names: Shrader, Matthew C., author. | Sweeney, Douglas A., foreword.

Title: Thoughtful Christianity : Alvah Hovey and the problem of authority within the context of nineteenth-century Northern Baptists / by Matthew C. Shrader; foreword by Douglas A. Sweeney.

Description: Eugene, OR: Pickwick Publications, 2021 | Series: Monographs in Baptist History | Includes bibliographical references and index.

Identifiers: ISBN 978-1-7252-8922-2 (paperback) | ISBN 978-1-7252-8923-9 (hardcover) | ISBN X978-1-7252-8924-6 (ebook)

Subjects: LCSH: Hovey, Alvah, 1820–1903 | Northern Baptist Convention | Church—Authority

Classification: BV4070.N87 S57 2021 (paperback) | BV4070.N87 (ebook)

04/13/21

For Tarah, my beloved

Contents

List of Tables | ix
Foreword by Douglas A. Sweeney | xi
Acknowledgments | xiii
Abbreviations | xv

    1. Introduction | 1
    2. Hovey within His Theological Context | 17
    3. The Ideal of Theological Education | 51
    4. Theological Method | 83
    5. Biblical Criticism | 134
    6. Practical Questions of Authority | 171
    7. Conclusion | 201

Bibliography | 211
Index | 233

Tables

Hovey's explanation of Biblical authority in 1867 | 111
Hovey's argument for the Bible as a supernatural revelation in 1870 | 111
Hovey's argument for the Bible as a supernatural revelation in 1877 | 111
Hovey's argument for the Bible as a supernatural revelation in 1900 | 111

Foreword

MORE THAN A QUARTER century ago, Nathan Hatch delivered a presidential address to the American Society of Church History that helped to realign the work of American historians. Reminding them of two hundred years of the Wesleyan churches' massive cultural influence on several different continents, he called for more attention to their history in the guild, especially in this country. In the wake of that address, the study of the Methodists became a major subfield of American church history.[1]

It is time for a similar call for scholarship on Baptists. Much larger than the Methodists, their history is older and their influence at home and overseas more impressive. The sources for the study of their people are vast. Yet precious few first-rate scholars have engaged them. The ratio of their size and cultural clout to the number of sophisticated studies devoted to their history is skewed quite severely—and far less balanced than the ratio for Anglicans, Puritans, Presbyterians, and Roman Catholics, for example.

Alvah Hovey (1820–1903) is the most important Baptist in America about whom few non-specialists have heard. He was a northern Baptist pastor, professor, and president of Newton Theological Institute in Newton Centre, a suburb of Boston. (Newton merged in 1965 with Andover Seminary to become the Andover Newton Theological School, and then again in 2016 with Yale Divinity School to become Andover Newton Seminary at Yale Divinity School.) A prolific author, preacher, and denominational statesman, he may have been the best-connected Baptist of his era.

The single most important topic to Hovey theologically was biblical authority. He had sojourned in Europe as a middle-aged professor and made a long stop in Germany as scholars in America debated the sources and critical study of the Bible. These travels and his own church's struggles with the issues of divine revelation and theological methodology haunted

---

1. See Hatch, "Puzzle of American Methodism"; Evans, "Reflections on the Methodist Historical Pie."

Hovey's work. And he was not alone in his concern for the Bible, which raises yet another key topic neglected by American historians. How perplexing it is given Scripture's significance to so many Christians that even specialists in American religion often ignore it. Most acknowledge that the Bible is important to believers. But few serious scholars have given this much time.[2]

For these reasons and more, Matt Shrader's book is welcome. It investigates the life of an intellectual leader whose impact on nineteenth-century American Christianity exceeds all previous attempts at comprehension. It does so, moreover, with more learning, judiciousness, and historiographical excellence than most other academic books published today. It deserves a wide hearing—and not just from Baptists.

May Shrader's tribe increase. May *Thoughtful Christianity* spur scores of younger scholars—from many different backgrounds—to research and write about the massive social, cultural, and theological import of Baptists in America, and all around the world.

Douglas A. Sweeney
Beeson Divinity School
Samford University

---

2. Jimmy Byrd, Jan Stievermann, and Mark A. Noll are important exceptions to this rule (among a small group of others). See esp. Noll, *In the Beginning Was the Word*, the first of what will be two volumes on this understudied subject by Noll.

Acknowledgments

THIS BOOK IS A reworking of my dissertation at Trinity Evangelical Divinity School, completed in 2019. There is no way to complete a dissertation without receiving significant help at many points along the way. I would mention the staff at Rolfing Memorial Library who provided expert assistance at several points while I was a student. I am also grateful to Diana Yount at the Franklin Trask Memorial Library of Andover Newton Theological Seminary who got me started in the Alvah Hovey special collection. And when the ANTS archives moved to Yale Divinity School, I received kind assistance from Christopher Anderson and Sara Azam with the Special Collections at the Divinity Library. I am also grateful to Pam Huttman and Kamil Halambiec who showed great kindness to me when I visited the archives at Yale and who provided a close place to stay at the Overseas Ministry Study Center. Since moving to Minnesota in 2019, I have also received help from the Central Baptist Theological Seminary library.

The cohort of fellow doctoral students at TEDS provided relentless encouragement along the way. Above all were my Historical Theology classmates who for some reason always appeared excited to hear about a Baptist who seemed lost to history. I must also give special thanks to the Church History faculty at TEDS, including Scott Manetsch and John Woodbridge, who kindly cared for and helped me and my family. My advisor Doug Sweeney shared his time, insights, and expertise above what I ever could have expected, both while a student and since both he and I have moved on to new work beyond TEDS. Those of us who have had him as our advisor and friend are the fortunate few, and I am humbled for him to write the foreword to this work. Since coming to Central Baptist Theological Seminary, I have received abundant encouragement and steady help to see the dissertation completed and then transformed into book form.

Many family and friends have also given help of various forms. Jeff Straub shared his friendship and his spectacular personal collection of

American Baptist primary sources with me without reservation. Our church families from multiple states and several Aunts and Uncles have shown kindness in many ways. My in-laws, my parents, and my brother always seemed to give encouragement when it was needed most. I am not sure what we would have done without so many who have lifted us along the way.

My children—Gabriel, Isaiah, and Eva—have made many sacrifices and have never ceased to give joy. I owe them. My wife Tarah, to whom the dissertation and this book is dedicated, has given much more than I have for this to happen. We married nearly fourteen years before the dissertation was completed, and I was an active student for all but one of those years. This has cost us more than we expected, and she has taken the brunt of that. The end of this journey has at last come and it is clear that it has drilled one thing into my thick skull: finishing is an accomplishment, but Tarah is the reward that has been mine the whole time.

Matthew C. Shrader
Plymouth, Minnesota

Abbreviations

AHP   Alvah Hovey Papers, Yale Divinity School Library

1

Introduction

"No one can be familiar with modern discussions about the possibility of knowing God or about the immanence of God—in a word, about thoroughgoing agnosticism, monism, or idealism—without seeing that these discussions reach to the very heart of religion and morality, or without desiring to contribute something, if possible, to a clear understanding of the truth by thoughtful Christians."[1]

THE MODERN DISCUSSIONS TO which the above epigraph refers reach further back than the 1892 date when it was penned and could be broadened beyond just knowledge of God to a host of theological, scientific, and social issues. Alec Vidler remarks, "In the nineteenth century there were developments in the natural and mechanical sciences, in the structure of society, and in the study of history, not least of the history which the Bible purports to be occupied, that were revolutionary in their consequences."[2] Theology in the wake of these progressions had to decide if it should follow suit and reconstruct itself according to the predominant trends. "As a result," states James Livingston, "theology faced a choice of either adjusting itself to the advances in modern science and philosophy and, in so doing, risking accommodation to secularization, or resisting all influences from culture and becoming largely reactionary and ineffectual in meeting the challenges of

---

1. Hovey, *Studies in Ethics and Religion*, iii.
2. Vidler, *Church in an Age of Revolution*, 9.

life in the modern world."³ As Sydney Ahlstrom succinctly summarizes: "The nineteenth century threw down a veritable gauntlet for the Church."⁴

Though historians recognize the importance of the nineteenth century for American religious history, there are still significant historiographical gaps. Writing in 2002 Mark Noll recognized one when he noted that, "The history of the Baptists in the eighteenth and nineteenth centuries is a subject as scandalously neglected as had been, until very recently, the history of early American Methodism."⁵ With the American revolution and the subsequent disestablishment of state-sponsored religion in the United States, the character of American theology faced a unique set of circumstances. It is generally understood that American theology influenced and was influenced by American culture. In particular, historians recognize that there was a growing change in religious authority away from institutional or creedal sources toward autonomy. The later nineteenth century saw further challenges face American religion, thus compounding the situation. A conundrum of American Baptist history is the lack of attention despite explosive growth and their centrality to the changing religious scene in the early republic. At the start of the nineteenth century Baptists were a small, struggling denomination. But by 1850 Baptists were the second most numerous of Protestant denominations in America at 750,000 adherents, a number which increased to 4.5 million by 1900.⁶

Though some has been done to fill Noll's lacuna, Northern Baptists have received significantly less historical attention than their Southern counterparts.⁷ A few major Northern figures from the latter part of the eighteenth

---

3. Livingston, *Modern Christian Thought*, 6.

4. Ahlstrom, "Theology in America," 286.

5. Noll, *America's God*, 149. Noll added that a major historiographical exception is the work of William McLoughlin. On American Methodism, in his 1994 presidential address to the American Society of Church History, Nathan O. Hatch addressed the dearth of Methodist studies (see Hatch, "Puzzle of American Methodism"). In the years after Hatch's address, several historians took up his call and have produced works exploring the development of Methodism in its American context following the pioneering ministry of Francis Asbury. A helpful synthesis of this historical work is given in Noll, *America's God*, 330–64. Also see Holifield, *Theology in America*, 256–72.

6. Gaustad and Barlow, *New Historical Atlas of Religion in America*, 374. Methodists were the largest at 1.25 million in 1850 and 5.5 million in 1900.

7. Scholarship on Southern Baptists has developed a healthy number of studies on key individuals as well as important theological movements such as the Primitive Baptists, Landmark Baptists, and Black Baptists. Examples could be multiplied, but a few include: Fitts, *History of Black Baptists*; Crowley, *Primitive Baptists of the Wiregrass South*; Gardner, *Decade of Debate and Division*; Wills, *Democratic Religion*; Tull, *High-Church Baptists in the South*; Rogers, *Richard Furman*; Mathis, *Making of the Primitive Baptists*; Chute, *Piety Above the Common Standard*; Patterson, *James Robinson Graves*.

century and the earlier part of the nineteenth century have been explored, such as Isaac Backus (1724–1806), John Leland (1754–1841), and Francis Wayland (1796–1865).[8] Likewise, some historians have studied figures from the latter part of the nineteenth century and earlier part of the twentieth century, such as Augustus Hopkins Strong (1836–1921),[9] Adoniram Judson Gordon (1836–1895),[10] and Walter Rauschenbusch (1861–1918).[11] Yet, this leaves understudied a significant theological development in the middle part of the century—specifically, the founding of Northern Baptist seminaries (beginning in 1825) and the early theology they produced (the first theology textbook *produced* was in the 1860s). These early seminary theologians have been almost entirely neglected save for mention in larger

---

8. For works on these figures and the general character of antebellum Northern Baptist life, see Backman Jr., "Isaac Backus"; Boyle, "Isaac Backus and His Ecclesial Thought"; Crane, "Francis Wayland and Brown University"; Fry, "Theological Principles of Isaac Backus"; Gaustad, "Backus-Leland Tradition"; Goen, *Revivalism and Separatism*; Grenz, *Isaac Backus*; "Isaac Backus"; Halbrooks, "Francis Wayland"; Maston, "Ethical and Social Attitudes of Isaac Backus"; *Isaac Backus*; McLoughlin, *Isaac Backus and the American Pietistic Tradition*; *New England Dissent*; *Soul Liberty*; Ohtsuka, "From Jonathan Edwards to Isaac Backus"; O'Brien, "Edwardsean Isaac Backus"; Page, "Francis Wayland."

9. Henry, *Personal Idealism and Strong's Theology*; Moore Jr., "Rise of Religious Liberalism"; Wacker, *Augustus H. Strong*; Houghton, "Examination and Evaluation"; Richardson, "Augustus Hopkins Strong"; Van Pelt "Examination of the Concept of the Atonement"; Massey, "Solidarity in Sin"; Thornbury, "Augustus Hopkins Strong"; "Legacy of Natural Theology"; Christian, "Theology of Augustus Hopkins Strong"; Aloisi, "Augustus Hopkins Strong and Ethical Monism."

10. Behney, "Conservatism and Liberalism"; Wilson, "Adoniram Judson Gordon"; Breton, "Inquiry into the Doctrine"; Houghton, "Contribution of Adoniram Judson Gordon"; Russell, "Adoniram Judson Gordon"; Robert, "Legacy of Adoniram Judson Gordon"; "Adoniram Judson Gordon 1836–1895"; Saxon, "Fundamentalist Bibliology 1870–1890"; Gibson, "A. J. Gordon and H. Grattan Guinness"; *A. J. Gordon*.

11. The number of those who have evaluated the thought and significance of Rauschenbusch is enormous; only a few will be listed here. For biographical treatments of Rauschenbusch, see Sharpe, *Walter Rauschenbusch*; Minus, *Walter Rauschenbusch*; Evans, *Kingdom Is Always but Coming*. For the significance of Rauschenbusch as a Baptist, see Patterson, "Walter Rauschenbusch"; Clipsham, "Englishman Looks as Rauschenbusch"; Tull, *Shapers of Baptist Thought*, 183–207; McBeth, *Baptist Heritage*, 598–99; Brachlow, "Walter Rauschenbusch"; Brackney, *Genetic History of Baptist Thought*, 333–37; Garrett Jr., *Baptist Theology*, 314–18. For Rauschenbusch's place in and significance for the social gospel movement, see especially Hopkins, *Rise of the Social Gospel*; Handy, *Social Gospel in America*; White Jr. and Bennett, *Social Gospel*; Lasch, "Religious Contributions to Social Movements"; Evans, *Perspectives on the Social Gospel*. For general consideration of Rauschenbusch's thought, see McGiffert Jr., "Walter Rauschenbusch"; "Church and Social Change"; Niebuhr, "Walter Rauschenbusch in Historical Perspective"; Handy, "Social Gospel in Historical Perspective"; "Walter Rauschenbusch"; Singer, *Walter Rauschenbusch and His Contribution to Social Christianity*.

historical surveys, a few essays, and a handful of dissertations. The early Baptist seminary professors provide an opportunity to look into the character of Baptist *seminary* theology during an important and understudied time. What kind of theology was taught in the early Baptist seminaries (having been founded in the context of a unique antebellum American theological scene) and how that theology was fit for the coming challenges of the later nineteenth century (particularly biblical criticism and the proliferation of theological liberalism) have not been adequately addressed.

The story of American Baptist higher education begins in the eighteenth century with the College of Rhode Island (1765), later to become Brown University.[12] Baptists continued to develop their theological education in a variety of forms, such as L & T (literary and theological) training schools and manual labor schools.[13] It was not until 1825 that Baptists began their first exclusively theological, graduate-level school, Newton Theological Institute, which was eventually joined by five other Baptist seminaries in the nineteenth century.[14] And, it was not until after the Civil War that the theologians of these Baptist seminaries began to publish in earnest.

When considering specific theologians, the figure of Alvah Hovey (1820–1903) of Newton Theological Institute occupies an interesting place in this story. This is because of his individual significance and because his career spans from antebellum America to the twentieth century (1849–1903). In a summary essay in a volume on Baptist theologians, David Dockery referred to Hovey as "the foremost theologian of the day."[15] Yet he is often neglected in surveys.[16] A closer look at this important figure can throw light on an obscure period of Baptist history.

---

12. Brackney, *Congregation and Campus*, 51–63.

13. Brackney, *Congregation and Campus*, 64–102.

14. The most significant Baptist seminaries that survived the nineteenth century were Newton Theological Institute (1825) in Newton Centre, MA; the Theological Seminary (1836) of Madison University in Madison, NY (renamed Colgate in 1890); Rochester Theological Seminary (1850) of Rochester University in Rochester, NY; the Southern Baptist Theological Seminary (1859) of Furman University in Greenville, SC (moved to Louisville, KY, and disconnected from Furman University in 1877); Baptist Union Theological Seminary (later Morgan Park Theological Seminary) of the Baptist Theological Union (1867) in Morgan Park, IL (became the Divinity School of the University of Chicago in 1892); and Crozer Theological Seminary (1867) in Upland, PA.

15. Dockery, "Looking Back, Looking Ahead," 342. One other indication of Hovey's influence comes from William Allison in his entry on Hovey to the *Dictionary of American Biography*: "Probably no other American Baptist ever spoke with more *ex cathedra* influence than he, yet he was the least assertive of any such authority" (Allison, "Hovey, Alvah," 270).

16. David Bebbington, in his survey of Baptists during the social and theological upheaval of 1870–1930, discusses the theological polarization brewing among Baptists

INTRODUCTION

The Figure of Alvah Hovey

Alvah Hovey was born on March 5, 1820, in Chenango County, New York.[17] Shortly after Alvah's birth the family moved to their long-time home in Thetford, Vermont. As a young farm boy Alvah received a solid education as well as a strong work ethic. At sixteen, he attended Brandon Literary and Scientific Institution in Brandon, Vermont, where he received further formal education in preparation for college. From 1839 to 1844, Hovey attended Dartmouth College, was provided with a liberal arts course of study, and was heavily involved in a number of societies.

Upon graduation from Dartmouth, Hovey served as president of a literary school for a year and then entered Newton Theological Institute. At Newton he acquired a biblical and theological education and mastered German. Evidently, he impressed his professor Barnas Sears so much that Sears wrote to his Andover Theological Seminary colleague Edwards Amasa Park, commenting: "I have a student named Alvah Hovey. He is a lion."[18] By Hovey's own account, three German-trained men stood out as the most important theological influences at Newton:[19] founder and architect Irah Chase (1793–1864) along with biblical scholars Barnas Sears (1802–1880) and Horatio Hackett (1808–1875). Norman Maring accurately notes the combined influence of Chase, Sears, and Hackett at Newton: "These men did much to promote the scientific study of the Bible, the spirit of inquiry and the keen regard for truth with which many graduates were to be stamped."[20] As later chapters will demonstrate, Hovey would certainly concur.[21]

---

and lists Augustus Strong and E. Y. Mullins as major voices conversant with contemporary theology but entirely leaves out Hovey. See Bebbington, *Baptists through the Centuries*, 83–120. Likewise, Thomas Nettles omits Hovey in his three-volume work, *The Baptists*, as do Thomas Kidd and Barry Hankins in their recent work, *Baptists in America*. See Nettles, *Baptists*; Kidd and Hankins, *Baptists in America*. As a counterexample, Bill Leonard includes Hovey in his telling of the narrative, albeit briefly. See Leonard, *Baptist Ways*, 398.

17. Biographical information is reliant upon Hovey, *Alvah Hovey*. Alvah Hovey also wrote a short treatise for his children, which is still extant in his collected papers: Hovey, "Narrative for My Children" (AHP). Several further sources are helpful, though to a significantly lesser degree, and will be discussed in the second chapter.

18. Sears quoted in Hovey, *Alvah Hovey*, 32.

19. More will be said about these men, the founding of Newton, and the character of Baptist education in subsequent chapters.

20. Maring, "Baptists and Changing Views of the Bible [I]," 56.

21. See Hovey, *Historical Address*. For views on Newton's success at their centennial, see Rowe, "Newton Theological Institution Historical Address"; English, "Newton Men in the Pastorate"; Barnes, "Newton Men and Missions"; DeBlois, "Newton Men in Education."

Hard economic times meant Hovey was unable to gather financial support for further study in Europe. Instead, Hovey took the pastorate at a church in New Gloucester, Maine but he only stayed for one year before accepting an invitation to teach at Newton. As it happened, Hovey taught at Newton until his death in 1903. The original contract was to teach Hebrew and to serve as librarian. But Hovey outgrew these teaching and administrative responsibilities during the more than fifty years he served at Newton. He variously held the posts of Instructor in Hebrew, Librarian, Professor of Bible Literature and Interpretation, Professor of Church History, Professor of Christian Theology, Professor of Theology and Christian Ethics, Professor of Biblical Interpretation of the New Testament, President (1868–1898), and Professor of Introductions and Apologetics.

During his teaching career, Hovey capped his own education by taking a ten-month trip (November 1861–September 1862) to Europe for the purposes of theological and cultural education with visits to major cities in England and continental Europe. He attended lectures by eminent thinkers including Ernst Hengstenberg, Leopold von Ranke, Isaak Dorner, Friedrich August Tholuck, Albrecht Ritschl, Johann Lange, Franz Delitzsch, and Gottfried Thomasius. He regularly called on these professors for private conversation, attended von Ranke's *Geburtstagfest*, had dinner at Dorner's home, and even squeezed in a trip to the Metropolitan Tabernacle in London to hear Charles Spurgeon preach. Hovey never earned a doctorate, but he was honored with the D.D. from Brown University in 1856 and the LL.D. from Richmond College and Denison University in 1876.

In America, Hovey had personal relationships with nearly every leading Baptist. These relationships were built primarily because of Hovey's thirty years of service as president of Newton. William Brackney remarks on the prominence of Newton: "To Hovey's credit, Newton became the most influential Baptist seminary of the mid-nineteenth century, counting four among five of the other Baptist seminary presidents as its alumni in 1868."[22] Hovey was also heavily involved in other activities, ranging from his church, to theological societies, to schools, to missionary associations and beyond.[23]

---

22. Brackney, *Genetic History of Baptist Thought*, 285.

23. Some of these include: deacon at the Baptist Church of Newton Centre, MA (of which Hovey participated, at different times, in the pastoral callings of William Newton Clarke and E. Y. Mullins); a trustee at Worcester Academy, Brown University, Wellesley College, and the New England Conservatory of Music; a corporate or board member of Boston's General Theological Library, American Tract Society, Massachusetts Bible Society, American Baptist Missionary Union, Watchman Publishing Company, National Divorce Reform League, Gardner Colby Ministerial Relief Fund, and the New England Centennial Commission; and member of the "Theological Circle," Harvard Biblical Club, Victoria Institute (London), and the Baptist Social Union of Boston.

By measure of importance, influence, and sheer volume, Hovey's publications are likewise significant. His major theological work was a multiple edition theological textbook.[24] He published books, articles, and pamphlets on a wide variety of biblical, theological, and practical subjects.[25] He also edited the American Commentary on the Old and New Testaments, contributing the introductory essay to the New Testament in the Matthew volume (authored by John Broadus) as well as authoring the commentaries on John and Galatians.[26] Of particular note, through his work as editor and as seminary president Hovey was involved in Baptist controversies surrounding biblical criticism at his seminary (Ezra Palmer Gould) and in the broader Baptist world (Crawford Howell Toy at Southern and William Newton Clarke at Madison).

Henry Burrage's 1894 comment on Hovey and his time at Newton nicely summarizes Hovey's place among nineteenth-century Baptists.

> Dr. Alvah Hovey, who was graduated at Newton in 1848, and was elected tutor in Hebrew in 1849, and professor of church history in 1853, became professor of theology and Christian ethics in 1855; and this position he still holds. In all these years his services in behalf of the institution have been of the highest

---

24. The three stages of Hovey's theological work are *Outlines of Christian Theology* (1870); *Manual of Systematic Theology and Christian Ethics* (1877); and *Manual of Christian Theology* (1900). The *Outlines* were intended and produced for classroom use only while the *Manuals* were published and made available to a wider audience. Also helpful for understanding Hovey's theology is a much shorter work that was prepared for young people to grasp the rudiments of theology, *Doctrines of the Bible* (1892). Though only a brief sixty-eight pages, this work follows the outline of his *Manuals* and offers an interesting look at the main points of his theology succinctly stated. Hovey also published an 1861 edition of his *Outlines* and an 1866 edition that had interleaved blank pages, both of which are exceptionally rare.

25. He published books on ethics and religion, the miracles of Christ, divorce, religion and the state, the Christian life, eschatology, as well as producing several unpublished classroom textbooks. Hovey also wrote two biographies, translated a German work on Chrysostom, and published numerous pamphlets on issues such as the value of church history, the pastor's work and preparation, the Baptist idea of "close" communion (originally at the request of Edwards Amasa Park), the state of humans after death, Baptist history, Christ's advent, future punishment, Old Testament offerings, Christian giving, and prayer. He also worked with John Broadus and H. G. Weston on an improved and revised translation of the New Testament for the American Bible Union. And, he delivered numerous speeches and addresses along with publishing articles in dictionaries and theological journals, including the *Christian Review*, *Baptist Quarterly*, *Bibliotheca Sacra*, *Biblical Student*, *Watchman*, *The American Journal of Theology*, *The Old Testament Student*, *The Biblical World*, and the *Examiner*.

26. Hovey, *Commentary on the Gospel of John*; "General Introduction to the New Testament"; *Commentary on the Epistle to the Galatians*.

value. Thorough scholarship, unfailing candor and willingness to follow whithersoever the truth leads, have characterized his career as an instructor; and his pupils have found in him not only a helpful teacher but a delightful friend. His published writings, which are numerous, have given him a wide reputation as a theologian and author. Since 1868, Dr. Hovey has been president of the institution. More than eleven hundred students have already availed themselves of the advantages that Newton affords. Three-fourths of this number have served as pastors of churches in our own land. Many of these have held, or are still holding, important positions, and most of them have proved themselves useful ministers of the Lord Jesus Christ. A large number have done heroic service as missionaries in foreign lands. Some have served as presidents of colleges and theological seminaries, or as professor in such institutions. The wisdom if the founders in establishing this school of the prophets has been abundantly justified.[27]

Hovey dwelt at the center of Baptist seminary life from the 1840s until the beginning of the twentieth century. He was personally connected to the earliest antebellum seminarians as well as the late nineteenth-century theologians advocating for biblical criticism and new formulations of theology. He also produced a prolific corpus. Quite simply, he provides an exceptional window into understanding nineteenth-century Baptist seminary theology.

Situating Hovey

Antebellum American Protestantism

As was mentioned above, historians recognize that there was a growing change in religious authority away from institutional or creedal sources toward autonomy. Nathan Hatch has explained the changing nature of antebellum American theology according to the concept of democratization. This speaks to the give and take between the church and the popular culture of the day that saw a downplaying of institutional authority in favor of the individual's ability and right to be his or her own authority.[28] Mark Noll has characterized the changing nature of antebellum theology as "Americanization" and explained it according to three central ideas: evangelical Protestant religion, republican political ideology, and commonsense moral

---

27. Burrage, *History of Baptists in New England*, 187–88.
28. Hatch, *Democratization of American Christianity*, 3–16.

reasoning.²⁹ E. Brooks Holifield has argued that antebellum American theology was essentially concerned to present a reasonable Christianity, which Christianity was worked out in concert with five other central themes: "The continued insistence on theology's 'practicality' and its ethical functions, the importance of Calvinism, the interplay between Americans and Europeans, the denominational setting of theology, and the distinction between academic and populist strands of thought."³⁰ In all three studies, Baptists are exemplars of the authors' theses. The authors argue that the American combination of ideas (theological, epistemological, and political) is unique when compared to other Western nations³¹ and it thus yielded not only a unique American culture, but a unique character to American theology, particularly in the years between the revolution and the Civil War.³²

Postbellum American Protestantism

While Hovey was educated and cut his theological teeth in antebellum America, his mature theology was produced after the Civil War where a new and large set of challenges appeared. Biblical criticism, theological liberalism,³³ and social justice, among others, all confronted American Protestants.

Conservatives, such as Hovey, have often been seen as holding on to an inherited "orthodox rationalism"³⁴ that was unable to cope with the modern

---

29. Noll, *America's God*, 9–13.

30. Holifield, *Theology in America*, 4.

31. See especially Howard, *God and the Atlantic*. Howard suggests that many Europeans see America as either an "erroneously religious society" or an "overly religious society."

32. Also important are Ahlstrom, "Scottish Philosophy and American Theology"; "Theology in America"; *Theology in America*, 23–91; McLoughlin, "Introduction"; Marsden, *Evangelical Mind*; Hatch, *Sacred Cause of Liberty*; Howe, *Political Culture of the American Whigs*; "Evangelical Movement and Political Culture"; Toulouse and Duke, "General Introduction"; Howe, *Making the American Self*; Bebbington, "Evangelicalism."

33. I am using "liberal" and "conservative" to denote a relative theological stance. "Liberal," "progressive," and "modernistic" are often used to describe the content of certain theologies during this time period. I will most often utilize the term "New Theology" to describe the theologies that are decidedly modernistic in their theological content. Though I will also use the term "liberal" when context clearly expresses the explanation offered here. On the general character of the theological stance(s) of the New Theology, see Averill, *American Theology in the Liberal Tradition*; Hutchison, *American Protestant Thought in the Liberal Era*; *Modernist Impulse in American Protestantism*; Williams, *Andover Liberals*; Cauthen, *Impact of American Religious Liberalism*; Dorrien, *Making of American Liberal Theology*.

34. This nomenclature goes back to at least Smyth, "Orthodox Rationalism."

mind (and its struggle with historicism)[35] because their epistemology was empirical at heart and thus, by necessity, destined to produce a modern theology.[36] Historians have regularly considered the American evangelical theologies of the eighteenth and nineteenth centuries to be influenced in their methodologies by the need to be reasonable and in most cases to allow a place in their theologies for empirical apologetics and maybe even natural theology. The philosophical school of Scottish Common Sense Realism (with its trust of the intellect and the senses) and the methodology of Baconianism (with its insistence on scientific gathering and use of data) purportedly influenced American theology.[37] According to this historiography, part of the crisis in the nineteenth century and beyond was that the insistence on the reasonableness of Christianity had enshrined a Christianity that gave evidential arguments a superficial place of authority. The philosophical and scientific revolutions of the era supposedly revealed as much and contributed to the exodus of educated people from traditional evangelical understandings of Christianity.[38] Normally it is an insistence on biblical inerrancy or some form of "biblical rationalism" that is seen as the primary indicator of such a maverick theological method. And, the finger is often pointed at the Princeton theologians[39] (or sometimes the post-Reformation

---

35. On historicism, see Howard, *Religion and the Rise of Historicism*. Howard argues that there are two kinds of historicism. One was a scholarly practice that gave pride of place to historical study over against conceptualizations of history. A second kind was the problem it created as a crisis of meaning in which all forms of knowledge are produced only by humans from within human history. It is the second that is of interest here.

36. Wacker, *Augustus Hopkins Strong and the Dilemma of Historical Consciousness*, 1–19. Wacker's book has been republished by Baylor University Press (2018) with an updated preface, but the text of the book remains exactly the same. Also see a few important works on the rationality of nineteenth-century conservative theology: Ahlstrom, "Scottish Philosophy and American Theology"; Smith, "Religion and Science in American Philosophy"; Bozeman, *Protestants in an Age of Science*; Stewart, "Tethered Theology." Though these primarily address Princeton, their conclusions are regularly applied to conservative theology of the nineteenth and twentieth centuries in general, as in the case of Wacker's study mentioned above. See also, for example, Holifield, *Gentlemen Theologians*; Hatch, "Sola Scripura and Novus Ordo Seclorum"; Szasz, *Divided Mind of Protestant America*; Noll, "Irony of the Enlightenment"; "Common Sense Traditions"; Marsden, "Everyone One's Own Interpreter?"; "Collapse of American Evangelical Academia"; *Fundamentalism and American Culture*, chapters 6, 13, 24.

37. See especially Bozeman, *Protestants in an Age of Science*; Ahlstrom, "Scottish Philosophy and American Theology"; Noll, *America's God*, 9–13.

38. Smith, "Religion and Science in American Philosophy." Smith argues this exodus continued in the twentieth century but expanded to be an exodus from any kind of Christianity at all.

39. Sandeen, *Roots of Fundamentalism*; Marsden, "Collapse of American Evangelical

dogmaticians)⁴⁰ as the progenitors or the quintessential representatives and thus the culpable party.

Recently, this historiography has been challenged by historians normally seeking to vindicate a particular individual or school of thought.⁴¹ The argument that is gaining traction is that the presence of forms of reasonableness or evidential apologetics is not controlling but only one piece within the greater theological superstructure. They argue that "presence of" does not equal "control by" when desiring reasonableness or utilizing Scottish Common Sense Realism.⁴² They argue that further theological categories, such as anthropology and soteriology, with their theological import on rationality, need to be simultaneously considered. In other words, these theologians were aware of problems vexing their times and sought to reconstruct theology to speak to the issues without also capitulating to its demands. Historians are now suggesting that nineteenth and early twentieth-century conservative (and mediating) theology in general was heterogeneous in its sources, content, methods, and motivations.⁴³ Historians are recognizing that multiple streams of thought significantly impacted non-liberal theology, thus these theologies were not merely a repeat of prior rational orthodox opinions nor a simple preview of later fundamentalist thinking. Consequently, designations such as "empirical," "rationalistic," "fundamentalistic," or "ahistorical" have been shown to have a shorter range of explanatory power.

Postbellum Northern Baptist Theology

Within postbellum American religion, the changing nature of Northern Baptist theology has only been somewhat charted.⁴⁴ While the standard

---

Academia," 238–47; *Fundamentalism and American Culture*, 109–18.

40. Rogers and McKim, *Authority and Interpretation of the Bible*.

41. E.g., Muller, *Prolegomena to Theology*; Woodbridge and Balmer, "Princetonians and Biblical Authority"; Helseth, *Right Reason and the Princeton Mind*. This prevailing historiography has also been challenged by some seeking to establish the historical continuity of inerrancy with the orthodox Christian tradition, e.g., Woodbridge, *Biblical Authority*.

42. See especially the essay by Helm, "Thomas Reid, Common Sense and Calvinism."

43. Hoffecker, *Piety and the Princeton Theologians*; Edwards, *New Spirits*, chapter 8; Helseth, *Right Reason and the Princeton Mind*; Aubert, *German Roots of Nineteenth-Century American Theology*; Gloege, "Gilded Age Modernist"; *Guaranteed Pure*; Wiard, "Gospel of Efficiency."

44. See, for example, Maring, "Baptists and Changing Views of the Bible [I]"; "Baptists and Changing Views of the Bible [II]"; Garrett Jr., "Sources of Authority in Baptist Thought"; Bush and Nettles, *Baptists and the Bible*.

Baptist history textbooks discuss Baptist growth and its significance, very few monographs have attempted to understand this time period at a deeper level. Studies on Augustus Hopkins Strong (showing how an educated and sophisticated conservative theologian came to terms with modern thought), A. J. Gordon (showing how an influential conservative conducted his ministry in the second half of the nineteenth century), and Walter Rauschenbusch (showing how a liberal Baptist utilized modern thinking) have already been mentioned above. A few studies have highlighted the growth of liberal thought at Northern Baptist seminaries, especially as it led up to the controversies of the 1910s and 1920s.[45] Gregory Thornbury's dissertation chronicled the place of natural theology in four significant Northern Baptist theologians in the nineteenth and early twentieth centuries, three of whom were from one seminary (Rochester).[46] Uniquely, David Priestley's dissertation compared the seminary theologians at all nineteenth-century Baptist seminaries. His concern was to see how they did or did not continue to uphold distinctive Baptist theological polemics. Hovey plays a part in Priestley's story, though Priestley is only concerned to show how Baptist seminary theology had placed Baptist distinctives merely as a subset of their theological ecclesiology rather than the driving force of a polemical Baptist theology.[47] This work differs from other studies by (1) looking primarily at Hovey and by (2) seeking to present Hovey's understanding of authority.

The literature surrounding Hovey himself is quite sparse. He was recognized in several of the older Baptist works, including William Cathcart's *Baptist Encyclopedia*,[48] Thomas Armitage's *A History of the Baptists*,[49] and A. H. Newman's *A History of the Baptist Churches in the United States*.[50] For example, Newman wrote, "Newton Theological Institution, though venerable with age, has lost nothing of the elasticity of youth. During the long presidency of Alvah Hovey, one of the foremost educators and theological authors of the denomination, it has maintained its position as one of the leading theological seminaries of the country."[51] Colleagues and former students on the occasion of Hovey's fiftieth anniversary of teaching in 1899, his

---

45. Moore Jr., "Rise of Religious Liberalism"; Hart, "True and the False"; Straub, *Making of a Battle Royal*.

46. Thornbury, "Legacy of Natural Theology." Thornbury looks at Francis Wayland, Ezekiel Gilman Robinson, Augustus Hopkins Strong, and Walter Rauschenbusch.

47. Priestley, "From Theological Polemic to Nonpolemical Theology," esp. 117–19, 154–66.

48. Cathcart, *Baptist Encyclopedia*, 546–7.

49. Armitage, *History of the Baptists*, 874–5.

50. Newman, *History of the Baptist Churches in the United States*, 480.

51. Newman, *History of the Baptist Churches in the United States*, 480.

INTRODUCTION

fiftieth wedding anniversary in 1902, and his death in 1903 also gave several shorter tributes.[52]

Despite his stature, the only monograph-length work on Alvah Hovey is the biography written by his son George Hovey in 1928: *Alvah Hovey: His Life and Letters*. The benefit of this work is the obvious firsthand knowledge that George Hovey had of his father and of Newton. In tone, the elder Hovey's life from a little boy through a distinguished scholarly career is lovingly chronicled, interspersed with a generous number of personal letters to and from Hovey. Alvah Hovey is presented as a well-known and significant Baptist theologian-churchman dedicated to a theological life that was informed and biblically based but also deeply practical.

Recent works on American Baptist history and theology have acknowledged the various contributions and influence of Hovey, though rarely in a focused way.[53] Norman Maring mentioned the influence of Hovey in emphatic terms. "Wide reading had made Hovey conversant in contemporary trends in Germany and England, and many Baptists considered him a veritable oracle. 'I have heard him called the Baptist pope of New England,' a friend was to say after Hovey's death. That title did not imply that he was autocratic, but that his scholarship commanded wide respect."[54] Others have considered Hovey within the tradition of Newton Theological Institute.[55] Hovey has also surfaced a few times within fundamentalism historiography. Jeffrey Straub's published dissertation on the growing hegemony of liberal influence within Northern Baptist life considered Hovey to be a significant conservative predecessor to the fundamentalist view of the Bible.[56] Fundamentalism historians George Dollar, David Beale, Kevin Bauder, and Robert Delnay have mentioned (only in passing) Hovey in connection to the Fundamentalist-Modernist controversy, describing him

---

52. English, "Alvah Hovey, D.D., LL.D."; "Dr. Hovey as a Teacher"; Newman, *Century of Baptist Achievement*; Horr, "Dr. Hovey and Educational Work"; Clarke, "Dr. Hovey as a Theologian"; Weston, "Dr. Hovey as an Author"; King, "Alvah Hovey and Foreign Missions"; "Alvah Hovey as Theologian and Teacher"; Crane, "Dr. Hovey with His Friends."

53. Nettles, *By His Grace and for His Glory*, 232–33; Brackney, *Baptists*, 28, 66, 194–95; *Historical Dictionary of the Baptists*, 217; McKibbens, "Hovey, Alvah (1820–1903)," 146–47; Leonard, *Baptist Ways*, 398; Garrett, *Baptist Theology*, 279–83; Chute et al., *Baptist Story*, 206.

54. Maring, "Baptists and Changing Views of the Bible [I]," 54. The quote comes from George Merrill, president of Colgate.

55. Brackney, *Genetic History of Baptist Thought*, 284–88; *Congregation and Campus*, 258–63, 293; Bendroth, *School of the Church*, 35–37.

56. Straub, *Making of a Battle Royal*, 45–46.

variously as the president of Newton Theological Institute when it slipped into liberal thought,[57] a scholarly conservative,[58] and a "proto-fundamentalist."[59]

Several further works have mentioned Hovey for his conservative stance on biblical authority.[60] Within this discussion there exists some disagreement on Hovey's precise position. In contrast to others, Maring, Brackney, and Winthrop Hudson have all asserted that Hovey felt the pressure of biblical criticism.[61] They have argued this showed in Hovey's later works on the inspiration of Scripture wherein he affirmed a religious dynamical theory of inspiration that seemed to allow infallibility in teaching but not necessarily in the words of scripture. This work will look at Hovey's conception of biblical authority, but this is only one part of the larger idea of authority within his theology and theological method.

This survey shows that work on Hovey has been done only briefly within tertiary sources or only indirectly within secondary sources and these studies are not always in total agreement with each other. A study of Alvah Hovey offers great insight into the much-neglected nineteenth-century American Baptist religious scene. He was a theologian and statesman important and influential in his day who has been variously explained, sometimes forgotten, but generally overlooked.

The Direction of This Study

American Protestantism experienced significant change and challenge in the nineteenth century. One of the primary areas of concern was the issue of authority. This was one area that experienced change in the early American republic and that experienced further change for Baptists with their explosive growth and the challenges of biblical criticism and theological liberalism. Thus, the driving question is: Granted that Hovey lived in a time of significant theological upheaval wherein theological and biblical authority were changing and contested concepts, in what ways did he, an early Baptist seminary theologian, understand, construct, and utilize theological and biblical authority?

57. Dollar, *History of Fundamentalism in America*, 146, 150.

58. Beale, *In Pursuit of Purity*, 176.

59. Bauder and Delnay, *One in Hope and Doctrine*, 6.

60. Garrett, "Sources of Authority in Baptist Thought"; Brackney, *Baptists*, 28; Kutilek, "Text and Translation of the Bible"; Bush and Nettles, *Baptists and the Bible*; Leonard, *Baptists in America*, 133.

61. Maring, "Baptists and Changing Views of the Bible [I]"; "Baptists and Changing Views of the Bible [II]"; Brackney, *Genetic History of Baptist Thought*, 284–88; Hudson, "Shifting Patterns of Church Order."

Subsidiary questions include: Did democratization and/or reasonableness drive Baptist thinking during the early nineteenth century and in what ways? In what ways did Hovey understand his place of authority especially as a pioneering seminary theologian in his tradition? What sources did Hovey find authoritative? What was the theological method of Hovey, particularly related to epistemology and confessionalism? What did Hovey understand the authority of the Bible to be? In what ways did Hovey address biblical criticism, especially as it pertains to biblical authority? How did Hovey's understanding of authority work out in practice?

This work argues that Hovey engaged critical views of the Bible yet clearly accepted the authority of the Bible based on its supernatural character as the dynamically inspired and inerrant Word of God. Hovey held to the reasonableness of Christianity and the scientific interpretation of the Bible. Human reasoning, however, had its limitations based on the problems of finitude and sinfulness. The Bible, rightly interpreted, was the supreme authority in all theological endeavors. Wherever theological issues were raised, and the Bible's authority was appealed to, Hovey resisted letting theological systems determine biblical interpretation. Yet, to adjudicate interpretive disagreements Hovey appealed to authoritative voices outside of the individual biblical interpreter, such as professional exegetes, professional theologians, and the orthodox tradition of the church in general. In sum, Hovey was in some ways a product of the nineteenth century's tendency toward democratization and reasonableness, particularly in his theological heritage, his exegesis, his theological method, and his baptistic views of confessions and individual soul liberty. Yet Hovey was not simply an "orthodox rationalist" or "democratized" for at least four reasons: (1) he advocated heavily for theological and exegetical education that would be the backbone of biblical and theological work, an education which was not only technical but also spiritual and which modified to what extent and how well anyone could simply read the Bible; (2) as a Baptist he had theological as opposed to merely philosophical/rational reasons for trusting human intellect and allowing individual decision making, yet he was quick to guard against individualism; (3) he regularly looked to authorities outside of the individual's reasoning ability, specifically in his appeals to exegetes and theologians and to the orthodox tradition of the church in general; and (4), most importantly, Hovey limited human rational ability, as evidenced in his epistemology, his understanding of the Creator/creature distinction, and his consistent requirement that the exegete and theologian understand and evidence the spiritual requirements of those disciplines.

This work provides a presentation of Hovey's intellectual, theological, and personal background through a historical survey of the nineteenth-century American theological scene, the nineteenth-century Baptist scene, Hovey's family history, his context at Newton, and the influence of his educational journey to Europe. Further, the theological formulations, controversies, and polemics Hovey engaged in and how they display his understanding of authority will be detailed.

Chapter two will look at Hovey's theological context in order to determine the theological and biblical sources that he inherited and was taught. Did Hovey's education in antebellum America pass on to him democratized sources of authority? Was he taught a need to be reasonable? More specifically, how was he taught to read the Bible and do theology, and what was authoritative in these exercises? While there is a difference between what someone is taught and what someone accepts for their own, it is important to consider the tools that Hovey had at his disposal and the context in which he dwelt.

2

Hovey within His Theological Context

OFTEN THE PERSPECTIVE OF a son lends unusual insight into the life of his father. In George Hovey's biography of his theologian-father, he recounts his family's 1873 transition into their newly built home. George relates how his mother thoughtfully planned the layout of the house with a particular interest in the office of her husband.

> The study and library was first located at the southwest corner of the house, warm in winter, and cooled in summer by the breezes of the hottest days; a room from which the student could catch glimpses of the sunsets which he enjoyed so much, as their golden, crimson, and purple light streamed through the great elms near the Rice house. The room with bay window was sixteen feet by fourteen feet. The writing-desk stood a little in from the west window; a large revolving bookcase with reference books was at the right hand; bookcases filled every available foot of wall space, extending upward about nine feet from the floor.[1]

George then provided this fascinating snapshot into the intellectual and theological world of his father:

> Above the bookcases were busts of Washington, Milton, Shakespeare, and Scott. Over the fireplace and in a corner where the uncovered wall permitted, there were, at least in later years, a picture of the Baptism of Christ, a photograph of Raphael's Head of Paul from his Saint Cecilia, a photograph of Sargent's

---

1. Hovey, *Alvah Hovey*, 157.

frieze of The Prophets in the Boston Public Library, a picture of Edwards A. Park, bas-reliefs of Neander and Schleiermacher.[2]

Alvah Hovey was and still is known for his Baptist theological conservatism.[3] So it may surprise some that the names of Edwards Amasa Park (1808–1900), Johann August Wilhelm Neander (1789–1850), and Friedrich Daniel Ernst Schleiermacher (1768–1834) appear to have been held in high regard. It helps to remember that Hovey was known to be well read, and he was highly revered for this learning even by those who rejected his conservative theology.[4] Hovey's awareness of a complex theological scene makes him a prime window into nineteenth-century American Baptist thought. As may be inferred, Hovey was influenced by a variety of viewpoints. A closer look at the people and institutions that influenced him will reveal much about his own theology.

A pious Baptist home in New England during the dynamic years of the early American republic provided the backdrop for Hovey's upbringing. This timeframe was important for all American Protestants, and especially for Hovey's own Baptist denomination. The unique American and New England theological context shaped many Protestants, including several crucial influences on Hovey such as Dartmouth College, Newton Theological Institute, and Andover Theological Seminary. In addition to his historical, denominational, and geographical contexts, Hovey was well aware of the seminal international discussions surrounding the Bible and theology. As the challenges of the later nineteenth century materialized, Hovey's responses are instructive. Hovey's theology evinces the diverse influences and attentions mentioned above. They deserve to be considered in turn.

Family Life and Early Education

Alvah Hovey was born on March 5, 1820, in the farmland of Chenango County, New York. His family was heavily influenced by its Puritan heritage.[5] His ancestors could point back to the 1630s as the time when the

---

2. Hovey, *Alvah Hovey*, 157.

3. See Cathcart, *Baptist Encyclopedia*, 546–47; Armitage, *History of the Baptists*, 874; Newman, *History of the Baptist Churches in the United States*, 480; Brackney, *Baptists*, 28, 66, 194–95; *Genetic History of Baptist Thought*, 285; Dockery, "Looking Back, Looking Ahead," 342; Garrett Jr., *Baptist Theology*, 279–83.

4. Shailer Mathews is a prime example of this. Mathews, *New Faith for Old*, 24–33.

5. Biographical information is reliant upon Hovey, *Alvah Hovey*. Hovey also wrote a short treatise for his children, which is still extant in his collected papers entitled "Narrative for My Children" (AHP). Other helpful, though limited, sources include

first Hovey, Daniel, immigrated to America from England.⁶ A century later, another relative, Amos Hovey, is said to have been "converted in the New Light movement under Whitefield."⁷ Alvah's family heritage evidently was self-conscious of its roots in early colonial America and the religious atmospheres of New England. Still, it was Alvah's parents, Alfred and Abigail, that had the most influence.⁸ Shortly after Alvah's birth the family moved to their long-time home in Thetford, Vermont. Hovey related that a combination of his own poor health as an infant and the fact that his parents only recently discovered they had been sold a fraudulent deed to their farm in New York were the motivators to move back to the town they knew well.⁹ The fifth child of eleven,¹⁰ Alvah began to help his father on the dairy and cattle farm at six years of age while attending school only a few months per year.

Cathcart, *Baptist Encyclopedia*, 546–47; Armitage, *History of the Baptists*, 874–75; English, "Alvah Hovey, D.D., LL.D."; "Dr. Hovey as a Teacher"; King, "Alvah Hovey and Foreign Missions"; "Alvah Hovey as Theologian and Teacher"; Weston, "Dr. Hovey as an Author"; Clarke, "Dr. Hovey as a Theologian"; Horr, "Dr. Hovey and Educational Work"; Crane, "Dr. Hovey with His Friends"; Newman, "Recent Changes in the Theology of the Baptists"; *Hovey Book*, 321–23; Pierce, *General Catalogue*, 65; Maring, "Baptists and Changing Views of the Bible [I]"; "Baptists and Changing Views of the Bible [II]"; Garrett Jr., "Sources of Authority in Baptist Thought"; Brackney, *Baptists*, 28, 66, 194–95; *Historical Dictionary of the Baptists*, 217; McKibbens, "Hovey, Alvah (1820–1903)"; Bendroth, *School of the Church*, 35–37; Hudson, "Shifting Patterns of Church Order"; Straub, *Making of a Battle Royal*, 45–46.

    6. Alvah Hovey is listed as entry 1081 in *Hovey Book*, 321–23.

    7. Hovey, *Alvah Hovey*, 3.

    8. See the short description in *Hovey Book*, 250–51. Alfred Hovey is listed as entry 596. The family originally lived in Thetford, Vermont, but moved to New York for a short three years, during which time Alvah was born, before moving back to Thetford when Alvah was very young. Alfred was said to be "of an inconstant disposition, desiring to move about and changing his business, but, through the influence of his wife, finally settled down to farming. He went in debt for his farm, worked hard, ran a large dairy, raised cattle and sheep, and paid for it." Abigail was described thus: "had a good common school education, and excelled in vocal music. Her voice had compass, purity and sweetness. She was a social favorite, especially among the Baptists." Abigail died in 1837. Alfred remarried (Sarah Hendricks) in 1839 and moved to Wisconsin where he lived until his death in 1872.

    9. Hovey, "Narrative for My Children," 2–3.

    10. Alvah had three older sisters: Clara Milly (1813–1851), Mary Ann (1814–1828), and Leantha (born 1816); one older brother: Amos White (born 1818, moved to Wisconsin as an adult); five younger brothers: William Ashley (born 1821, moved to California as an adult), Leland Aaron (born 1823, moved to Illinois as an adult), Oramal Fletcher (born 1825, moved to Iowa as an adult), Charles Edward (1827–1897, served as Brigadier and Brevet Major-General in the Civil War and is buried in Arlington National Cemetery, Washington, DC), Eleazar (born 1829, moved to Wisconsin as an adult); and one younger sister: Frances Mary Ann (born 1834). See entries 596 and 1080–86 in *Hovey Book*.

Alvah's son, George, related that despite the limited school exposure during his early years his father developed an interest in studying, particularly during the cold winter evenings. At fifteen Alvah began more serious study at the nearby Thetford Academy. He proved to be gifted in these general education studies as well as sensitive to the strong religious education he received at home. His principal and primary teacher, Mr. Richards (who went on to teach at the University of Alabama), first taught Alvah how to study and write.

Alvah mentioned that his religious education at home came primarily from his father: "So far as I now recollect my earliest impression of a religious nature was one of awe and fear of God. I was taught that he was very great and holy, and I was at times much afraid that he would punish me for my sins. My father was at times very earnest and solemn in warning us, the children, of the terrible nature and penalty of sin."[11] George Hovey recounted that Alfred Hovey "was fairly well educated for a farmer, and taught a district school when a young man."[12] Further, "he was a sound Calvinist, able to give a reason for the faith that was in him. But he was a slave neither to forms nor creeds. It was his custom to omit the regular family prayers when he felt that his spirit was not sincerely prayerful."[13]

Conversion came for Alvah at about fifteen years of age after a process of uncertainty over the changes he believed had happened in his own soul. By his own record, his conversion story began with conviction of his sin and the just punishment of God upon him: "When I was twelve years old there was a revival in the town and two of my sisters, with some other young people whom I knew, began to entertain a hope that their sins were forgiven. My own thoughts had often been directed to my sinfulness and need of pardon. Awe and fear troubled me when I thought of God as a holy Sovereign."[14] Hovey did not describe his conversion process as a radical moment of crisis, but a recognizable change over time: "And far from the time when my sisters were baptized, I experienced a great change in my spirit. It brought me no special joy; but it did include a more abiding sense of my sinfulness, more reverence for the name and worship of God, more satisfaction in meeting with Christians and listening to their prayers and exhortations, if indeed I had any satisfaction in these before. My fear of God as a holy Judge became a different feeling, embracing an element of

---

11. Hovey, *Alvah Hovey*, 12.
12. Hovey, *Alvah Hovey*, 3.
13. Hovey, *Alvah Hovey*, 4.
14. Hovey, "Narrative for My Children," 15.

gratitude and admiration."[15] This conviction and the beginning of change was through regular Gospel presentations by his father and not just through the revival that was in town. Alvah relates that: "I did think of God as a holy and merciful Father, and I knew that his mercy was through Christ alone, but somehow I did not lay hold of Christ as my Savior with a confiding faith. This was my state of mind for about three years."[16] Alvah stayed in this state until he felt that a true sense of conversion had happened to his soul: "The new vision of God remained with him and gradually after months of uncertainty he came to believe that a permanent change had been wrought in his soul. From that time he sought to know and serve his Creator."[17] After this, Alvah steadily grew in his faith, but it was not until he was seventeen that he publicly confessed this belief and was baptized.[18]

When Alvah turned sixteen his father released him from family farming duties so that he could attempt to raise money for continuing education. He attended Brandon Literary and Scientific Institution in Brandon, Vermont. While there, Hovey had his first experience of an academic atmosphere, and he thrived. George Hovey noted the influence of a recent Newton Theological Institute graduate over his father at the time. This man, Cornelius A. Thomas, D.D., was pastoring the Baptist church in Brandon.[19] Alvah felt the desire to enter Christian ministry and made this remark, evidently of Thomas, at the fiftieth anniversary of Newton in 1875: "By the advice of a country pastor, who studied in this institution, my own purpose to obtain a liberal education before entering the ministry was fixed, and words are wanting to express the gratitude which I have sometimes felt to him, while studying the Scriptures in the very words employed by the Saviour and his Apostles."[20] Hovey's early decision to obtain a liberal arts education set a course of lifelong advocating for thorough education. As Hovey finished his early education, he returned home to Thetford only to leave the

---

15. Hovey, "Narrative for My Children," 16.

16. Hovey, "Narrative for My Children," 17.

17. Hovey, *Alvah Hovey*, 13. Alvah related that he was confident of his conversion by June or July 1836 and so was baptized at that time (Hovey, "Narrative for My Children," 17).

18. Hovey, *Alvah Hovey*, 13. This pattern of conviction of sin, struggle, and conversion to the joys of salvation resembles the normal pattern of "revival theologies" in New England during the First and Second Great Awakenings, and among Baptists in particular. See Caldwell III, *Theologies of the American Revivalists*, 11–42, 101–26, 145–63.

19. Alvah noted that what made an impression on him about his pastor was "His sterling integrity, his good understanding, his spotless character, his catholicity and kindness, his love to his own people and their Lord" (Hovey, *Alvah Hovey*, 17).

20. Hovey, *Historical Address*, 42.

following day to travel the short distance to Hanover, New Hampshire and Dartmouth College.

Dartmouth College

When Hovey left his home to pursue post-secondary education, he entered a complex intellectual scene that provided the backdrop for his own education and theological construction. After the Great Awakening[21] and the American Revolution (with the subsequent disestablishment of state-sponsored religion),[22] a new vista of possibilities opened to American Protestants. Part of this was due to a significant growth in numbers that came along with population growth and the continuation of revivals. The population of the country itself multiplied by a factor of eight between 1780 and 1860, with growth among Protestant religions greatly surpassing that factor.[23]

The open religious market place and the proliferation of revivals meant the renunciation of the former ways of influencing society, the growth of voluntary means, and the invention of new forms (denominations,

---

21. On Baptists in the Great Awakening, see vol. 1 of Benedict, *General History of the Baptist Denomination in America*; Backus, *History of New England*, chapters 14–18; Armitage, *History of the Baptists*, 619–775; Newman, *History of the Baptist Churches in the United States*, 239–332; Vedder, *Short History of the Baptists*, chapter 20; Goen, *Revivalism and Separatism in New England*; McBeth, *Baptist Heritage*, 200–251; Leonard, "Baptist Revivals"; Kidd, *Great Awakening*, chapters 12, 15–17; Bebbington, *Baptists through the Centuries*, chapter 5; Kidd and Hankins, *Baptists in America*, chapter 2.

22. On Baptists and the Revolution/Disestablishment, see vol. 2 of Benedict, *General History of the Baptist Denomination*, chapters 7–12; Backus, *History of New England*, chapters 23–33; Armitage, *History of the Baptists*, 776–813; Newman, *History of the Baptist Churches in the United States*, 333–75; Vedder, *Short History of the Baptists*, chapter 20; McLoughlin, *New England Dissent*; *Soul Liberty*; Lovejoy, *Religious Enthusiasm in the New World*, 215–30; Goen, *Revivalism and Separatism in New England*; McBeth, *Baptist Heritage*, 252–88; Creed, "Baptist Freedom"; Ragosta, *Wellspring of Liberty*; Kidd, *God of Liberty*; Kidd and Hankins, *Baptists in America*, chapters 3–4.

23. In 1780, the largest denomination in America was Congregationalism with over 700 churches and Presbyterians were the second most numerous with a little less than 500. Baptists came third with about 450 and Anglicans were right around 400 churches. Importantly, Methodists had only a couple dozen itinerant preachers by 1776. And, these church numbers reflect a sharp increase for all denominations after the First Great Awakening in the mid-1700s. However, Protestant numbers increased much more dramatically in the nineteenth century. By 1850, Methodists had the most churches with over 13,300 and Baptists were second at over 9,300. Presbyterians had over 4,800 and then came Restoration Churches (over 1,800), Congregationalists (1,700), Episcopalians (1,400), and Lutherans (1,200), all which continued to grow during the later nineteenth century. See Gaustad and Barlow, *New Historical Atlas of Religion in America*, 1–10, 219, 390.

organizations, programs, and schools)[24] for what religion looked like.[25] As was mentioned in the first chapter, democratization reshaped much of the authority structure within American Protestantism. Popular interest was shaping religion after their own interests and concerns.[26] "Paradoxically, the establishment of firmer lines of spiritual authority and the bureaucratization of belief were made easier by religion's partial expulsion from the political domain."[27] More than just a demographic explosion and a new church-state relationship, the early republic faced an intriguing set of new ideas that offered new possibilities for theology. Alvah Hovey received his theological training in this American environment. The new opportunities and conceptions of authority that came with this new landscape certainly influenced his education. The extent to which this is the case remains to be seen.[28]

From 1839 to 1844, Hovey attended Dartmouth College, which was only nine miles down the Connecticut River from his father's home.[29] The growing college in Hanover, New Hampshire had an entirely prescribed liberal arts course of study centered on mathematics and the classics.[30] He was involved in an anti-slavery society, a temperance society, a "social friends" society, two literary societies, Phi Beta Kappa, and the Dartmouth College Theological Society, becoming its president his senior year. Finances were difficult while attending Dartmouth. He worked summers farming and winters teaching in various literary and scientific institutes while he also found the occasional opportunity to preach in order to pay for school. Because of

---

24. See Marty, *Protestantism in the United States*, 67–75. Daniel Walker Howe argues that, "The evangelical reinvigoration of New England culture proceeded along two dimensions, the social and the intellectual. The social dimension was the 'evangelical united front' of interdenominational benevolent associations; the intellectual dimension was represented by New Haven Theology, otherwise known as New School Calvinism" (Howe, *Political Culture of the American Whigs*, 159).

25. McLoughlin, "Introduction," 1–2; Noll, *America's God*, 174–75.

26. See Hatch, *Democratization of American Christianity*.

27. Bayly, *Birth of the Modern World*, 336.

28. This environment certainly describes Baptists. Simply put, the nineteenth-century Baptist story is one of explosive growth and significant adaptation and fragmentation. See Brackney, "Turn Toward a Doctrinal Christianity"; Holmes, *Baptist Theology*, 32–37.

29. Hovey remarked that "Dartmouth College was but nine miles from my father's house, and was selected by me, principally on that account. Had Brown University or Waterville College (now Colby) been as near my home or even as well known to me as Dartmouth, I should without doubt have selected one of them" (Hovey, "Narrative for My Children," 29).

30. Hovey, *Alvah Hovey*, 19. The curriculum included physical sciences, mathematics, natural philosophy, languages, rhetoric, composition, philosophy, politics, history, and theology. See Lord, *History of Dartmouth College*, 2:261–66.

his finances his junior year took two years to complete and he was not able to attend classes. Instead, he completed the required reading and work to gain credit for the junior year of college.[31]

Dartmouth struggled during Hovey's time as a student. The numbers dropped some and the students had a reputation for being rather unruly. According to one historian, "The early and middle forties were especially a period of noisy disturbance."[32] Dancing, bowling, cards, and "ardent spirits" were several of the ways in which students found themselves in trouble.[33] The suppression of such activities were "in accordance with the strict ideas of the times" and had the effect that "the spirit of mischief found expression in uncharted ways and often developed into lawlessness and insubordination."[34] Vandalism was rampant as was the offence of "horn-blowing" (this was normally during the night, a class, or some other gathering and could last an hour or more). Several students were expelled on various occasions on these grounds, which was often met with widespread student protest or riot.[35]

Hovey's connections to these behaviors are unrecorded, but we do know that he built a relationship with Dartmouth's president, Nathan Lord (1792–1870), who was known as a strict disciplinarian, indicating that Hovey was most likely distanced from the disturbances. One interesting note provided by George Hovey is that Alvah twice received funds for anti-slavery participation from the Northern Baptist Education Society while at Dartmouth: "'1839, November 19, gave for assisting a slave to Canada, fifteen cents'; and '1840, July 4, for anti-slavery society, one dollar.'"[36] Debates over slavery were exceptionally tense during Hovey's time at Dartmouth and participation in a temperance society, an anti-slavery society and assisting a slave (an action which was evidently known enough to win him monetary support) show willingness to enter controversy.[37] During Hovey's time as student, President Lord was a staunch and convinced abolitionist who supported such activities. However, Lord changed his views from abolitionist to pro-slavery around 1847, much to the disappointment of many

---

31. Hovey related to his children that, in hindsight, the inability to take the junior year courses was not the best of options. See Hovey, "Narrative for My Children," 36–37.

32. Lord, *History of Dartmouth College*, 2:279.

33. Lord, *History of Dartmouth College*, 2:267, 276.

34. Lord, *History of Dartmouth College*, 2:276.

35. Lord, *History of Dartmouth College*, 2:279–83.

36. Hovey, *Alvah Hovey*, 20.

37. Lord, *History of Dartmouth College*, 2:251–55.

of Dartmouth's constituency.[38] For his part, Hovey did not follow Lord's example and remained an abolitionist his entire life.[39]

From 1830–1849 there was no person to fill the Phillips professorship of divinity or the pastor of the College church. The responsibilities were filled by either an ordained faculty member or, as was more often true, President Lord. Several men were hired in either role but only lasted a short while. Evidently the high standards, poor reputation of the town, growing tendency to have brief hires, and the issue of slavery was so divisive as to render appointment of a theology professor too difficult. Some glimpse of the theological content can be seen when Daniel J. Noyes, former pastor of the South Congregational Church in Concord, New Hampshire, was finally appointed to the theology professorship in 1849. The agreement was that his "religious sentiments are in accordance with the compend of Christian doctrine set forth by the Westminster Assembly of Divines in their Shorter

---

38. In fact, in 1863, Lord cast the deciding vote which stopped the awarding of an honorary degree to Abraham Lincoln. This upset many to the point that the Trustees (including a man named Amos Tuck, who was a close friend of Lincoln) moved to terminate Lord. Before they were able to, Lord offered his resignation. Lord, *History of Dartmouth College*, 2:321–26.

39. One tantalizing story that has survived recalls that on a Sunday in April, 1865, Alvah Hovey was called in to the First African Baptist Church in Richmond, Virginia, as a member of the Christian Commission of the Federal Army. Richmond had only just fallen to the Union and there was much change happening quickly with the end of the war. However, amid the stir, the church's white pastor, named Robert Ryland, was pro-slavery and instructed his members to return to their masters instead of joining the Union Army. This comment nearly got Ryland arrested by several black Union soldiers (who had captured the city), except his parishioners stepped in on his behalf. Hovey was reportedly called to be an intermediary and he suggested the church vote on whether to retain their pastor or not, a suggestion that pleased everyone present. The church voted to retain Ryland, but he resigned within a few weeks knowing that he could not effectively minister given the events and his own pro-slavery views. For this story and the events surrounding the freeing of Richmond and its impact on the black churches there, see chapter 6 in Billingsley, *Mighty Like a River*, esp. 65–67. The story is tantalizing because it is impossible to substantiate in Hovey's own papers. Hovey's pocket diary for 1865 contains several entries concerning the Civil War. Monday, April 3, Hovey notes that "Richmond is taken!" Saturday, April 15, notes the assassination of President Lincoln the day before. Further notes on the war, as well as his own busy schedule of teaching and preaching, fill the days during April and May, but there is no mention of a trip to Richmond as told in the above story. Hovey, "Personal Journal (1865)" (AHP). Hovey's journal does clearly show his affection for the Union and the abolition of slavery. Further, one of Hovey's younger brothers, Charles Edward Hovey, was a Brigadier General for the Union, was seriously wounded serving under General William T. Sherman at the Battle of Arkansas Post, and is buried in Arlington National Cemetery.

Catechism, and that any material departure from that platform is deemed by the Board a sufficient ground of removal from office."[40]

Not much is known of Lord's theological stance. He graduated from Bowdoin College (1809) and Andover Theological Seminary (1815) and served as Dartmouth's president from 1828–1863. He was "well acquainted with the Hovey family, owning a neighboring farm. He used to speak of Alvah to the neighbors as his 'brag scholar.' The friendly interest of such a man was a force not to be overlooked in studying the formative influences in a young man's life."[41] Not only Lord but also his appointees to the theological chair were graduates of Andover Theological Seminary, which suggests that Hovey would have received some theological teaching in that tradition. Lord's method of theological teaching was incompletely described in this way: "His appeal was always first to the conscience, then to reason, rather to reason first and conscience afterword, and as conscience was in his view the only individual witness to the truth of God, whose final expression was the Bible, he made the Bible the basis of every appeal to conscience and enforced it under a literal interpretation as a rule of life. From its teachings, as he believed them, he never swerved, no matter where they led him."[42]

Among the Alvah Hovey papers only a few notes survive of Hovey's theological education at Dartmouth.[43] There are less than thirty short pages of lecture notes written in Hovey's hand. These notes have to do with the nature of religion, the relation of will to affections, the theoretical organization of theology, and Scripture. Though brief, there is a clear understanding of theology as a science which organizes the Bible. The data of theology are gathered from the Bible and then organized. They are assumed to agree with each other, thus, the theologian is to understand the more difficult by the clearer and is to resist the urge to leave out difficult notions. Logic and the powers of the mind are then meant to organize and construct theology. As one note remarks: "The elements of theology, as a science, are exegetical and logical, the former furnishing the material, the latter the instrument."[44] On the relation of philosophy, which was also referred to as reason, Hovey listed five important principles:

1. Science cannot be overruled by theology.

---

40. Lord, *History of Dartmouth College*, 2:291.
41. Hovey, *Alvah Hovey*, 25. See Lord, *History of Dartmouth College*, 2:218–333.
42. Lord, *History of Dartmouth College*, 2:332.
43. Hovey, "Student Notebook: Lectures on Theology (1843–1844) (Dartmouth College)" (AHP).
44. Hovey, "Student Notebook: Lectures on Theology (1843–1844) (Dartmouth College)," 7 (AHP).

2. Necessary consequences of established principles cannot be disregarded.

3. Reason is a guide in those lower matters which are presupposed by the Scriptures.

4. Speculation on the highest questions respecting God and the invisible world can never be the basis of a sound theology.

5. Those spiritual principles which are common to all systems of philosophy must be admitted by the theologian.[45]

Hovey's notes went on to say that natural theology is presupposed in theology but is vague and insufficient. The evidences of Christianity are useful but need more theological training to be properly utilized. In other words, the Bible was the basis for theology and reason would help to understand and expound this theology. But there was also something in theology that was not readily apparent to reason. Hovey recorded it this way: "There can be no theology without a respectable degree of metaphysical, or logical (philosophical) talent. On the other hand a dry logical theology is not the most perfect. Theology must have life and breath; and must leave a place at least for many things which cannot be reduced to the form of a syllogism."[46]

Interestingly, the way that Hovey noted the theological method began with a presupposition: "A student must have some established views at the outset, e.g., that the Christian religion is of divine authority, and that the Bible teaches evangelical religion."[47] One does not come without any assumptions to the Bible. The full theological method was summarized in this way: "Begin with the elementary principles of each topic in orthodox theology. 1. Examine the Scriptures and think for yourselves. 2. Read those authors in which you expect most truth in the best form; 3. Look at the leading positions of others of different views. Thus you will always carry with some set of text, something positive, to guide and aid you in your inquiries."[48] The exegetical task of biblical interpretation was presupposed as well as the historical task of understanding the major orthodox views. The theologian was tasked with organizing these doctrines in an understandable and logical way. They were also to give attention to the major issues of the day, though with caution not to be over-focused on the present.

---

45. Hovey, "Student Notebook: Lectures on Theology (1843–1844) (Dartmouth College)," 9 (AHP).

46. Hovey, "Student Notebook: Lectures on Theology (1843–1844) (Dartmouth College)," 12 (AHP).

47. Hovey, "Student Notebook: Lectures on Theology (1843–1844) (Dartmouth College)," 13 (AHP).

48. Hovey, "Student Notebook: Lectures on Theology (1843–1844) (Dartmouth College)," 13 (AHP).

When Hovey's notes transition to speak of the character of the Scriptures, there is discussion of the authenticity, authority, and inspiration of the Scriptures. Hovey listed six points of belief: "(1) the divine character of the NT; (2) the promise of inspired aid to the apostles; (3) the profession of inspiration by the apostles; (4) the consistent views of the early church; (5) the inspiration of the OT according to Christ and the apostles; and (6) the apostolical character, directly or indirectly, of the NT writings."[49] Hovey does not provide any notes on the details of how this inspiration happened, but he does note that the materialistic theories and critiques of the Bible are unconvincing. There are also notes on the canon and textual criticism. Both of which provide a few bullet points as to why the current books and texts are trustworthy. In summary, the notebook from Hovey's student days at Dartmouth show a few glimpses into his early education surrounding theological method and the authority of the Bible. However, the measure to which Hovey accepted these and made them his own are not noted in these books or elsewhere.

Several points can be observed about the upbringing and early education of Hovey that carry significance for his future years. His spiritual environment was Calvinistic and quite serious, both at home and probably at Dartmouth. Through his connection to Nathan Lord, and the other ministers and faculty in and around Dartmouth, Hovey would have had his first introduction to the theology that was characteristic of New England. The details of this Calvinism at Dartmouth are mostly absent, however. This absence is significant, as Hovey takes several opportunities during his life to reflect on other theological influences upon himself but leaves out mention of Lord or of Dartmouth in general. As such, the influence of Andover at this point in his life is relatively unknown; though, as will be shown below, Andover will prove to be a significant influence in Hovey's later education and thinking. What we do know about the theological training of Hovey is that he was drilled in a theological method that was biblically based (because the Bible was trustworthy) but also left a high place for human reasoning. Also important to note is that his class notes reflect that he was taught to have a pre-conceived notion of one's theology as you begin the theological task. This particular method was certainly not followed at Newton. Though how much Hovey accepted this as his own will have to be seen in his own theological writings. Hovey felt a serious burden to utilize his studies as best he could for the purpose that God had called him. Baptist ideas over

---

49. Hovey, "Student Notebook: Lectures on Theology (1843–1844) (Dartmouth College)," 19 (AHP).

the proper course of ministerial education were[50] (and are) perennial hot topics and Hovey was convinced early on for a liberal arts foundation upon which a seminary education would build. A consequence of this education was that Hovey obtained solid language training and through the course of his life he would teach Latin, German, Hebrew, and Greek (plus he learned proficiency in French while at Dartmouth).

Newton Theological Institute

Upon graduation from Dartmouth in 1844 Hovey served as president of a literary school for a year and then entered Newton Theological Institute, which was located on the outskirts of Boston in Newton Centre, Massachusetts. Newton was the first Baptist seminary founded in America (1825),[51] and it was highly influential. Augustus Strong once commented about Newton: "To Newton belongs the glory of being the first exclusively theological institution established in this country by Baptists. For eighty-four years she has furnished our denomination with the best of training, and with many of our noblest preachers and pastors."[52] Hovey spent almost the entirety of his adult life at Newton and so it is no wonder it would be influential upon him (and he upon it). Three men were the most influential on Hovey: founder and architect Irah Chase (1793–1864) along with biblical scholars Barnas Sears (1802–1880) and Horatio Hackett (1808–1875).

Irah Chase and the Founding of the School

Irah Chase was trained at Andover Theological Seminary and then spent part of 1823–1824 at the Universities of Halle, Leipzig, and Göttingen.[53] At Andover he revered the biblical studies teaching of Moses Stuart.[54] Con-

---

50. As will be seen below, with the founding of the Baptists' first seminary, Newton Theological Institute (1825), Baptists began debating on the needs and preferred course of theological education.

51. "Newton was the ninth denominational seminary opened in the United States behind Andover, Princeton, Harvard, Bangor, Hartwick, Auburn, General, Yale, and Virginia" (Brackney, *Congregation and Campus*, 260).

52. Strong, *Miscellanies*, 1:278. The title of the essay is "Schools of the Prophets." It was an "Address at the inauguration of the Rev. George E. Horr, D.D., as president of the Newton Theological Institution, Newton Center, MA, June 9, 1909."

53. On Chase, see, Chase, "Rev. Irah Chase, D.D."; Hague, *Christian Greatness in the Scholar*; Maring, "Baptists and Changing Views of the Bible [I]," 55–58; Brackney, *Historical Dictionary of the Baptists*, 97; *Genetic History of Baptist Thought*, 279–82.

54. More will be said about Stuart below. For more details, see Giltner, *Moses Stuart*.

vinced of the need for educated clergy, Chase was burdened with providing a similar seminary for Baptists based on the Andover model.[55] He believed that the traditional idea of a pastor training his apprentice could not provide the fully rounded course like a seminary and so he joined the founding of Newton Theological Seminary.[56] The three-year course of study was determined by Chase to include biblical languages, ecclesiastical history, biblical theology, and pastoral duties.[57] In a significant move, the place of systematic theology was severely downplayed in favor of biblical theology. Whereas Andover had a central place for systematic theology during their second year, Newton originally only had biblical studies.[58] The idea was that the school would not let systematic theology (or any theological system) influence the interpretation of the Bible. By downplaying a "pre-conceived" set of doctrines (such as Calvin or Turretin) that would supposedly predetermine what the Bible would need to mean, Chase hoped to instill in their graduates a particular relation of biblical theology to systematic theology with biblical theology having the obvious pride of placement. William Hague, Chase's biographer, remarked:

> Now, let it be here observed that it was the cherished aim and the main end of Professor Chase, in his plan of a theological institution, directly to reverse this order; to upturn the foundations of an established method which could plead for itself the prestige of a venerable Past; and instead of allowing the student to have his mind subjected to the power of a logically-compacted system anticipatory of what he would find in Scriptures, and thus prejudging what he *ought* to find, to constrain him to become thoroughly grounded in the original Scriptures themselves, and to make him, like Apollos, "mighty" in those Scriptures by a conscious mastery of their meaning, their scope, and of their applications, according to those, fixed principles of interpretation that would stand the test of the severest scrutiny like pure gold tried by the fiery crucible.[59]

---

55. Bendroth, *School of the Church*, 25–42.

56. On the founding of Newton as the first Baptist post-undergraduate ministerial school and its general character, see Brackney, *Congregation and Campus*, 258–62.

57. Hovey, *Historical Address*, 13–23.

58. Margaret Bendroth recognizes this change as well and also remarks that the scheme of Chase required four full-time professors, which was not accomplished until 1839. See Bendroth, *School of the Church*, 29–35.

59. Hague, *Christian Greatness in the Scholar*, 23.

It must be simultaneously recognized that Newton declined to accept a confessional standard for their seminary.[60] Margaret Bendroth notes: "Newton had no constitution, and its leaders made no attempt to set forth a faculty creed, course curricula, or any means of doctrinal oversight of the school."[61] The downplaying of systematics and the absence of a confession certainly had long-term consequences.[62] Considering the place of Newton within Baptist life, this was a significant move and not one that went without notice.[63] Nearly a century later Strong recognized Newton's reputation surrounding their method of instruction and commented: "Doctor Chase taught a theology so unlike that of Princeton that some of our extremely orthodox ministers refused to put their sons under what they regarded as heterodox teaching."[64] The theological climate was one of high academic standards, free inquiry, no confessional standard, and biblicist theological reasoning.[65] What Irah Chase created at Newton, Alvah Hovey inherited.

Barnas Sears

Sears replaced Chase as Professor of Christian Theology in 1835. He studied in Germany under August Tholuck and Wilhelm Gesenius at Halle in 1833–1835, and he returned to German universities on several other occasions for continued study.[66] Sears thoroughly enjoyed his German education and

60. Glenn Miller describes it thus: "Newton had one peculiarity. Unlike Andover or Princeton, the school had no creed and recognized no authority but the Bible. Newton replaced Andover's traditional second-year course in Systematics with a year of biblical theology" (Miller, *Piety and Intellect*, 326).

61. Bendroth, *School of the Church*, 31. Also, "Newton Theological Institute"; *Newton Theological Institution*.

62. Brackney comments: "Here he followed Moses Stuart, but was freed from Andover's confessional requirements" (Brackney, *Genetic History of Baptist Thought*, 281n80). For the place of Andover's creed within their founding, see Giltner, "Fragmentation of New England Congregationalism"; Williams, *Andover Liberals*, 1–7.

63. Brackney notes that Chase's model was "a model that influenced all of the other Baptist schools of the nineteenth century" (Brackney, *Genetic History of Baptist Thought*, 281). It was not until 1913 and the founding of Northern Baptist Theological Seminary that any Baptist seminary in the North accepted a confessional position; see Brackney, *Congregation and Campus*, 293–94.

64. Strong, *Miscellanies*, 2:60.

65. I am using the phrase "biblicist theological reasoning" to refer to the tendency in Chase (and others) to (1) utilize a scientific approach to Scripture, to (2) resist allowing any theological system or statement to influence biblical interpretation, to (3) utilize any source of truth, and to (4) build a positive theology from this basis.

66. Hovey wrote the biography of Sears: Hovey, *Barnas Sears, a Christian Educator*. Also see Brackney, *Historical Dictionary of the Baptists*, 372–73; *Genetic History of Baptist Thought*, 282–84.

even developed a close friendship with Tholuck.[67] Sears's method of teaching was not to utilize a textbook but to encourage students to build their own theology. Hovey described Sears in this way:

> The theology taught by Doctor Sears was biblical in its source and evangelical in its tone. It was clear to those who sat at his feet that he was not in search of new opinions because they were new, or of old opinions because they were old, but rather of the truth, whether new or old. But, though his theology was biblical in its source, he did not shut his eyes to the lessons of nature. While he believed in Jesus Christ, as the highest and perfect revelation of God the Father, his mind was evermore hospitable to truth from any source.[68]

Sears gave his students a comprehensive bibliography for reading, encouraged their interaction with European scholarship, and sought merely to furnish them with the ability to think. Hovey appreciated that Sears "would lead [students] to answers founded on reason, rather than authority."[69]

Among Hovey's papers, he kept a notebook from his theology classes with Barnas Sears. "Theological Lectures by Barnas Sears, or rather, Essays by A. Hovey" was written on the inside cover.[70] The content of the notebook covered the topics of theological writers, regeneration, theological reasoning, inspiration, the existence and attributes of God, sin, and the atonement. The notes provided only brief glimpses of what was taught, but some idea of what Hovey took from Sears is still possible.

When it came to theological reasoning, Hovey noted that science and reason are to be trusted and that theology cannot be contradictory to either, though he did allow that science may be only partially established, and the biblical witness may be vindicated after a time. When it came to inspiration, Hovey's notes show that it was not merely the thoughts of the authors that were inspired but also the words. Also, the idea that the words were dictated was rejected in favor of the view that the human authors' personality and style are retained. The existence of God is reasonable and natural but not necessarily a logically conclusive truth. The discussions of God's attributes (personality, spirituality, aseity, immutability, eternity, omnipresence, and omniscience) followed classical theistic explanations and definitions. Under the doctrine of sin, Hovey noted that depravity is universal among all

67. Hovey, *Barnas Sears*, 33–53.
68. Hovey, *Barnas Sears*, 64.
69. Hovey, *Historical Address*, 36.
70. Hovey, "Theological Lectures by Barnas Sears, or Rather, Essays by A. Hovey (Newton Theological Institute)" (AHP).

humans. Interestingly, Hovey's notes on the propagation of sin indicated that Sears followed some of the contemporaneous explanations in that the inclination to sin was propagated but not the guilt for the sin itself.[71] On the issue of the atonement, Hovey could only describe the deity of Christ before the notes end. The notes are certainly brief, but something of the content of the theology taught by Sears as well as the theological method is clearly seen. Though educated at Newton and not Andover as was Chase and Hackett, Sears clearly stood in line with the ideal of high scholarship, free inquiry, and a biblicist theological reasoning.[72] Hovey discussed the progress of Baptist education on a few occasions and he clearly followed the lead of Chase and Sears,[73] even pointing out his clear acceptance of Sears's position.[74]

Horatio Hackett

Horatio Hackett, like Chase, attended Andover Theological Seminary and studied under Moses Stuart. Hackett arrived at Newton in 1839 as Professor of Biblical Literature and Interpretation. His travels to Germany in 1841–1842 took him to Halle where he studied under Tholuck and Gesenius and then to Berlin where he studied under Ernst Hengstenberg and August Neander.[75] A well-respected biblical scholar, Hackett was known far beyond the Baptist or even the American world.[76] Hovey's admiration for Hackett is revealed in his 1876 comments: "For a considerable period, at least, his was the name that attracted young men to this school, and his the ability which retained them here. Not only by the accuracy of his knowledge, but also by the singular beauty of his language, did he charm and inspire the classes under his charge, and wield a potent influence in favor of Christian culture."[77]

---

71. The discussion surrounding original sin and its propagation and contemporaneous debates will be covered below.

72. One famous instance is remembered by a former student, J. B. Gough Pidge, and recorded by Alvah Hovey: "On one occasion [Sears] remarked, *I do not care to have you remember what I say; I am simply anxious to teach you how to think. If you learn that, you may burn my lectures if you will*" (Hovey, *Barnas Sears*, 102).

73. Hovey, "Doctrinal Theology for Christian Pastors"; *Historical Address*, 57–58; "Progress of a Century"; *Studies in Ethics and Religion*, 440–75.

74. Hovey, "Doctrinal Theology for Christian Pastors," 663–69.

75. Hackett also travelled to Europe on more than one occasion. Hovey spoke at Hackett's funeral, which address is still extant. See Hovey, "Dr. Hackett at Newton."

76. At his death, tributes came in from several sources, including Tholuck at Halle, B. F. Westcott at Cambridge, and Joseph Angus at Regent's Park College in London. All these tributes are included in Whittemore, *Memorials of Horatio Balch Hackett*.

77. Hovey, *Historical Address*, 37.

Hovey remarked that Hackett consistently held Scripture supreme, which was an indication of his spiritual life: "The depth of his Christian life was also revealed by treatment of the Holy Scriptures. For it is not too much for me to say, that he manifested an absolute and unwavering confidence in their divine character and authority. The word of a sacred writer was to him the word of the living God, and he paid to it the homage of unqualified faith."[78] Hovey remembered Hackett as one who gave his life to interpretation of Scripture, which he did with reverence, sureness, joy, and familiarity.[79] Known for instilling into his students the need for rigorous scientific understanding of the Bible, the need to learn how to think, and a sincere reverence for Scripture, Hackett continued the legacy of Newton, and with a new level of academic respectability.

As was quoted in the previous chapter, Norman Maring explained the combined influence of Chase, Sears, and Hackett at Newton: "These men did much to promote the scientific study of the Bible, the spirit of inquiry and the keen regard for truth with which many graduates were to be stamped."[80] Considering his own words, Hovey would concur.[81]

The Andover Influence

Each of Hovey's works attests to his wide reading, his theology textbooks above all. An extremely wide range of theologians informed his theology. Yet, as a theologian living in New England during the nineteenth century it forces the question as to whether Edwardsianism influenced Hovey. Newton was only a matter of miles from the campus of Andover. Newton was modeled after Andover in several ways. And, as has been shown, several of Hovey's teachers and predecessors (Lord, Chase, and Hackett) were educated at Andover.

Andover was heavily involved in the Calvinist debates among Congregationalists and Presbyterians in the early nineteenth century. Following the

78. Hovey, "Dr. Hackett at Newton," 237.

79. Hovey, "Dr. Hackett at Newton," 230, 237. Hovey remarks that Hackett considered command of biblical languages to be critical. "But in prosecuting his inquiries, the literature of Germany on Biblical subjects was indispensable, and that of France useful, a personal inspection of places in the Holy Land was important, and familiarity with modern Greek desirable" (Hovey, "Dr. Hackett at Newton," 230).

80. Maring, "Baptists and Changing Views of the Bible [I]," 56.

81. See, Hovey, *Historical Address*. For views on Newton's success at their centennial, see Rowe, "Newton Theological Institution Historical Address"; English, "Newton Men in the Pastorate"; Barnes, "Newton Men and Missions"; DeBlois, "Newton Men in Education."

death of Jonathan Edwards (1703–1758), a new theological tradition was formed in New England that sought to utilize Edwards.[82] Douglas Sweeney has summarized this tradition well: "Technically speaking, 'the New England Theology' was the tradition of Protestant thought that stemmed from the work of Jonathan Edwards and flourished in New England during the first half of the nineteenth century. As distinguished from the rest of New England theology, 'the New England Theology' was uniquely Edwardsian. A tradition of variations on certain key Edwardsian themes, it represented the first indigenous theological movement in America."[83] The New England Theology, then, refers to a long and broad stream of theological reasoning. Within this broader stream there are other, more specific streams that have more precise referents. These include the "New Divinity," "Tasters," "Exercisers," and "New Haven Theology."[84] The major issues were how to understand and appropriate Edwards's theology of original sin, Edwards's idea of the will (and human moral accountability), and how this affects atonement theology.[85] And, broader than the stream of New England Theology, there were the general categories of "New School" and "Old School,"[86] which applied to wider geographical and denominational boundaries. Old School referred to more traditional forms of Calvinism (as they are found in the Post-Reformation dogmaticians and Princeton in particular) that "formed its identity in reaction against the innovations of New England, but it was selective in its attitudes toward Edwardeans."[87] New School referred to

---

82. For general surveys of the various parties and an explanation of the issues, see Noll, *America's God*, 253–329, esp. 264; Sweeney, *Nathaniel Taylor*; Holifield, *Theology in America*, 341–94; Crisp and Sweeney, *After Jonathan Edwards*, 130–207. For a wider view of nineteenth-century atonement theologies and their significance in denominational differences, see the four-part article by Wells, "Debate over the Atonement in Nineteenth-Century America."

83. Sweeney, "Edwards and His Mantle," 97n1. Sweeney's essay is an essential overview of the historiography. For further explanations of the New England Theology, see Sweeney and Guelzo, *New England Theology*, 13–24; Crisp and Sweeney, "Introduction."

84. For overviews of each of these movements (and others), see the essays in Crisp and Sweeney, *After Jonathan Edwards*.

85. Holifield lists five assertions characteristic of New England Theology, though they can fit under the three broad categories listed here (Holifield, *Theology in America*, 343). Several works are important on these themes and are listed here. Also consider their place within the historiography of the New England Theology, as discussed in the article by Sweeney: Fiering, *Jonathan Edwards's Moral Thought*; Conforti, *Samuel Hopkins and the New Divinity Movement*; Guelzo, *Edwards on the Will*; Conforti, *Jonathan Edwards*; Sweeney, "Edwards and His Mantle"; *Nathaniel Taylor*.

86. Marsden, *Evangelical Mind*.

87. Holifield, *Theology in America*, 372. They were selective toward Edwards's followers because they also tried to claim Edwards in most cases.

Calvinism that modified Calvinism along the three main theological issues mentioned above.[88]

When surveying the writings of Hovey, one can see that he was very much aware of the various "schools" of theological thought within early America. And it was the New England Theology, particularly as it was associated with Andover,[89] by which Hovey was most influenced.[90] This can be seen in Hovey's comments on Moses Stuart and Edwards Amasa Park.

Moses Stuart

Mention has already been made of Moses Stuart (1780–1852) in regard to his influence on Chase and Hackett. Stuart is often called the "Father of Biblical Science in America."[91] Trained at Yale under Nathaniel William Taylor, he was Professor of Sacred Literature at Andover Theological Seminary from 1810 until his death in 1852. Stuart is significant for his understanding and transmitting of German trends in exegesis and for advocating the historical-grammatical method of exegesis.[92] Stuart was grateful for the critical exegetical tools that the Germans could give to study the Bible, but this led him to have a few doubts and his students to have even more.[93] He created some controversy when he openly questioned the plenary inspiration of the Bible in class. Though Stuart doubted the Bible's full inspiration for a time he never fully relinquished it and he always considered the Bible to be authoritative even if it could be interpreted according to modern principles of exegesis.[94] For Stuart, the Bible could be read like any other book: "We come then, after canvassing these principal objections against the position

---

88. Most historians recognize that "New School" is difficult to define and to delimit. See Holifield, *Theology in America*, 341–94, esp. 370–77. Noll summarizes them as "those which welcomed New England insights," and those "which did not" (Noll, *America's God*, 262–63).

89. On the connection of the New England Theology and the origins of Andover, see Giltner, "Fragmentation of New England Congregationalism"; Bendroth, *School of the Church*, 1–24. On the connection to Park, see Phillips, "Edwards Amasa Park"; Cooley, "New England Theology and the Atonement."

90. For a more extended and pointed treatment of Hovey's connections to Edwardsianism, see Shrader, "New England Baptist Alvah Hovey."

91. The epithet "The Father of Biblical Science" was carved on Stuart's gravestone (Giltner, *Moses Stuart*, 135).

92. Stuart was mostly self-trained in German biblical criticism but nevertheless became a leader in America in understanding it. See Giltner, *Moses Stuart*, 1–17.

93. Williams, *Andover Liberals*, 17–18.

94. See John Giltner: "Stuart never questioned the propriety of the claim that historical criticism and biblical authority should march hand in hand. It was fundamental to his work that they were united" (Giltner, *Moses Stuart*, 55).

which has been advanced, to the conclusion before stated, viz. that the rules of interpretation applied to other books, are applicable to the Scriptures."[95]

Stuart's influence on Hovey is fairly apparent. While there was the indirect influence of Stuart's pupils who became Hovey's teachers, there is also the fact that Hovey himself wrote a tribute to Stuart at his death. Hovey considered Stuart to be "a great and good man: whose history is worthy of being studied by all who love the Bible."[96] Hovey admired how he combined the exactness and thoroughness of study with a deep reverence for God and his word. In his eulogy, Hovey noted that Stuart believed in "the full inspiration of the Scriptures" and that "the principles taught by it are never treated as doubtful of excellence or authority. They are pronounced holy, and just, and good, with such vigor and emphasis of language, as plainly declare the heart of the writer to be in his words."[97] Hovey noted that Stuart followed the "grammatico-historical method" which "avails itself of just such a critical examination of words and phrases as must be employed in the study of Homer or Plato."[98] In this, Hovey agreed with Stuart's assertion that the Bible should be read much like any other book. Hovey clarified that this does not make illumination superfluous, but it also does not make the requirements of exegesis null and void. Interpretation was an inductive science that needed illumination. Hovey's comments here are especially helpful to see precisely how he worked out exegesis and illumination, learning from Stuart:

> The Holy Spirit may remove prejudice from the heart—may give a humble, docile temper—may guide the mind more rapidly and surely to a just view of what is taught—may quicken its energies, and unfold to it the wider and deeper religious truths involved in many passages; but it will never perform the work of the Lexicon or Grammar; much less will it make language signify what these, perfected by all available means, forbid it to signify. For in that case the written Word would lose its value. The trumpet would give an uncertain sound. One could never rely upon the results of study, however patient and candid, unless by some infallible criterion he could be sure they were suggested or sanctioned by a special act of the Divine Spirit.[99]

---

95. Stuart, "Same Principles of Interpretation," 137. See Brown, *Rise of Biblical Criticism in America*, 94–110; Kuklick, *Churchmen and Philosophers*, 89–91.

96. Hovey, "Moses Stuart," 288.

97. Hovey, "Moses Stuart," 290.

98. Hovey, "Moses Stuart," 291.

99. Hovey, "Moses Stuart," 292.

Hovey evidently believed that the work of exegesis was necessary, and that the grammatical-historical meaning was determinative, but it also required an assurance that the Holy Spirit had indeed revealed what was being exegeted.

While Hovey admired Stuart's method, and considered it essentially correct, he made it clear that he did not think Stuart's conclusions were always correct. Sometimes Stuart was wrong when "endeavoring to carry a point."[100] In other words, Hovey thought Stuart let his doctrinal or confessional commitments get in the way of honest interpretation. And so, in terms of method, other than giving undue place to outside theological commitments, Stuart was essentially correct, and Hovey sought to emulate him. Hovey also appreciated that Stuart awakened an interest in "Biblical Criticism" in his students and in those who read him. "[Stuart] was a reformer. He called those about to enter the Christian ministry to the study of the Bible, and taught them how to engage in the work."[101]

Edwards Amasa Park

A later presence at Andover Theological Seminary was the imposing figure of Edwards Amasa Park (1808–1900). Park began teaching at Andover in 1847 and, as Douglas Sweeney has commented, from the very first he "had been won over to New Haven Theology."[102] Charles Phillips describes Park's Calvinism as a "synthesis of Edwardsian natural ability, New Divinity moral government, and a Hopkinsian exercise scheme."[103] Park is often recognized as the last of the Edwardsians because the train of Edwardsian thought that moved through Samuel Hopkins and Nathaniel Taylor mostly ended with Park.[104] When Park retired in 1881, the liberal New Theology had overrun Andover and effectively silenced further adherence to the Edwardsianism that Park had held.[105]

At the death of Park in 1900, Hovey offered a memorial address concerning the "Substance and Manner of Professor Park's Teachings."[106] In this

---

100. Hovey, "Moses Stuart," 292. Hovey also mentions the verbosity of Stuart was a great detriment, though by no means limited to him alone.

101. Hovey, "Moses Stuart," 294.

102. Sweeney, *Nathaniel Taylor*, 147.

103. Phillips, "Edwards Amasa Park," 152.

104. Foster, *Genetic History of the New England Theology*, 471–540; Sweeney, *Nathaniel Taylor*, 145–51; Phillips, "Edwards Amasa Park."

105. Williams, *Andover Liberals*, 26–30; Bendroth, *School of the Church*, 76–82; Phillips, "Edwards Amasa Park," 160.

106. Hovey's essay is the first half (338–47) of the co-published work: Hovey and

essay, Hovey reveals the depth of their personal relationship. For nearly half a century the two taught in outskirts of Boston. Both served on the Board of Fellows at Brown University for several decades together and enjoyed each other's conversation during the hour-long commute from Boston to Providence (a trip which evidently also often included Adoniram Judson Gordon). Hovey also mentioned that he closely studied the whole outline of Park's course of theology as copied from two students, read nearly all of Park's published writings with interest, listened to lectures by Park at Newton on the atonement, and learned much from Park in private discourse.[107] Hovey greatly admired Park's ability to speak, his commanding demeanor, and his humor, considering these all to be confirmation of the greatness of Park and his thought.

As to Park's theology, Hovey elucidated several points central to Park's theology: the benevolence of God as fundamental in creation and redemption, freedom of choice in the moral government of God so that humans could possess moral freedom, "every sinner a sinner by choice," Jesus' sacrifice showed God's estimate of the law, and the doctrine that the Bible is true and the only perfect rule of faith and practice.[108] After this able summarization, Hovey then commented:

> In a word, the substance of Dr. Park's theological teaching was not a system of philosophy, though it was closely reasoned and profoundly philosophical; nor was it a system of ethics, though it was closely united with moral law and profoundly ethical in spirit; but it was the gospel of Jesus Christ, lustrous and vital throughout with the living and loving personality of God, and appealing to reason, to feeling, to imagination, and to will—that is, to the whole spiritual nature of man—thus proving itself to be in our own day, as in Paul's, the power of God unto salvation to every one that believeth.[109]

Hovey also admired that Park considered truth as it came from the Bible or from nature and as a teacher he encouraged freedom of inquiry. When truth was found, whether in Scripture or in nature, it was to be rigorously related to the rest of Christian understanding. Hovey also noted that: "Of the New

---

Cook, "Professor Park as Preacher and Teacher." Joseph Cook's essay is entitled: "The Tone of Awe and Self-Effacement in Professor Park's Discourses" (347–59).

    107. Hovey and Cook, "Professor Park as Preacher and Teacher," 339–41.

    108. Hovey and Cook, "Professor Park as Preacher and Teacher," 341–43.

    109. Hovey and Cook, "Professor Park as Preacher and Teacher," 343–44.

England Theology, as a scheme of religious thought, he knew all that was worth knowing, from the time of the elder Edwards to his own day."[110]

For Hovey, the most impressive and essential feature of Park was that there was a real faith behind his teaching authority. Again, Hovey's estimation of the man on this point was a significant influence on his own approach and must be quoted in full:

> He charged his pupils to call for evidence, instead of assertion; and insisted upon their bowing to the authority of universal principles and well-attested facts, rather than to his own dicta, however honest or beautiful. The personal factor however, could not be eliminated wholly. The enlightened intellect could not divorce itself from the regal conscience or the glowing heart. The teacher's experience of religious truth must affect the glance of his eye, the tones of his voice, and the place of emphasis in his speech. This is as it ought to be. There is heat as well as light in the spiritual world; and no one can lead others into the deepest life of that world, until he has felt, as well as seen, the goodness of God. No reasoning of man about spiritual things will represent the fullness of the truth as it is in Jesus, unless he has known it by the touch of faith, and learned it by the life of love. A bad man cannot be a good teacher of theology, for he does not appreciate the best part of it—the love of God which passeth knowledge. Neander was looking in the right direction when he chose for his motto: "It is the heart which makes the theologian." And in the person and life of Dr. Park, we have seen a teacher of theology whose bodily presence answered in some degree to his powerful mind and abundant knowledge; while his simple faith and ever-growing love multiplied a hundred-fold the value of his service to mankind.[111]

The indivisible connection of faith and knowledge was central to the theologian and the teacher. To understand the things of God and communicate them, one must have a vital relationship with God. This eulogy shows, and it will be evidenced in Hovey's own theology in subsequent chapters, that both in terms of theology and in method Hovey's estimation of Park can hardly be over-appreciated.[112]

---

110. Hovey and Cook, "Professor Park as Preacher and Teacher," 345.

111. Hovey and Cook, "Professor Park as Preacher and Teacher," 346.

112. For more information on how the Andover influence played out in specific Edwardsian themes, see Shrader, "New England Baptist Alvah Hovey."

European and Continuing Self-Education

When Hovey finished his studies at Newton in 1848, he took a church in New Gloucester, Maine, though he only stayed for one year.[113] He attempted to gather financial support to study in Europe but was unable due to the difficult economic times. In 1849, he accepted a call to teach at Newton, where he would end up teaching for the rest of his life. Hovey began his teaching career as Instructor in Hebrew (1849–1854) and Librarian (1849–1862). When other professors retired or took trips to Europe, Hovey often filled in and at different times became Acting Professor of Bible Literature and Interpretation (1851–1852, 1858–1859) as well as Professor of Church History (1853–1854). He began his longest-tenured position of Professor of Christian Theology in 1854.[114] Along with the changing responsibilities at the school, Hovey was ordained in Boston on January 13, 1850, and then married Augusta Rice, the daughter of the Methodist minister in town in whose home Hovey had boarded for three years, on September 24, 1852. By every account, their marriage was rich and happy and lasted until Alvah died in 1903.[115]

In the 1860s, Hovey at last gathered the finances required and took a ten-month trip (November 1861–September 1862) to Europe for the purposes of theological and cultural education with visits to Liverpool, London, Hamburg, Berlin, Göttingen, Halle, Prague, Vienna, Rome, Bologna, Geneva, Bonn, Erlangen, Tübingen, Paris, and Zurich, among others. He

---

113. This year was probably as a supply, with an eye toward possibly extending a call to pastor. See Hovey, "Narrative for My Children," 47–49. Not much is known of this church or of Hovey's time there. Joshua Millet notes that the Baptist church in New Gloucester was founded around 1780, was at times a member of the Bowdoinham Association and Cumberland Association. At the time of Millet's publication (1845), the church had their second meeting house and 114 members (Millet, *History of the Baptists in Maine*, 101, 147–49, 406, 419). See also Burrage, *History of Baptists in New England*, 196–209; *History of the Baptists in Maine*, 65, 98–101. Burrage refers to the church simply as New Gloucester Baptist Church.

114. Hovey held this until 1870 when it was broadened to the title of Professor of Theology and Christian Ethics (1870–1899). He was also President from 1868–1898, acting President (1898–1899), and Professor of Introductions and Apologetics (1899–1903). Hovey, *Alvah Hovey*, 257.

115. Augusta Maria Rice was born in Newton Centre on February 19, 1831. Her Methodist father and the Baptist minister both performed the wedding. Alvah and Augusta had five children together, though one tragically died at only a few hours old: George Rice (born January 17, 1860), Agnes Curtis (August 23, 1861–August 23, 1861), Helen Augusta (born May 13, 1863), Hattie Lee (born March 22, 1865), and Frederick Howard (born October 7, 1868). Alvah and Augusta had seven grandchildren born by the time of Alvah's death, though one of those also tragically died in childhood. See Hovey, *Alvah Hovey*, 42–43; *Hovey Book*, entries 1081, 1631, 1635.

stayed at some for several weeks (Berlin and Rome) and others for only days at a time. One major purpose to the trip was "to study the methods of management and of teaching practised [sic] at the best universities and by the most famous professors. It was to get as definite an impression of the personality of the great Biblical scholars as would be possible from an attendance in their classes for a few weeks, and from personal acquaintance with them."[116] As has been mentioned, he attended lectures by academics such as Ernst Hengstenberg, Leopold von Ranke, Isaak Dorner, Friedrich August Tholuck, Albrecht Ritschl, Johann Lange, Franz Delitzsch, Gottfried Thomasius, and Merle d'Aubigne. He regularly called on these professors for private conversation both inside and outside the universities, attended von Ranke's *Geburtstagfest*, attended multiple dinner parties at Dorner's home, and even squeezed in a trip to the Metropolitan Tabernacle in London to hear Charles Spurgeon preach.[117] Large portion of the trip was spent travelling around the major cities of Europe and observing the culture. However, in several German and Swiss cities Hovey was able to sit and listen to the lectures of theologians for extended periods of time.

Hovey's take on the trip was mixed. Margaret Bendroth rightly notes "his Vermont Baptist discomfort with the pipe smoking and snuff dipping he witnessed among the German professors. He worried about their want of piety, the lack of private and family prayer, and believed 'as never before the importance of deep and earnest love to God in all who preach the gospel.'"[118] Hovey wrote a letter back to his students of Newton dated April 17, 1862, and was careful to describe the importance of piety amid intense study:

> Doubtless I may be mistaken; but it seems to me that there is very little practical piety in the German universities. I have not had the satisfaction of hearing a theological professor or student

---

116. Hovey, *Alvah Hovey*, 76.

117. One of Hovey's journals from his trip records his thoughts about the trip to the Tabernacle: "Aug. 24, This morning we rose at the usual hour and after a good English steak went over the Thames and found the Tabernacle. There was a great crowd, 1,500 perhaps, in waiting at the doors. The house was filled. All the aisles below were crowded with persons standing. The pressure on entering was almost dangerous. The discourse of Mr. Spurgeon was plain, earnest direct, and sufficiently instructive to be profitable. . . . Mr. Spurgeon appeared to find no difficulty in making himself heard by all in the house. The members of the congregation seemed to be respectable people and to listen attentively to the words of the preacher. May he do great good!" (Hovey, "Personal Journal (Europe 1861–1862)" [AHP]).

118. Bendroth, *School of the Church*, 37. Hovey's own diary remarks: "The tobacco used in Germany is said to be not very good; but any defect in the quality seems to be made up by an increase of the quantity. Several of the professors not only smoke but take snuff" (Hovey, *Alvah Hovey*, 78).

offer prayer except in the pulpit. In Berlin and Göttingen the students have no meetings for social worship, nor do the professors ever address them, so far as I could learn, in a simple way, for the purpose of leading them nearer to Christ. The scholastic interest is not only supreme but exclusive, at least so far as I could learn.... In my intercourse with German scholars I have been made to feel as never before the importance of deep and earnest love to Christ in all who preach the gospel. Knowledge and faith should grow up together in the soul. If some men have zeal without knowledge, it is equally true that some have knowledge without love or zeal.[119]

Despite his disappointment at the lack of outward piety among the professors, Hovey took the time to note several evangelical professors and his appreciation for what he perceived to be their more conservative or evangelical stance.[120] In this category he placed Hengstenberg, Dorner, and Delitzsch. Interestingly, while in Bonn, Hovey remarked concerning Albrecht Ritschl: "Formerly a rationalist of the Rothe and Schenkel stamp he is tending steadily, I am told, toward evangelical views."[121] Hovey's estimation of Ritschl perhaps overestimated how far toward evangelical views Ritschl was moving at the time and how far he ultimately moved during his mature theological life. It does, however, fit well with the tendency with many German theologians (including some that Hovey admired much, like Dorner, though this tendency was not true of Ritschl) of the middle-nineteenth century to move away from the more rationalist theologies without travelling as far as the traditional confessional theologies and thus eventually finding mediating theological positions (*Vermittlungstheologie*).[122]

---

119. Hovey, *Alvah Hovey*, 83.

120. Hovey regularly used both the terms "evangelical" and "conservative" in this context.

121. Hovey, "Personal Journal (Europe 1861–1862)" (AHP).

122. On German mediating theology, see Schott, "Vermittlungstheologie"; Holte, *Die Vermittlungstheologie*; Aubert, *German Roots of Nineteenth-Century American Theology*, esp. chapter 3. Claude Welch has noted that to understand where Ritschl is coming from it is important to remember that he was educated by several leading mediating theologians during the most influential period of mediating theology. In sum, Welch sees Ritschl as certainly more liberal than the preceding *Vermittlungstheologen*, but still a mediating theologian of a sort who decried the pure rational approach to theology devoid of personal faith and ethical demands. By expressing the impulses of late-nineteenth-century Protestant liberalism, Ritschl became the major representative voice. See Welch, *Protestant Thought in the Nineteenth Century*, 2:1–30.

If he was not impressed by the personal life of German professors (though he admired Isaak Dorner very much)[123] Hovey certainly was by their learning and their theological influence. Indeed, he always felt the enormous responsibility to be aware of and respond to new trends in theology. This was instilled in him as a student and young professor at Newton and confirmed by his trip to Europe. Midway through his trip, when he left Tübingen, he reflected upon his time studying under eminent theologians and upon his own task as theological teacher:

> On the whole, I have found the hearing of theological lectures in this land of universities very stimulating. Occasionally, to be sure, a feeling of discouragement possessed me as I have thought of the vast amount of work which I wish to do in order to be a good teacher of the truth as it is in Christ; but this feeling has soon given place to another, namely, the feeling that I will do with my might what my hands find to do, remembering that God often takes the weak things of the world to confound the mighty. He will accept of earnest endeavors, even though the power be as nothing. I have also become satisfied that it is by no means necessary for me to restrict myself to a single department. The ablest and most successful of the German professors deliver generally two courses of lectures. Perhaps they study as much as if they delivered just one. At any rate they take a broader view of truth than they would if limited to a single department. . . . My conclusion, then, is, that I have been too anxious about the large extent of my labors, too desirous of having them restricted to a single course. Providence has seemed to require me to spread out my labors over a somewhat extended territory, and I am beginning to feel that providence is wiser than I.[124]

Hovey benefited much from the trip, but was clearly ready to return home, get to his family and work, and implement what he had learned. As he was preparing to leave Liverpool and cross the Atlantic, he noted: "Home and home duties are now getting fast hold of my thought. I wish to make a great

---

123. "Dorner is profound and earnest, a true Christian—the ablest professor whom I have met in Germany. Not less than seventy (which is nearly all the theological students in the University) attended his lectures daily. He is perhaps fifty years old, of a light complexion, rather slight, but erect and full of dignity" (Hovey, *Alvah Hovey*, 80). Hovey also relates a lengthy toast given at a dinner party to Hovey "that he might be prospered in accomplishing the purposes for which he had come to Europe, return to his own land in safety, find it in a state of peace, with liberty and law established, and labor long and usefully as a teacher of theology."

124. Hovey, "Personal Journal (Europe 1861–1862)" (AHP).

many changes in my lectures—Theology, Ethics, History. I must improve my course in each."[125]

It has been made clear by now that the importance of balancing true piety alongside serious scholarship was not lost on Hovey. He often communicated his frustration at the lack of piety among the professors, which he took to be indicative of the state of European nations.[126] Another of the lasting impressions of the trip seems to be the clear awareness of the scale of work that was left to him to do as a theology teacher in the nineteenth century. At one point on the trip Hovey opined: "As I now look forward to my return home and back over the few months which I have passed in Europe a feeling of regret arises that I have done so little, learned so little. In fact to speak the truth, I have only learned a little more thoroughly my own ignorance and the great amount of labor to be performed in making my course of instruction what it should be."[127] Hovey had read many of the professors that he sat under before he went, but the impression of sitting under their teaching and seeing their intellectual ability firsthand combined with the apparent downturn in visible piety drove Hovey to think anew of the importance of his profession.

After this trip, Hovey continued his own education through consistent reading, teaching, speaking, and writing. Because of his excellent education in languages, Hovey was able to read German, French, and Latin theological works. His own works demonstrate his familiarity with European theology, and he was also known for his reviews of contemporary European theology.[128] During his academic career Hovey was a member of several theological and literary societies wherein he was able to interact with a host of variant viewpoints. He was a part of a club for Baptist preachers in the 1850s and a club called the "Theological Circle" from 1869–1895 (affectionately referred to as the "CC"), which met to discuss book and papers.

---

125. Hovey, *Alvah Hovey*, 91.

126. Hovey made this remark about the European professors: "The higher classes of Europe are afraid of America either because they heartily believe our system of government too republican, too democratic for the good of the people, or because they fear its influence will prove in the end adverse to their particular interests" (Hovey, *Alvah Hovey*, 85).

127. Hovey, "Personal Journal (1861a)" (AHP). Hovey continued: "Have I gained the impulse which will carry me through that labor? Have I seen enough to make me consecrate myself anew to a good work and by the grace of God persist in it to the end? I am ready to flatter myself that the year has not be wholly lost in this respect. And I am anxious to believe that my future efforts will be more successful than the past."

128. In the *Baptist Quarterly*, Hovey often provided book reviews in groups of three or more. These sections were titled "Foreign Literary Intelligence," wherein Hovey would review European scholarship.

He also became a member of more prestigious clubs such as the Victoria Institute, London, and the Semitic Club of Cambridge (1881, later named the Harvard Biblical Club), which was run by liberal thinkers C. H. Toy and D. G. Lyons.[129] His students included famous liberals such as Ezra Gould and Shailer Mathews, both of whom Hovey continued correspondence with for years after. Throughout his life's work as a theologian, professor, and statesman Hovey remained aware of the international theological scene and activity worked to meet the dual need for genuine, measurable faith combined to substantive scholarship.

Hovey and the Challenges of Postbellum American Protestantism

Hovey took his European trip during the beginning of the Civil War. Prior to that point he had published a handful of articles and pamphlets as well as a biography of Isaac Backus. But it was not until he returned that he began to publish his more substantive theological works. Hovey stayed in Newton until his death, but he had several opportunities to leave. All of Hovey's siblings, and his father and step-mother, moved West by the mid-1850s. Hovey himself felt the urge to go West as he thought that was where the future theological battles would be fought. George Hovey relates several instances where institutions either asked Hovey to come or nearly did: Brown University gave consideration to calling Hovey as president in 1867; Madison (Colgate) University voted him president in 1865, which Hovey declined; and the new Crozer Theological Seminary (Upland, PA) elected him to the chair of the Interpretation of the Bible in 1867. Hovey actually accepted Crozer's call, resigned from Newton on October 1, 1867, but then rescinded his resignation a few weeks later having decided to stay in Newton. Crozer called again in 1869 offering a position, which Hovey again declined after more consideration. It was around that time (1868) that Hovey was made President of Newton, a post he stayed in for three decades.[130]

During his tenure, Hovey responded to a host of theological and practical issues that troubled his school and his denomination. In addition to being President of a seminary, Hovey published dozens of articles, books, and pamphlets and delivered many papers and speeches on topics of controversy. As his son relates, "The position of Doctor Hovey in the denomination had gradually come to be unique. In New England among Baptists he had long been a kind of authority on all difficult religious questions. To

---

129. Hovey, *Alvah Hovey*, 150–53.
130. Hovey, *Alvah Hovey*, 116–27.

a large degree this confidence in his breadth of information and soundness of judgment had now spread far beyond New England."[131] Based on his reputation, it was suggested by several other Baptists, including John Broadus, that Hovey should be the general editor of a Commentary on the New Testament, to which he agreed in 1876. Over the next two decades, this commentary set created several controversies related to biblical criticism. Despite these controversies, and his age, Hovey was still asked to be General Editor of the Old Testament commentary beginning in 1893 (a task which was still in process at the time of his death in 1903).[132]

Outside of his editing, Hovey dealt directly with biblical criticism when he published a book defending the miracles of Christ. His first book after returning from his European educational trip was *The Miracles of Christ As Attested by the Evangelists* (1864) in which he strongly argued the case for each of the miracles of Jesus to be authentic (responding chiefly to Baruch Spinoza and David Friedrich Strauss).[133] He also provided several reasons that had been given for rejecting the testimonies for miracles and then responded to each objection (responding mainly to David Hume).

In addition to biblical criticism, Hovey was aware of the theological climate that was changing, especially as challenges to more conservative views surfaced. In 1872, Hovey published *God With Us: Or, The Person and Work of Christ, with an Examination of "The Vicarious Sacrifice" of Dr. Bushnell*. As the subtitle suggests, Hovey provides a ninety-page review of Bushnell's famous book of 1866 (and republished in 1871) wherein he heavily critiqued Bushnell's view of Christ and his work.[134] Hovey was also the chairman of

---

131. Hovey, *Alvah Hovey*, 173.

132. The Old Testament commentary set was long planned before 1893. In a letter from 1890, John Broadus wrote to Hovey indicating why he and Professor Manly from Southern wanted Hovey to be the editor of the Old Testament as well: "It would seem a natural thing, and in itself appropriate, that you should go on to this after doing the other. You have made a decided success of the other, and would carry prestige to the new enterprise, besides the hold which you so justly have upon the confidence of the whole Baptist brotherhood. Your assured orthodoxy, sound judgement, and kindly tact in dealing with men would find an especially important field for exercise in this undertaking. I have talked the matter over with Dr. Manly, who thinks well of the scheme, and thinks most decidedly that you are the man to carry it through" (John A. Broadus to Alvah Hovey, July 16, 1890 [AHP]).

133. Hovey, *Miracles of Christ*.

134. Bushnell, *Vicarious Sacrifice*. Christology remained one of the primary foci of Hovey's theological corpus to the end of his life. Anticipating those who may charge him with a lack of charity, Hovey provided an apology for his response to Bushnell. Hovey saw his response not as a desire to stir up religious controversy, nor as demeaning criticism against a distinguished author, but as an issue of truth. In Hovey's mind, "both the precept and the example of Paul authorize the servants of Christ to contend earnestly

the pulpit committee that called William Newton Clarke to be the pastor of the First Baptist Church in 1869.[135] Clarke famously struggled with the New Theology during his decade in Newton, eventually moving to Canada where he published several books evidencing liberal theology.[136] Certainly aware of Clarke's liberal theology, in contrast to his own conservatism, Hovey and Clarke remained especially close friends up until Hovey's death in 1903.[137] Hovey was also good friends with Augustus Hopkins Strong, who famously proposed a controversial idea for how to understand God's interaction with the world, which he called "ethical monism,"[138] a view which Hovey consistently rejected.[139]

With biblical criticism and more progressive theological views, several theological doctrines were at stake. At the heart of each, the authority of the Bible, the nature of revelation, and the how to come to terms with the changing theological and philosophical world around them were of critical importance.[140] But these were not the only places where questions

for the faith once delivered to the saints" (Hovey, *God With Us*, viii). Bushnell's work failed in an essential point. "The teaching of 'The Vicarious Sacrifice,' if defective, as I think, by denying any reaction of the Atonement upon the mind of God, is profoundly erroneous, and its influence must be even more hurtful, in many respects, than it would be if it embraced less truth and uttered it with less power." Christology was particularly important to Hovey both as a matter of theological importance and as religious duty.

135. He also later chaired the committee that called E. Y. Mullins to the same pulpit in the 1890s.

136. See especially, Clarke, *Sixty Years with the Bible*; *William Newton Clarke*; *Outline of Christian Theology*.

137. The theological method of Hovey will be addressed in subsequent chapters and will take note of the differences between Hovey and his contemporary Baptists. On Hovey and Clarke's friendship, see the memorial address that Clarke delivered at Hovey's funeral, Clarke, "Dr. Hovey as a Theologian."

138. The clearest statement of Strong's ethical monism appears in his final *Systematic Theology*: "Ethical Monism is that method of thought which holds to a single substance, ground, or principle of being, namely, God, but which also holds to the ethical facts of God's transcendence as well as his immanence, and of God's personality as distinct from, and as guaranteeing, the personality of man" (Strong, *Systematic Theology* [8th ed.], 105).

139. An extended discussion of the back and forth between Hovey and Strong on the issue of monism is given in chapter 6.

140. On these issues in Strong and Clarke, see Brown, "Theology of William Newton Clarke"; Henry, *Personal Idealism and Strong's Theology*; Howe Jr., "William Newton Clarke"; Moore Jr., "Rise of Religious Liberalism"; Wacker, *Augustus H. Strong*; Priestley, "From Theological Polemic to Nonpolemical Theology"; Richardson, "Augustus Hopkins Strong"; Van Pelt "Examination of the Concept of the Atonement"; Thornbury, "Augustus Hopkins Strong"; "Legacy of Natural Theology"; Christian, "Theology of Augustus Hopkins Strong"; Aloisi, "Augustus Hopkins Strong"; Straub, *Making of a Battle Royal*.

surrounding authority surfaced in Hovey's life. There were several denominational challenges that Hovey addressed as a President and statesmen of Baptist life.[141] For instance, later in the nineteenth century, when Bible training schools were founded, the issue of the intellectual life for Baptists re-emerged, and Hovey continued to hold for higher educational standards.[142] Without question, Hovey faced a wide spectrum of challenges in the last third of the nineteenth century.

The Question of Authority

This chapter has considered the theological context of Hovey as it is important to consider the theological tools he had at his disposal as he faced the new theological challenges. In his early family life and education Hovey was instilled with a solid Calvinistic upbringing and conversion and he received a solid educational base and work ethic. As Hovey went to school, the major challenges were how to establish authority within the theological enterprise based on the tendency to democratized sources and methods and how to construct a theology with this new tendency toward the need to be reasonable. At Dartmouth, Hovey received a solid liberal arts and language preparation with perhaps some theological content in the New England Theology tradition as well as a distinct theological method that suggested a foundational position for a preconceived theological system. When he went to Newton, he inherited an atmosphere of high academic standards, free inquiry, no confessional standard, biblicist theological reasoning,[143] an emphasis on education, as well as Baptist theology. Andover influenced Hovey through Moses Stuart's scientific interpretation of the Bible (though Hovey's insistence on biblicist reasoning still holds), Edwards Park's vital connection of learning and faith, as well as more explicit exposure to the New England

---

141. Some other foci include his works on eschatology, ethics, and denominational distinctives. See Hovey, *State of the Impenitent Dead*; *State of Men after Death*; *Biblical Eschatology*; *Manual of Systematic Theology*; *Studies in Ethics and Religion*; *Close Communion*; *Restatement of Denominational Principles*; *Commentary on the Gospel of John*; *Commentary on the Epistle to the Galatians*.

142. More can and will be said about this subject. Chapter 3 of this work will explore this and other themes related to Hovey and education. Chapter 5 will look at select theological challenges. On Hovey, Newton, and the Boston Missionary Training School (the A. J. Gordon school), see Gibson, *A. J. Gordon*, 131–42; Brackney, *Congregation and Campus*, 345–53; Bendroth, *School of the Church*, 105–9.

143. Again, I am using the phrase "biblicist theological reasoning" to refer to the tendency to (1) utilize a scientific approach to Scripture, to (2) resist allowing any theological system or statement to influence biblical interpretation, to (3) utilize any source of truth, and to (4) build a positive theology from this basis.

Theology. Hovey's trip to Europe and his continuing efforts at self-education reinforced the requirement for deep scholarship and also the importance of faith for the theologian.

Hovey addressed several theological challenges in several different ways during his time at Newton. Education, his constructive theology, biblical criticism, progressive theology, and various denominational squabbles all received his attention. In each of these the challenge of authority appears and provides explicit windows into the ways he used his training to answer these challenges. Again, the primary question this book is asking is: Granted that Hovey lived in a time of significant theological upheaval wherein theological and biblical authority were changing and contested concepts, in what ways did he, an early Baptist seminary theologian, understand theological and biblical authority?

When considering the challenges that Hovey faced in the later nineteenth century, a few points by way of summary help as they lead into the primary questions that the subsequent chapters will address:

First, education is an important topic and speaks directly to the question of authority. Hovey clearly taught within the Baptist stream that put a lot of emphasis on educational training. This produces several questions: what role or authority did additional education provide that the less educated did not have? Was the educated pastor and/or professor more authoritative than the less educated and on what grounds? Not all Baptists found extensive education necessary, and the resulting discussions provide some evidence of Hovey's view of authority.

Second, Hovey's theological method is important to delineate as it is the most explicit place in which Hovey speaks to the issues of biblical and theological authority. His anthropology, epistemology, bibliology, soteriology, and where they locate authority need to be discussed, especially considering the historiographical import of Hovey's conservative theology.

Third, seeing that Hovey engaged with biblical criticism in his personal life and his scholarly writing, in what ways did he understand biblical trustworthiness and authority in relation to the projects of biblical criticism?

Finally, Hovey faced the issue of authority in several different situations within his denominational life as a Baptist. In these situations, in what ways did Hovey understand and appeal to authority?

3

The Ideal of Theological Education

"But as these old members passed off the stage, and a new race took their places, who required more cultivation in their preachers, and as these preachers themselves became more and more sensible of their deficiencies in mental culture, they began to cast around them for the best means of attaining it."[1]

WRITING IN 1860, DAVID Benedict penned the above words in an effort to explain the differences between the common Baptist attitude toward education in the early nineteenth century and that of the mid-century. According to Benedict, the "old members" were those who were converted during the New Light Stir of the late eighteenth century.[2] They valued extemporaneous preaching and felt that the only qualification needed was a call to preach. With a new generation of Baptists came a new concern for education. Benedict noted and discussed the new forms of education that were present by 1860, but even more forms appeared by the end of the century.

1. Benedict, *Fifty Years Among the Baptists*, 298–99.
2. The New Light Stir of the 1780s was one major revival event that bridged the so-called First and Second Great Awakenings. Thomas Kidd and Barry Hankins are correct when they assert: "For Baptists and other evangelicals, the First Great Awakening bled into the Second" (Kidd and Hankins, *Baptists in America*, 78). There is no definitive history of the New Light Stir. For Baptist involvement in this time period and especially involvement in the late eighteenth-century revivals, see Marini, *Radical Sects in Revolutionary New England*; Goen, *Revivalism and Separatism in New England*; Lindman, *Bodies of Belief*; Bebbington, *Baptists through the Centuries*, chapter 6; Kidd and Hankins, *Baptists in America*, chapter 5.

This chapter will offer a brief exposition of nineteenth-century Baptist educational history before providing a detailed discussion of Hovey's personal understanding of Baptist education. The purpose is to present in what ways Baptists, and Hovey in particular, understood theological education to affect authority. In other words, did the more theologically educated person have more theological or pastoral authority than the less (or non-) educated?

Baptists and Theological Education in Nineteenth-Century America

Several models of theological education were utilized by Baptists in the nineteenth century. After David Benedict wrote the comment above he went on to say: "Some of them engaged in a course of self-teaching, some obtained the aid of ministers and men of other callings near them, while others went to neighboring academies, and a few, by dint of effort, pursued a college course, even after they had become settled pastors, and had families growing up around them."[3] Much of the educational standards that Baptists held to in the early nineteenth century were inherited from the previous century. Thus, while it is correct to say (along with Benedict) that the nineteenth century brought a fresh demand for more Baptist education, it is also true that Baptists have strong educational roots in the eighteenth century. As Robert Torbet has noted about "the formative period of education to 1850":

> While Baptists traditionally have not placed education foremost in the requirement of their ministers, insisting first of all upon personal piety and the leading of the Spirit in preaching, they have not disregarded education and many have devoted themselves diligently to its promotion. While the majority have regarded it sufficient for laymen to know how to read the Bible for themselves, many have realized the importance of a trained ministry. Hence, Baptists were participants in the academy movement that began in the Colonies in the eighteenth century.[4]

Prior to any institutional forms of Baptist education, there were limited choices. Leon McBeth noted that "Baptist ministers who desired education had three choices. They could return to England, which a few did before the Revolution made that less feasible; they could read on their own;

---

3. Benedict, *Fifty Years Among the Baptists*, 299.
4. Torbet, *History of the Baptists*, 305.

or they could attend Harvard or Yale, especially later in the century."[5] Self-taught ministers were most prevalent as this method was "the oldest form of ministerial formation"[6] in the first couple centuries of Baptist history. And it should be understood that not all who took this route were contrary to education. It was simply a matter of opportunity and means.

Mentoring was another common method of ministerial training, especially for those who sought to fulfill the legal requirements to be recognized as a minister.[7] This method could take anywhere from one to five years to obtain the necessary experience. American Baptists owe much to their British counterparts in this regard, as the British dissenters looked to mentoring as a means to educate, which eventually developed into several well-organized schools where mentoring was performed.[8] But on the whole, American Baptists did not develop the academies for ministerial training as the British did. Rather, formal ministerial and theological education mostly imitated other American denominational standards. "In the American Colonies a different culture of learning and accompanying institutional development ensued. The model became the establishment of Harvard as a college with pretensions to be a university like Oxford or Cambridge."[9] The self-taught and mentoring models enjoyed great success, particularly on the frontier, but as the need grew for more educational opportunities for ministers and for laypeople alike, Baptists utilized several institutional models.[10]

5. McBeth, *Baptist Heritage*, 235. McBeth goes on to say: "However, Baptists faced harassment and second-class treatment at these schools. Further, many were proselyted to the state religion before graduation, giving rise to the saying that you could send a Baptist to Harvard but could not get one out."

6. Brackney, "Development of Baptist Theological Education," 86.

7. Benedict, *Fifty Years Among the Baptists*, 299; Brackney, "Development of Baptist Theological Education," 86–87.

8. Brackney, "Development of Baptist Theological Education," 87–88; *Congregation and Campus*, 47–51.

9. Brackney, *Congregation and Campus*, 51. That American Baptists imitated the educational models of other denominations is well-attested. Sweet, "Rise of Theological Schools in America," 271–72; Short, "Baptist Training for the Ministry," 227–34; Torbet, *History of the Baptists*, 305; McBeth, *Baptist Heritage*, 235; Leonard, *Baptist Ways*, 128, 171–74.

10. William Brackney has written much on the history of American Baptist education and has provided a few lists of Baptist educational institutional types. In his 1999 article he listed five types of historical models for theological education: classical college, the William Staughton school (mentoring school), the manual labor school, the literary and theological school, and the theological seminary (Brackney, "Development of Baptist Theological Education"). In his 2008 book, Brackney expanded his considerations to more than only theological education to any type of Baptist educational institution, wherein he presents six models: the classical college, literary and theological schools (along with manual labor schools), schools for special interest groups (such

The Rhode Island College (chartered in 1764) was the first Baptist college in America.[11] In an era of established churches, Rhode Island was chosen by the school's founders (who were mostly from the Philadelphia Association) because it was "practical and expedient" since the colony had more ability to attain educational charters "free of any sectarian religious tests."[12] The purpose of the Rhode Island College (which was renamed Brown University after a monetary gift from alumnus Nicholas Brown Jr. in 1804) was to train pastors, clearly imitating other colonial, denominational models. The heart of these models of education was an emphasis on a general education with an emphasis on Latin and Greek (classical education). Through the leadership of James Manning, Jonathan Maxcy, Asa Messer, Francis Wayland, and Barnas Sears the school matured and became well established.[13] Many other colleges followed the example of Brown in the establishment of a classical model of education and then evolving into a university. This model "wanted more than a theological college, both in breadth and recognition."[14]

While Brown was the major producer of Baptist leadership, Baptists started many more colleges and also attended several of the other denominational colleges, especially Yale, Princeton, and Dartmouth. Among Baptist denominational colleges, William Brackney has suggested that there were essentially four prongs.[15] The first prong was the Northern schools, which generally followed the pattern of one school per state. The second prong was the Southern schools, which generally followed the pattern of regional schools. The third prong was the colleges established for various special interest groups, such as freed slaves, women, and Native Americans. The

---

as women, freed slaves, and Native Americans), Baptist universities, seminaries, and Bible colleges (Brackney, *Congregation and Campus*, 44–46). Brackney also discusses theological schools in America in his 2004 book, but his purposes are not to outline various specific models but to trace discernible and genetic theological traditions (Brackney, *Genetic History of Baptist Thought*, 251–54). My presentation is interested in theological education as it overlaps with Hovey's life and so my presentation will look most like his 1999 list, though I will include some discussions of the Baptist universities and Bible colleges. In any case, I am indebted to Brackney's scholarship in the content of my presentation.

11. Glenn Miller has argued that it would be more proper to call it a "public" institution and not a Baptist school because it was quite liberal or free from religious tests (Miller, *Piety and Intellect*, 317). William Brackney counters this argument and describes it as unsubstantiated in Brackney, *Congregation and Campus*, 53–54.

12. Backus, *History of New England*, 2:137.

13. On the history of Brown, see Guild, *History of Brown University*; Bronson, *History of Brown University 1764–1914*; Phillips, *Brown University*.

14. Brackney, *Congregation and Campus*, 62.

15. Brackney, *Congregation and Campus*, chapter 4.

fourth prong was the various colleges that were organized by smaller Baptist denominational groups, such as Swedish Baptists, Landmark Baptists, and Freewill Baptists. In summary, Brackney commented: "To the credit of tenacious schools, the support of thousands of congregations, and the contribution of astute administrators, by the early twentieth century various sections of the Baptist family created the most expansive and comprehensive system of higher education of any religious group in the United States or Canada."[16] Baptist colleges proliferated during the nineteenth century and provided a variegated source of education for pastors and laypeople alike.

While the college model helped to produce a more general college education in preparation for ministry, Baptists utilized additional forms of education to provide more specifically theological education, often without the educational requirements of a college. Two of these models were aimed at elementary and secondary education, particularly in more rural locations. The Manual Labor School model was popular in the 1830s and 1840s. It was European in origin and it aimed at providing skilled-labor training combined with theological education. This model proved popular to many as it provided mental, physical, spiritual, and economic preparation.[17] The South claimed more manual labor schools than the North. Schools started in this model often saw themselves as college preparatory schools and so it is no wonder that manual labor schools sometimes developed into colleges and universities.[18] Manual labor schools were eventually superseded by colleges and by a more successful college preparatory model, the Literary and Theological Institute.

The "L&T" model "was a hybrid of a ministerial training school that focused upon theological courses for the training of Baptist ministers plus a program of courses of a general literary kind for both ministers and other students." In other words, "It was an amalgam of the philosophy that a liberal education was preferred for pastors and those who after 1815 would advocate a professional and focused type of ministerial training."[19] This model raised the long-standing question of whether ministry preparation should be more literary or more theological. Some, especially on the frontier, considered this form of education to be sufficient for ministry preparation, while many others did not. From its beginning, the purpose of the L&T school

16. Brackney, *Congregation and Campus*, 138.

17. See Graham, "From Patriarchy to Paternalism."

18. Brackney notes that among Baptists, "those post-secondary schools with a manual labor heritage are Colby, Colgate, Newton, Wake Forest, Furman, Denison, Franklin, Kalamazoo, Shurtleff, and Richmond" (Brackney, *Congregation and Campus*, 71).

19. Brackney, *Congregation and Campus*, 86.

was temporary. In many cases they were designed to be the beginnings of a college or university. The fact that the L&T schools had state charters was highly beneficial for an aspiring college that wanted to grant degrees. The most normal course of development was for the literary side of the L&T to develop into a college[20] and the theological side of the L&T to develop separately (which could mean an independent seminary department at a university, transfer their programs elsewhere, or close altogether).[21]

Baptists began utilizing the university model in the North first (with Brown University) and then the South. In actuality, the Northern Baptists were behind other Northern denominations while the Southern Baptists were ahead of other Southern denominations. Rochester University (1850) was a major success story as it was the first Baptist university that was founded as a university;[22] and, due to its location in a booming industrial city and its leading faculty, thrived financially and developed a strong reputation. Several further universities were founded across the United States with mixed successes. Funding and denominational support (both in terms of money and students) were the main hurdles to survival. The "new" University of Chicago (1892)[23] was the first truly research university that Baptists started.[24] The combination of gifted leadership under William Rainey Harper and huge financial support from John D. Rockefeller helped spawn a new era of Baptist education. Though beyond the purview of this work, with the founding of the new University of Chicago and further developments of other Baptist universities in the early twentieth century, there was a steady move away from explicitly Baptist identity among many of the historically Baptist schools.[25] Within nineteenth-century Baptist life, the university model was followed in various ways with various levels of success.

The model of theological education to which Hovey was most connected was the post-graduate school that was designed with the specific purpose of theological training of ministers. This theological school was

20. More development and tendencies arose from the L&T schools, such as the development of "religion" majors that were a natural outflow of the combination of literary and theological studies but that had not been part of the classical college structure. On these further developments, see Brackney, *Congregation and Campus*, 86–102.

21. Brackney, "Development of Baptist Theological Education," 90.

22. Rosenberger, *Rochester and Colgate*; *Making of a University*.

23. The "old" University of Chicago was started in 1856, though it was plagued with the Great Fire of 1871, financial downturn in 1873, and another fire in 1874 that left the school in financial ruin. The "new" University of Chicago enjoyed much different success. See Storr, *Harper's University*; Brackney, *Congregation and Campus*, 216–25; Straub, *Making of a Battle Royal*, chapter 4.

24. Brackney, "Baptists Turn Toward Education," 133–35.

25. Brackney, *Congregation and Campus*, 250–51.

sometimes attached to a university (such as at Rochester and Madison) or sometimes a stand-alone theological school (such as Newton). "Technically speaking a theological school is a post-graduate institution that offers courses toward degrees, diplomas, or certificates for the professional training of ministers."[26] Several reasons have been given for why Baptists started their post-secondary theological schools and a few points are generally agreed upon.[27] First, there was a strong desire to imitate the other denominations around them, particularly in the North. Second, there was a need for more sophisticated clergy to meet the challenges of the day, especially as first-rate theological production was becoming more and more of a specialized task. As the options for theological training multiplied, the debate surrounding the inherent worth and necessity intensified. Each model was considered for its thoroughness of ministry preparation, its financial feasibility, and the length of preparation time.

One historical example of the place of education within Baptist life is important. Barnas Sears, who was discussed in the previous chapter as having taken the mantle of Irah Chase at Newton Theological Institute, was outspoken in the area of education. In 1853, The New York Baptist Union for Ministerial Education met in Rochester, New York, for a week of meetings and for a celebration of the recent (1850) founding of the Rochester University and Seminary. What most people came for was an expected confrontation of ministerial training views. Francis Wayland, the president of Brown University at the time, stood and delivered a passionate (three-hour!) appeal. He argued that while seminary education was good, it was not the sole method needed and it needed to guard from becoming a specialist's degree. Rather, because there was such a need for pastors on the frontier, more expedient means must be also utilized, such as pastoral apprenticeship or a solid undergraduate degree. As a contrary voice, Barnas Sears stood and gave a no less passionate (though only two-hour) speech. Sears saw the coming wave of higher education in America as a greater need than mass-producing ministers. He felt that if Baptists could not produce top-flight thinkers then they would sink under the rising tide of intellectual questions facing them. The Wayland-Sears debate was not the only or the last time Baptists disagreed over education, but it was perhaps the paradigmatic

---

26. Brackney, *Congregation and Campus*, 254.

27. For various reasons, see Sweet, "Rise of Theological Schools in America," 271–72; Torbet, *History of the Baptists*, 305–19; Leonard, *Baptist Ways*, 173; Brackney, "Development of Baptist Theological Education," 90; "Baptists Turn Toward Education," 130–32; *Congregation and Campus*, 253–56. Though a few variants are offered, all recognize the desire to imitate other denominations and the desire for more educated/specialized clergy.

confrontation.[28] Benedict, in the same passage cited at the opening of this chapter, clearly takes the side of Wayland and argues strongly against stand-alone theological seminaries, though he does think there is a place for seminaries attached to Baptist universities.[29] In contrast, as will be seen in more detail below, Hovey explicitly accepted the position of Sears.[30]

Toward the end of the nineteenth century another institutional form of theological education surfaced among Baptists: the missionary or pastoral training school.[31] These schools were designed to meet a specific need to train pastors and missionaries in a more expedient manner than in a theological seminary. The Freewill Baptists had a school beginning in the 1840s where they trained their ministers. This school was loosely organized and eventually joined Bates College in 1870.[32] This model of training workers for a pressing ministry need under a curriculum that was heavily concentrated on ministerial preparation rather than any kind of classical model is also seen in later training schools. Baptist pastor Adoniram Judson Gordon started the Boston Missionary and Training School in 1889. This school followed the nondenominational model of Nyack Missionary Training College (1882) and Moody Bible Institute (1886) in its organization. And, it was followed by further such schools (Baptist and not) in the twentieth century.[33] This model generated much discussion and controversy, even in the nineteenth century. Again, the discussion surrounded the stretching of limited

---

28. For a great overview of this debate, see Short, "Baptist Training for the Ministry." Short's take is that Sears and Wayland saw differing needs but both felt the pinch of Baptist finances. Thus, while they remained cordial friends (Sears actually succeeded Wayland as President of Brown in 1855), they were aware that Baptist education could not have it both ways.

29. Benedict, *Fifty Years Among the Baptists*, 302–4. Benedict's primary concern was twofold: the high cost of stand-alone schools, which he believed could be alleviated by attaching to a university; and the general superfluity of advanced theological study that will only benefit a few. He suggested a finishing school for those who would be presidents of colleges and/or professors.

30. Hovey, "Doctrinal Theology for Christian Pastors."

31. Brackney provides an entire chapter on "Baptists and the Bible College." He sees four categories of Bible colleges: "The pastoral training school, the congregation-based institutes/colleges, the denominationally sponsored post-secondary institutions, and interdenominational Bible schools in which a significant number of Baptists have been trained" (Brackney, *Congregation and Campus*, 344). Of these categories, the only one that has roots in the nineteenth-century is the pastoral training school. This model was also called the missionary training school in the contemporaneous literature.

32. Brackney, *Congregation and Campus*, 345–47.

33. On the Gordon school as well as other Baptist Bible schools, see Houghton, "Contribution of Adoniram Judson Gordon," chapter 6; Gibson, *A. J. Gordon*, chapter 7; Brackney, *Congregation and Campus*, chapter 9.

educational finances to support further schools, the necessary education for a minister, and the debate about the scarcity of ministers.[34]

Brackney is certainly correct to say that "the Baptist pilgrimage in higher education has been an impressive struggle against the odds of an unlearned ministry, too many experiments for a fledgling denominational tradition, and inadequate financial resources. Yet, overall the Baptist accomplishment is without question and worthy of comment."[35] Baptists found multiple ways to provide theological education to their people. This development was never without disagreement or controversy. From the very beginning, Baptists pushed back against the need for any theological education. And with each successive step of further education, the debate on the educational requirements on ministers surfaced. Many of these debates were about the practicality of executing such endeavors, but there were also clear discussions that more education was dangerous because it could lead to false pride and a false sense of authority. Hovey lived within this ongoing debate and he often lent his not inconsiderable opinion. The brief history outlined above intersects at many points with Hovey's life. Further, on several occasions he was intimately faced with the question of education which couched within them the question of theological and institutional authority. It is to Hovey's personal interactions with Baptist education and how these evince his understanding of theological education that we now turn.

Hovey and the Authority of Education

As the second chapter showed, Hovey personally experienced several of the above educational models, but it was his long tenure at a post-undergraduate seminary that deserves the most attention, especially since he served as a president for three decades. Within his time in Baptist theological education, Hovey interacted with the Baptist debate over education several times and in several different ways, all of which provide understanding to his view on the authority of theological education.

There was remarkable consistency over Hovey's career when he wrote about education. Hovey began his teaching career in 1849 and as early as 1856 he was publishing his discussions on the necessary preparation for ministry. Toward the end of his life in his 1892 work, *Studies in Ethics and Religion: Or, Discourses, Essays, and Reviews Pertaining to Theism,*

---

34. See, for example, Johnson et al., "Missionary Training Schools"; Vedder, "Editorial Department."

35. Brackney, "Baptists Turn Toward Education," 128.

Inspiration, Christian Ethics, and Education for the Ministry,[36] as the subtitle makes plain, Hovey collected and wrote essays on several topics. The section on "Education for the Ministry" contained five essays on the subject, some of which had been published or presented at some point prior.[37]

The first essay, "Preparation for the Christian Ministry"[38] was first delivered on October 29, 1856, at North Adams, Massachusetts.[39] The second essay, "Value of Systematic Theology to Pastors,"[40] has an interesting history. This essay was first published in 1863. Shortly after returning from his European education, Hovey wrote the article for *The Christian Review* and titled it: "Doctrinal Theology for Christian Pastors."[41] An introductory note to that article explains that it is "a Discourse preached before the New York Baptist Union for Ministerial Education, May 13, 1863, at Rochester." Further than these two published versions, the Alvah Hovey Papers contain a lecture entitled: "The Study of Theology by Pastors," which document also notes that this lecture was delivered as part of his theology class under the "Benefits of this Course of Study."[42] The 1863 article, the 1892 essay, and the hand-written lecture are nearly identical manuscripts. The difference is that they have different introductions and conclusions (each tailored to their audiences) along with some minor stylistic variances. The one major difference is the 1863 article, which has a six-page addendum that discusses specifically how the theological school is ideal in accomplishing the proper theological training needed for pastors. The hand-written lecture has a few differences in word choice, such as utilizing the phrase "Systematic Theology" whereas the published versions have "Christian Theology."[43] This rather inconsequential difference does not change the substance of the argument but it does suggest that the hand-written lecture predates the 1863 essay,[44] which is plausible since Hovey first began to lecture on theology in

---

36. Hovey, *Studies in Ethics and Religion*.

37. For the sake of clarity in regard to which essay within *Studies in Ethics and Religion* is being referred, I will note each essay with a separate title rather than simply pages within the collected work.

38. Hovey, "Preparation for the Christian Ministry."

39. This historical note is in an endnote in the 1892 version. Hovey, "Preparation for the Christian Ministry," 475.

40. Hovey, "Value of Systematic Theology to Pastors."

41. Hovey, "Doctrinal Theology for Christian Pastors."

42. Hovey, "Study of Theology by Pastors" (AHP).

43. Hovey, "Study of Theology by Pastors," 13 (AHP); cf. Hovey, "Doctrinal Theology for Christian Pastors," 654; "Value of Systematic Theology to Pastors," 486.

44. In other words, it is more likely that Hovey used "Systematic Theology" before the 1863 and 1892 versions and then changed the phrase to "Christian Theology" in

1854. Whenever Hovey first began utilizing this lecture within his theology lectures, the important point is simply to say that from the early days of Hovey's theology lecturing through the latter years of his teaching career his arguments presented within these three versions remain nearly identical in the words themselves, let alone substance, thus showing consistency of view across his career.

The third essay in the 1892 book provided no indication that it was written previously, but the fourth essay was. These are entitled "Character Tested by Religious Inquiry"[45] and "Post-Graduate Fellowships."[46] The fifth essay, "A Good Church History,"[47] was first delivered on June 28, 1854 as: "An Inaugural Address to the Trustees and Friends of the Newton Theological Institute."[48] The church history essay does not provide so much of a defense of theological education in general as an explanation of what the content of the church history department should look like.

Though the five essays published together in 1892 provide a detailed picture of Hovey's view of education, they are not the only places he spoke to the subject. In 1876 he published an essay in *The Baptist Quarterly* entitled "Progress of a Century: The Baptists in 1776 and in 1876,"[49] wherein he discussed several places where the American Baptists have not changed and several places they have changed over the first century of the United States of America. The article has a section on education and, not surprisingly, Hovey sees this as one place that American Baptists have progressed. Also, in 1885, Hovey participated in a journal forum discussing "Reforms in Theological Education."[50] *The Baptist Quarterly* again asked Hovey (along with other leading Baptist theological educators Augustus Hopkins Strong of Rochester

---

the 1863 edition, rather than changing the phraseology between 1863 and 1892, or even after those dates. This phraseology change from "Systematic Theology" to "Christian Theology" also occurred in the titles of his published Theology textbooks: Hovey, *Manual of Systematic Theology and Christian Ethics* (1877); *Manual of Christian Theology* (1900).

45. Hovey, "Character Tested by Religious Inquiry."

46. Hovey, "Post-Graduate Fellowships." This essay was originally delivered in April 1870 before the National Baptist Educational Convention, held in Pierrepont Street Baptist Church in Brooklyn, New York. The substance of the essays published in 1870 and 1892 do not change. A few word changes exist as well as some changes under the final main point where Hovey discusses the particulars of the fellowships. Hovey reworded and rearranged this section, though the substance remains the same. The 1870 essay was published as Hovey, "Fellowships," 56–65.

47. Hovey, "Good Church History," 533–60.

48. Hovey, "Good Church History," 533n1.

49. Hovey, "Progress of a Century."

50. Hovey et al., "Reforms in Theological Education." Hovey's essay is pages 407–15.

Theological Seminary, William Newton Clarke of Toronto Baptist College, and John Broadus of the Southern Baptist Theological Seminary) to discuss the state of theological education, the necessary educational requirements for pastoral work, and if an elective system of education is preferable.[51]

Across the decades of Hovey's teaching career, he addressed the need of theological education, how it should look, how it should be reformed, and how it fits within the Christian life. In the various places he addressed the subject, Hovey displayed remarkable consistency of opinion even as he was willing to admit weaknesses and offer suggestions for improvements. In order to understand his view with some nuance, the major points of his arguments will be presented in the remaining sections of this chapter.

The Training Required for the Ministry

Throughout his writings on education, Hovey consistently argued that there were biblical requirements for the ministry which necessitated substantial theological training. He accepted that training and theological knowledge were not enough, but they could not be overlooked. His most succinct statement on pastoral requirements came in 1863: "After good natural parts—a sound mind and aptness to teach—the first qualification for the ministry, is deep piety; the second, a call from God to enter upon this work; and the third, education in its best sense, culminating in a thorough study of divine truth."[52] This three-fold qualification appears throughout his writings on education. While he certainly spends the majority of his time discussing the third part, what should be kept in mind is that Hovey refused to let the study of theology become divorced from other requirements and from the larger purpose of becoming an effective minister according to biblical standards.

Hovey exegeted several New Testament passages and concluded that a pastor has to be sufficiently mature not only spiritually but also intellectually. To take one example: "The Epistle to the Hebrews speaks of certain persons

---

51. The elective system refers to the program that some Baptist schools adapted where a student could choose which classes to take, in what order to take them, and how long they would be enrolled in school. This system was more conducive to the student who had financial struggles or the student who wanted to specialize their studies. The older system had an entirely prescribed three-year program with the more focused goal of preparing a man for the pastorate with all the tools the school felt were essential to this task. As it happened, Hovey largely stayed away from the question of electives and simply defended the older system.

52. Hovey, "Doctrinal Theology for Christian Pastors," 669. As was explained above, this 1863 article contains a six-page addendum wherein Hovey explains why he believes the theological seminary provides the best place to obtain the necessary preparation. This quote is from the end of that addendum.

The Ideal of Theological Education

who had been believers long enough to be teachers, but who still needed to be taught the first principles of Christian doctrine, to be fed with milk and not with meat. The implication is plain: one who is not sufficiently mature in knowledge and experience to profit by the deeper truths of our holy religion is not mature enough to become at once a pastor and a teacher."[53] What is implicit in this statement is that a pastor must be a teacher, and a mature one at that. Hovey found that the New Testament frequently either alluded to or explicitly said that one of the requirements of ministry was the ability to hold "fast the faithful word" to as to be able to "both exhort and to convince the gainsayers" (Titus 1:9). Further, they should be able to commit their own teaching "to faithful men, who shall be able to teach others also" (2 Tim 2:2). On this passage, Hovey argued that "if the 'others' here contemplated are faithful men looking forward to the pastoral office, the teaching here enjoined must be somewhat over and above that which is necessary to qualify one for the Christian duties of ordinary life, something indeed which may be fitly called a ministerial or a theological education."[54] Beyond these passages, Hovey looked to Matthew 10:34; Acts 4:12, 33; 20:28; 1 Corinthians 15:5; Galatians 1:7–9; 2:11; Ephesians 4:11; Colossians 1:28; 1 Timothy 4:11–13; 5:17; 2 Timothy 2:15; 3:16–17; 4:2–3; Hebrews 5:12; 2 Peter 1:16; and 2 John 10 as all giving descriptions of what the pastor needed to be able to do with their theology.[55] Hovey was adamant that a pastor needed to be a competent theologian in order to fulfill the pastoral requirement of teacher.

But it should be remembered that in nearly every place where Hovey described the need for theological training, he tempered the discussion with the need to mingle this knowledge with faith. "He must be one who clings, not to human speculation or intuition, but to revealed truth, which is sure, and worthy of all acceptance. He must be, not a rationalist, who leans to his own understanding, nor a mystic, who surrenders himself to the impulses of his own fancy or feeling, but an educated Christian, who knows and loves, and retains with the grasp of *intelligent faith*, that system of truth which was taught by Christ and his apostles."[56] He believed that the voices in the world that were contrary to Christianity were pervasive and had to be met with sound theology, but this knowledge was to be bound to the Christian life: "It is enough for any one to look abroad, and note the influences which control thought and determine conduct in the world. Men effect very little in the pastorate, unless sustained by *intelligent piety* in their

---

53. Hovey, "Value of Systematic Theology to Pastors," 485.
54. Hovey, "Preparation for the Christian Ministry," 441.
55. Hovey, "Preparation for the Christian Ministry," 447–55.
56. Hovey, "Preparation for the Christian Ministry," 440 (emphasis added).

churches; and those who succeed, by the grace of God, in transferring their own knowledge, and infusing their own spirit into a considerable number of their flock, act through them far more powerfully than they could alone."[57] The personal abilities of a pastor that would qualify him for the pastorate reached to the entire person.

Not only the personal character qualifications but also the work required of a pastor was properly understood for Hovey as multi-faceted. He described this in a few different ways. In one place he argued that the pastor's preaching should be doctrinal, polemical, evidential, and ethical.[58] This was not meant to be comprehensive, but rather a representative list designed to show the multi-faceted needs of a congregation to which the pastor's preaching must speak. In another place he argued that theology would meet rational, moral, and spiritual needs of pastors.[59] This was simply to say that the pastor is a multi-faceted being and needed to feed their own person properly in order to be able to feed others. And Hovey also argued that theology was essential in many ways: it helped pastors themselves; it helped their people; it helped evangelization of the lost; it helped in the edification of believers; it helped guard against wandering and deception; and it helped promote the usefulness of believers.[60] Pastors had a responsibility also to the wider world, according to Hovey. This was because "Christianity enlarges the heart, and makes one a citizen of the world. It unites by true charity those whom oceans separate, and pronounces every man a neighbor to his fellow. It fires the soul for action, and converts far-seeing benevolence into far-reaching beneficence."[61] This could take the form of mission work, Bible and tract distribution, education, or other benevolent ministries.

Between the responsibilities to their own flock, to the unbelievers around them, and to the general well-being of the world around them, the pastor was to attend to himself since he was called to a high office that necessitated proper preparation. Before the student became a pastor, Hovey was adamant that "His views of the cardinal doctrines should be settled."[62] This would take a thorough training in languages, history, biblical theology, and systematic theology. The pastor should be adequately settled in their views to keep them from floating away from the faith under the stresses of the job. More than just the solidification of conviction, Hovey argued that

57. Hovey, "Value of Systematic Theology to Pastors," 495–96 (emphasis added).
58. Hovey, "Preparation for the Christian Ministry," 450–58.
59. Hovey, "Value of Systematic Theology to Pastors," 478–85.
60. Hovey, "Value of Systematic Theology to Pastors," 487–96.
61. Hovey, "Preparation for the Christian Ministry," 463.
62. Hovey, "Value of Systematic Theology to Pastors," 482.

the pastor needs to have this training because he is to have as much or more ability as his parishioners. "A proper discharge of this great duty required deeper insight, larger comprehension, superior knowledge, in the realm of spiritual truth, on the part of him who teaches, than are possessed by his people."[63] The theological training of the pastor was a necessary requirement to meet the basic needs of the office and to properly elevate the pastor to be the proper theological leader and authority for the people to whom he ministered. This is authority in piety and in knowledge.

As shown above, "intelligent faith" and "intelligent piety" were phrases Hovey used to describe succinctly the pastoral requirements. This encompassed the abilities to build up believers, defend the faith, better the world, and even destroy Christianity's critics. In Hovey's 1863 article on "Doctrinal Theology for Christian Pastors" there is a paragraph that also appears verbatim in his archived lecture and his 1892 reprint. It captures well Hovey's overarching vision of ministerial qualification:

> It may be assumed that nearly all who are looking forward to the work of preaching the gospel in a Christian land expect to do this in the pastoral office. And a large share of those who are called to enter the ministry will spend their days in such a land. They ought, therefore, to be qualified for the pastoral office; and to be qualified for this office, they ought to be not only zealous and of ready-speech, but also sound in the faith, well-instructed, and able rightly to divide the word of truth. As guides and teachers they should be enriched with knowledge, scribes ready in the law, prepared to instruct the people of God, to feed the flock of Christ with heavenly food. The treasures of sacred learning should be at their command; and whatever study may be necessary to secure this should be cheerfully undertaken. In the best sense of the expression, pastors should be learned as well as devout.[64]

As has been hinted, Hovey believed that the best place one could attain the necessary theological training was at a theological training school (seminary). Why that is so, and how that school should look and function, is addressed in the following section.

---

63. Hovey, "Preparation for the Christian Ministry," 448.

64. Hovey, "Study of Theology by Pastors" (AHP); "Doctrinal Theology for Christian Pastors," 646–47; "Value of Systematic Theology to Pastors," 476.

The Preferability of Training in a Theological School

Superior to other options of training, Hovey felt that a theological school afforded the best system and opportunity for the aspiring pastor to attain the required skills. He felt this not because other systems did not have their value, but because the theological school offered the best training that could be afforded and was concentrated in its course of study.

> I do not, therefore, hesitate to say, that, in view of their contemplated work and of the time given to preparation, candidates for the sacred office need and should have the best instruction possible; nor will I withhold an expression of my belief, that our leading schools of theology do furnish instruction far more thorough and reliable than could be given by any single pastor. In this respect their utility should never be questioned. If they fail in this respect, it must be due to the grossest incompetency, or unfaithfulness on the part of teachers. And Christian knowledge, be it observed, is the first object of pursuit in ministerial education. To seek it with a proper aim is the most wholesome mental and spiritual discipline. It increases one's faith, humility, love of truth, and power to grasp and wield it in the services of the church.[65]

The expertise of school instructors was superior to the ordinary pastor because they could concentrate their attention to their areas of expertise more than a pastor could. Further, multiple professors can multiply the influence of a single pastor.[66] When one considers the arduous preparation that Hovey felt was necessary for the pastor it is not difficult to see why Hovey would advocate for what he considered the best preparation possible. While previous generations may not have had an option for such a thorough education, Hovey felt the contemporary needs demanded this training. "If the duties of a Christian pastor have been modified at all by the lapse of time and the changes of society, it is certain that they have become, not less, but more arduous than at first, demanding greater intellectual and spiritual power for their performance than ever before."[67]

It was mentioned above that Hovey felt that not only were the students required to have a multi-faceted skillset, they were also to have the

---

65. Hovey, "Doctrinal Theology for Christian Pastors," 667.

66. "It would be absurd to doubt that three or four men, devoting themselves with zeal to particular branches of sacred study must be able to communicate more knowledge than one man giving his attention for the most part to other labors" (Hovey, "Doctrinal Theology for Christian Pastors," 666).

67. Hovey, "Preparation for the Christian Ministry," 442.

major doctrines of the Christian faith largely settled by the time that they left the school. To be sure this was accomplished, and the students were sufficiently prepared, Hovey explained at length the major departments of the theological school and how they fulfilled this goal. In his contribution to the symposium in *The Baptist Quarterly Review* of 1885, Hovey listed out and explained that there were five central areas of training received at a theological school.[68] First was a study of the scriptures in the original languages. While he recognized that not all could sufficiently master the biblical languages he felt that the benefit of being able to understand better the Bible as well as the theological debates based on nuanced arguments made the original languages an invaluable tool. The second area was Christian Theology. He simply argued that, "It is difficult to see how this part of theological education can be omitted, how a young man, without a carefully formed creed as to the principle verities of religion, can be prepared to teach the way of life. It is easy to decry dogmas and systems of truth, but every man who thinks to any purpose, or teaches with any clearness, must have a system, a creed, more or less self-consistent and worthy of confidence."[69] Hovey readily admitted that the study of the Bible was more important than the construction of a theological system, but he was clear that systematic study was required.[70] This is a departure from Newton's original curriculum established by Irah Chase, who did not originally have a place for systematics, as was discussed in chapter 2. Though it does follow that of Barnas Sears.

The third area was the history of Christianity. The benefits of seeing God's work in history as well as the development of doctrine through history was too important to omit. Hovey felt that God was at work in history and the Christian historian could parse out that work through practicing history well. "By it the ways of Providence are made manifest."[71] Hovey's longer essay on "A Good Church History" provides further explanation of this point. "For, 'God is in history,' and especially in the history of his people. His presence is their 'cloud by day and pillar of fire by night.' His favor is their life, and his benediction their pledge of victory. The story of their achievements is the record of what God has wrought. And next to the infallible Word, this record brings us nearest the Holy One, and points out

---

68. Hovey et al., "Reforms in Theological Education," 410–13.

69. Hovey et al., "Reforms in Theological Education," 411–12.

70. "For, according to the present use of the expression, Biblical theology would neither embrace the evidences of Christianity, nor the Christian doctrines in a complete and orderly view, nor a full exhibition of the coherence and certainty of these doctrines" (Hovey et al., "Reforms in Theological Education," 412).

71. Hovey et al., "Reforms in Theological Education," 412.

most distinctly his way among men."[72] The fourth area was "preaching and pastoral service." The primary directive and purpose of this area is built on the idea that, "Knowledge is not enough; a minister cannot be useful unless he knows how to use his knowledge."[73] Hovey admits that many learn to preach by preaching, but he asserts that becoming an effective preacher will only by augmented by skilled instruction. The final area that Hovey listed out was elocution, by which he meant homiletics as well as general speaking ability.[74] He felt that preachers were often justly criticized for poor reading and speaking. "Everything possible, therefore, should be done to improve their speaking in regard to quality of voice, distinctness of utterance, variety of tone, and correctness of emphasis, but with the utmost care not to destroy the personal characteristics which distinguish every human voice from every other."[75]

---

72. Hovey, "Good Church History," 547. Hovey argued that the manifestation of God's work in church history reveals the great things God has done for Christianity and it makes known the "actual law of progress in Christianity" (Hovey, "Good Church History," 553). To Hovey, this means that a good study of church history would show the methods and agencies that God has used for the advancement of his purposes. Church history is also able to "foster a charitable spirit," help increase the church's "soundness of judgment upon religious questions," and it could provide wonderful examples from history for the benefit of "spiritual bearing and worth" (Hovey, "Good Church History," 558–59). In sum, church history has much value, and one of those values is the ability to see how God works and builds his church through his providence. The way to determine this working is through tracing the historical examples and seeing if they are built truly on the Word of God or on a false foundation. Hovey's postmillennialism certainly shows in his positive view of the progress of history. See Hovey, "Messianic Power in History (Incomplete Manuscript)" (AHP); *Biblical Eschatology*, 1888. Hovey accepted what would now be termed "providential" church history. This usually refers to attempts by historians to categorically label and describe moments in church history as the actual working of God's providence. The contemporary discussion surrounding the place of providential explanations of history is extensive. For a few warnings on the use of providential history, see Trueman, *Histories and Fallacies*, 166–67; Fea, *Why Study History?*, chapter 4. The debate about providence is part of the larger debate about how much a Christian ought to let his or her Christianity affect the historical practice. For a few viewpoints on such a Christian history, see Marsden, "Common Sense and the Spiritual Vision of History"; Noll, "And the Lion"; Kuklick, "On Critical History"; Bradley and Muller, *Church History*, chapters 1–2. Also see the preface and intro as well as the essays in Fea et al., *Confessing History*. For a helpful Christian debate on the place of supernatural explanations within Christian history, see Marsden and Woodbridge, "Christian History Today."

73. Hovey et al., "Reforms in Theological Education," 412.

74. In one manuscript in Hovey's papers, he refers to this as "Homiletics and Pulpit Elocution" (Hovey, "Lecture [on the Purpose of the Curriculum of Newton Theological Institute]," 2 [AHP]).

75. Hovey et al., "Reforms in Theological Education," 413.

Outside of the five main areas of the theological school curriculum, Hovey felt that there were several other benefits to this course of study. One of these benefits was the opportunity to meet and develop lasting friendships with other future ministerial laborers. "Many who are now covered with the dust of toil can bear witness to the comfort and strength which they owe to friendships formed in the Seminary, and many more to the precious results in their own characters of fraternal friction with students preparing for the ministry."[76] Hovey likewise felt that the student could find plenty of opportunities to preach and become active in local churches during their three years in seminary. Hovey also saw the possibility of including an apprenticeship for those students who needed it.[77] But the primary responsibility was the preparation of the future pastor to be theologically grounded and practically equipped to deliver that knowledge to their people. "It may, therefore, be safely affirmed that a course of theological study will ultimately assist the minister of Christ in discharging his pastoral duties, in speaking to the hearts of men as a spiritual counsellor, reprover, or comforter."[78]

Just as the office of pastor was understood to be a multi-faceted work, so also the training must be rigorous and thorough enough to prepare for this work. In sum, Hovey felt that "the work of a Christian pastor is one of surpassing magnitude and sacredness; that it calls for the deepest piety, the ripest wisdom, and the most abundant knowledge in him who would perform it well; and that a course of theological study is exceedingly desirable, is an advantage above all price, to those who are set apart to this work."[79]

Theological training by itself was inadequate, but lack of theological training was similarly inadequate. Proper theological education increased the usefulness of the pastor which provided the authority to perform their duties. Despite Hovey's feelings toward theological education, he was certainly aware of objections, and he was acutely aware of potential deficiencies in the theological school.

Caveats and Objections

Hovey clearly had very high opinions of the post-undergraduate theological education that Baptists could offer. This is not to say that he did not qualify these opinions. As a veteran educator, Hovey was well aware of the deficiencies of theological education and of the common objections that

---

76. Hovey, "Doctrinal Theology for Christian Pastors," 667–68.
77. Hovey, "Doctrinal Theology for Christian Pastors," 668.
78. Hovey, "Preparation for the Christian Ministry," 461.
79. Hovey, "Preparation for the Christian Ministry," 466–67.

critics would put forth. Sprinkled throughout his various writings on education are caveats that clarify his viewpoints as well as answers to the potential objections.

While writing about the progress that Baptists had made in the first century of the nation, Hovey admitted that education was one of the areas that saw good progress. Yet this was somewhat tempered:

> This [progress], however, is no more than might have been expected. Any other result would have been out of keeping with this age. But I cannot say that their progress in this direction has corresponded fully with the growth of the denominations. Looking at the change with the best light I have I can speak of it as an occasion for gratitude, but not for glorying. For the progress has been quite irregular, and efforts in the right direction have been limited to a small number of men. Not until recently have laymen of intelligence and influence taken hold of this work with a will, resolved to make our schools equal to the best.[80]

The lack of finances meant that Baptists were behind other denominations that had a plethora of endowed schools and could thus focus more on the quality of the education.[81] Baptists had done much good work, but without the backing of more lay people there could not be the progress to match the growth.

The limited educational development was one caveat and was closely tied to another, namely, that theological education was always bound to be an incomplete exercise. The purpose of theological education was to present a very well-rounded and mature individual, ready for pastoral duties.[82] But part of the message in the several essays he wrote was to say that

---

80. Hovey, "Progress of a Century," 479.

81. The troubled finances of Newton during the entirety of Hovey's tenure is a constant theme of his son's biography, Hovey, *Alvah Hovey*. It is also documented in Bendroth, *School of the Church*, 35–42.

82. "Human wisdom will never so perfectly balance and adjust the influences brought to bear on students for the ministry, as to give them the best conceivable culture in every direction, in thought, reason, imagination, speech, feeling and taste. To quicken the religious sensibilities and secure for them a free and full expression; to bring the imagination into vigorous use without permitting it to disturb the relations of truth; to stimulate and employ the reason, making it at the same time the ally of faith and the servant of a renewed will; to keep the mind alert, the heart open, the conscious tender; to fill the soul with enthusiasm for a lowly, self-denying, but glorious work; to call into action every power for good, and repress every tendency to evil, and to put the student in possession of all possible resources for the mission before him, is a task which no body of men yet in the flesh can be supposed to perform" (Hovey, "Doctrinal Theology for Christian Pastors," 664).

theological education in a seminary was to lay the groundwork for a lifetime of theological education.[83] This progress in theological education mirrored the progress of the Christian life (sanctification), which is to say that it was always incomplete. For this reason, Hovey was open to modification and to suggestions for how to better the seminary system.[84] Speaking to the nature of theological study and "religious inquiry," Hovey was satisfied to admit that there was an element of mystery or partial knowledge: "Partial knowledge is all we can now obtain in regard to any subject. Partial knowledge is all we can now have in matters of religion. And it is wholesome for us to bear this in mind while we investigate doctrines of surpassing interest."[85] This mystery was not a reason to lose faith or to give up on theological study, but it was a necessary limitation to keep in mind.[86]

And so, when he anticipated the charge that the pursuit of knowledge or reason could easily lead to an inordinate conception of truth, Hovey simply stated that: "Learning is not grace, scholarship is not godliness; but learning may be made the handmaid of piety, and true scholarship may be joined with faith. The vain boast of ungodly men, that they are the only fearless disciples of truth, and the pernicious doubt whether this be not so, which has been infused into the hearts of timid believers by the strange assurance of pantheists, should be met and neutralized by the education of Christian men."[87] There were limitations of theological education based on the nature of doctrine, the nature of the pastorate, and the nature of knowledge. The reality of mystery within Christian doctrine, the lifelong development needed for the pastor, and the fact that learning and reason were limited and combined with faith, all provided helpful caveats to his call for better theological education.

Beyond the caveats were specific objections that Hovey directly addressed. In some cases, Hovey felt the objections had helpful points to make, but he also felt his overall notion of theological education (with its caveats)

---

83. See Hovey, "Doctrinal Theology for Christian Pastors," 664–65; "Value of Systematic Theology to Pastors," 478.

84. He offered a few of his own, which will be discussed below.

85. Hovey, "Character Tested by Religious Inquiry," 508.

86. On the idea of mystery, Hovey worked through several theological loci and noted the points of mystery inherent in each of them. To give one example, when speaking about understanding the being and nature of God, Hovey concluded: "Thus human reason is unable to comprehend the modes of his existence, and we fall down and worship a Being whom we know but in part, whom we see through a glass darkly" (Hovey, "Character Tested by Religious Inquiry," 502–3). This notion of mystery and the limitation of reason will play heavily into Hovey's epistemology, which will be discussed in the following chapter.

87. Hovey, "Post-Graduate Fellowships," 531.

guarded against the negative aspects of these objections. In other cases, Hovey felt the objections simply did not carry the weight their proponents felt they did.

When he advocated for extended theological education, Hovey was aware that many able pastors, and many of his readers, had not had the education he was calling essential. Hovey was careful to be appreciative to many of these pastors who had neither seminary nor college education while also calling attention to why they were useful. His extended explanation of this point is important to read:

> Let me be well understood. To depreciate the usefulness of ministers who have never taken such a course is no part of my design in the present discussion. Many of this class have been signally honored by the Saviour. Their sound judgment, practical energy, deep experience, fervent piety, and persuasive eloquence, have placed them in the front rank of champions for the truth, and have endeared them to all genuine believers. We venerate the names of John Bunyan, Andrew Fuller, and Thomas Baldwin. We believe with all the heart that "Christ Jesus counted them faithful, putting them into the ministry." We recognize also with grateful joy the wisdom and efficiency of numerous pastors in our own land who have been led to omit all preparatory study, whether classical or theological, and to enter at once upon their holy work. They will, it cannot be doubted, have many able successors; and the ministry of our denomination will be largely augmented by noble men who pass directly from other callings to its blessed service. Not a few of these will be justified, we believe, by their advanced age and domestic relations, and superior intelligence in omitting a course of preparatory study. Their action in this matter will not result from any reluctance to put forth the self-denying, persistent efforts required of a faithful student, but from a conviction that the sum of their usefulness will be made the greatest by entering at once upon their ministerial work.
>
> Whether, however, some by taking this course may not neglect a more excellent way, and so fail of the greatest possible usefulness, is a question worthy of patient thought. For although one may be very efficient in his Master's service, we are not thereby forbidden to suppose that he might have been still more efficient. Although his labors may be attended by the blessing of God, we are not therefore to conclude that his way has been perfect and all his decisions right.[88]

88. Hovey, "Preparation for the Christian Ministry," 442–43.

This quotation shows that Hovey was quick to admit that there are certain times and situations where theological education has not been necessary. He further admitted that there were several noteworthy Baptist pastors who did not have the education but were still great pastors. However, hidden within these concessions Hovey made the point that that these highly useful pastors carried on the necessary theological self-education, thus fulfilling, in a roundabout way, Hovey's recommendation for lifelong theological education necessitated by the pastorate. Hovey also admitted that some pastors are called later in life or are called after they have started a family, thus making theological education quite difficult. Hovey recognized these exceptions to his rule, but he still questioned whether the lack of education was the best course. This was why he affirmed that theological education at a seminary was "exceedingly desirable for those who are about to enter the Christian ministry."[89]

Accompanied to the prior objection that God has used many pastors without formal theological education is the objection that: "Not those of superior intelligence and theological culture, it is said, have been honored most highly in preaching the Word, but those who were called directly from secular business into the service, and who possessed an amount of knowledge scarcely greater than their hearers."[90] Hovey argued that the historical record simply does not support this assertion. Hovey spent several pages walking through church history and explaining how the apostles, Paul, the apostolic companions, Polycarp, Irenaeus, Cyprian, Tertullian, the Cappadocians, Wycliffe, Huss, Luther, Melanchthon, Zwingli, Calvin, Knox, Pascal, Whitefield, Wesley, Edwards, and others all were bettered by education.[91] Hovey concluded: "It is evident from such a survey that no preachers have been more signally useful than those who have prepared themselves by much study for their work. It is evident that, in making use of human agency for the spiritual good of men, God has honored the general laws of action and influence established by himself. Knowledge and utterance have been prerequisite to success in teaching."[92] Exceptions may be found, but the best way to fulfill the Scriptural requirement to teach and pass on the faith to others is to obtain theological education.

A more realistic objection was that: "They are not practical. They do not enable students to improve their gifts. One can never learn to preach in the closet. Were these young men to read theology with a pastor, he would

---

89. Hovey, "Preparation for the Christian Ministry," 445.
90. Hovey, "Preparation for the Christian Ministry," 467.
91. Hovey, "Preparation for the Christian Ministry," 467–72.
92. Hovey, "Preparation for the Christian Ministry," 472.

call upon the now and then to stand in his pulpit, and still oftener to conduct an evening service; and their increase of practical skill would more than compensate them for the knowledge which they would forego."[93] Hovey felt that there was something to this critique, but it mostly rang hollow. The theological schools all had a sufficient number of local churches within travelling distance which allowed students to preach throughout the year by filling these empty pulpits. The summer months away from school also allowed time for pulpit experience. Hovey thought that a short time of pastoral apprenticeship was not beyond the question. This was not necessary, and it would be much shorter than the pastoral apprenticeship that many Baptists had historically pursued, but it could be helpful to some.[94]

A more serious objection was the charge that a system of theological education cannot make a pastor.[95] To this Hovey readily agreed. He felt that the calling of a preacher was the duty of the Holy Spirit to call and the duty of the church to recognize and prepare the student. Hovey felt that this charge was tied to the critique that the seminary often failed to produce adequate pastors, which Hovey felt was completely off the mark. "Do the seminaries make the ministry? Have not the churches, and the colleges, and the Spirit of the living God, something to do in this matter? We fear that theological education is held responsible for more than its share in making ministers. Let no man suppose that by any system, new or old, education can do the work of the Holy Spirit, or of the Christian churches in preparing our youth for the pulpit."[96] In other words, not only did Hovey agree that the seminary could not make the minister, but he felt that those who were charging seminaries with usurping this work were actually failing to do this work themselves. The churches needed to be intimately involved with the prospective pastor in preparation. Theological education was one piece, albeit an important one to Hovey, of the preparation.

One further objection that Hovey anticipated was that theological study tended to make reason supreme[97] or tended to turn pastors away from the Spirit toward philosophizing.[98] Hovey essentially agreed that this was

---

93. Hovey, "Doctrinal Theology for Christian Pastors," 668.

94. "It is quite possible, however, that besides a full course of study in the Seminary, many students would do well to spend a few months with a pastor, before undertaking the responsibilities of the gospel ministry over a church, especially if they are still young and without much experience in public labor" (Hovey, "Doctrinal Theology for Christian Pastors," 668).

95. Hovey et al., "Reforms in Theological Education," 409–10.

96. Hovey et al., "Reforms in Theological Education," 410.

97. Hovey, "Character Tested by Religious Inquiry," 500.

98. Hovey, "Value of Systematic Theology to Pastors," 477–78.

possible but did not agree that it was necessary. He argued that the mistake inherent in this danger was to forget the limitations of reason, particularly in regard to theological issues.[99] "For no man is wise enough to solve all the riddles of the universe. Whoever seriously undertakes to do this, will find, as John Foster well said, that the small spheres of light in which he moves about is encompassed by darkness, and that the surface of the surrounding darkness increases just as rapidly as the sphere of light increases."[100] Hovey also spoke to the claim that this led to a "philosophizing spirit" or "to quench the flame of Christian zeal."[101] Hovey agreed there was a danger that too much study could lead to pride or to the neglect of the Spirit, though he felt they did not have to. Further, there was a tendency to overreact to this danger and neglect needed study. "Let it also be remembered that, in the Christian, knowledge and faith are homogenous and inseparable."[102]

Hovey was willing to defend his conception of theological education against those who disagreed, and he recognized that providing caveats and addressing objections was a helpful way to do this. His conception of theological education was nuanced and well-developed. Beyond defending and describing what theological education was, Hovey also described further needs for theological education.

Envisioning Well-Rounded Baptist Theological Education

It has been shown that Hovey expected much from theological education because he believed much was required of a pastor. The needs of the day required that the pastor be able to communicate on multiple levels. Thus, more than a simple exposition of the theological facts of the gospel was required.[103] Pastors needed to be able to address multiple concerns based on the needs of those to whom they ministered.

---

99. Hovey also related two dangers of this "critical spirit": "They will either close their eyes to all signs of divine ways and judgments which transcend their modicum of reason, and, making themselves the measure of all things will be lifted up with vanity, or they will be troubled and humbled by the mysteries of truth, and only after many a conflict enter the paths of peace" (Hovey, "Character Tested by Religious Inquiry," 500).

100. Hovey, "Character Tested by Religious Inquiry," 500.

101. Hovey, "Value of Systematic Theology to Pastors," 477.

102. Hovey, "Value of Systematic Theology to Pastors," 479–80.

103. "Hence if the preaching of such a message is to be of any real service in leading men to Christ, this preaching must consist of something more than a bare announcement of pardon. It must appeal to intellect, reason, and conscience; it must instruct, convince, and alarm" (Hovey, "Preparation for the Christian Ministry," 446).

Some hear his message with the ear, but give no heed to its meaning. Some admit its weight, but defer action for the present. Some deny its truth, or attempt to pervert its language. Some reject the gospel of peace and devise a plan of their own. Some are careless, some busy, some reckless, and all with one consent begin to make excuse. It is therefore necessary for the ambassadors of Christ to urge their message upon reason, conscience, and heart, to depict the majesty of their King, the guilt of those who trample on his authority, the ruin which persistent rebellion will bring on them, the blessedness in store for all who accept of pardon through Christ, the nature of this act of acceptance, and the danger unspeakable of postponing it for an hour. To do this they should know, if possible, all the weapons in the armory of truth, and be able to conquer reason, pierce the conscience, alarm the fears, and touch the sensibilities. They should be able to follow up their work from week to week, giving the sinner no rest from argument, admonition, entreaty, till he is brought to cry for pardon. Swiftness of foot and strength of lungs, though moved by zeal, will not suffice for this work. Great faith, rich experience, and abundant knowledge are in full request.[104]

Hovey also believed that Baptist education had indeed improved,[105] but he thought more could be done. Interestingly, he wrote one essay calling for post-graduate fellowships for gifted students.[106] Hovey pointed out that the English universities have an admirable fellowship system that American Baptists should consider copying on at least two points. "The Fellows of a college in Oxford or Cambridge *owe their position to the eminent scholarship*, and they *draw their support from the revenues of the college*. Thus men of approved capacity are enabled to advance their knowledge and culture, by a life of study prolonged far beyond the usual limits; and from this body of scholars, go forth, year by year, accomplished teachers, preachers, and writers, to positions of the highest influence."[107] Hovey went on to argue that Baptists had this "very evident" need. Devout Christian scholars are needed in fields such as physical science, linguistic science, and indeed all areas

---

104. Hovey, "Value of Systematic Theology to Pastors," 491.

105. Hovey, "Progress of a Century," 479; Hovey et al., "Reforms in Theological Education," 410.

106. Hovey, "Post-Graduate Fellowships." In the educational symposium with Strong, Clarke, and Broadus, Hovey also was willing to allow for some elective courses "for the ablest scholars," so that they could develop areas of specialty for the benefit of the denomination (Hovey et al., "Reforms in Theological Education," 413).

107. Hovey, "Post-Graduate Fellowships," 513.

of human knowledge.[108] This was, according to Hovey, because unbelievers simply do not see things as Christians do.

The need for funding and the need to be sure that too much study does not lead to impiety were also noted by Hovey.[109] He anticipated that many young men would be tempted to go directly into ministry and not wait to gain the further preparation about which he was speaking. Therefore, encouragement was needed so they would enter this study, just as funding was needed so the students could afford this additional course and make it worth the additional time. The objection that too much study could lead to impiety was one that Hovey had previously rejected, which he did again here. He simply noted that any pursuit could "divert the mind unduly from direct efforts to save men and honor God."[110]

On the whole the need for further education for the most educated was necessary and Hovey felt there was an adequate model to follow.[111] His consistent theme was: "But whatever may be said in favor of entering the ministry with little mental culture, there can nothing be said in favor of unlearned men for teachers in the higher branches of knowledge."[112] There was a need for learned clergy and for specialists of the highest caliber.

Again, amid all the deep learning, and suggestions for how to deepen this scholarship Hovey never divorced learning from true piety. In fact, Hovey consistently wrote that one of the most serious needs was for more spiritual nurture in theological learning. Hovey ended his essay on "Reforms in Theological Education" with this: "Yet there is one thing that would do more for theological students than any change in their studies, namely, a deeper consecration to the Lord. They need just what the churches need, a fresh outpouring of the Holy Spirit, that they may go into the work of the ministry 'in the fulness of the blessing of the gospel of Christ.' The reforms to be sought in educating men for the ministry are chiefly spiritual rather than intellectual."[113] It was important that the students understand that one major purpose of theological education was to learn to use their minds properly as they studied the things of God. In other words, "It must teach—for many are they who need this instruction—the way in which a

---

108. Hovey, "Post-Graduate Fellowships," 517.

109. Hovey, "Post-Graduate Fellowships," 520.

110. Hovey, "Post-Graduate Fellowships," 520.

111. Hovey gave several further explanatory details about the post-graduate fellowships, such as suggested length, suggested areas, qualifications of these students, how they should use their time, and how much of a stipend they should receive for this task. See Hovey, "Post-Graduate Fellowships," 524–31.

112. Hovey, "Post-Graduate Fellowships," 523.

113. Hovey et al., "Reforms in Theological Education," 415.

Christian may lawfully use and refresh the faculties of his mind; so that reason, memory, imagination, conscience, and will, may all be trained to the highest perfection and made subservient in every act to the glory of God."[114]

The students' spiritual life was more important than the studies to which they gave themselves. "And if the spiritual life is not sustained by daily communion with God there is a danger of profaning the work of investigation, and of falling into the snare of intellectual pride or into the abyss of despondency."[115] It is important to note Hovey's admission here not only that study can lead to either pride or despondency, but also that study can be profaned. In another place, Hovey noted that personal character influences conclusions. This is because sin and darkness can cloud the mind.[116] Further, without the light that Christianity brings, Hovey felt that unbelievers simply did not see things as they should. Thus, Christians sensitive to the Spirit and highly trained were sorely needed.

> It cannot, then, be safe for us to neglect this vast domain [physical sciences]; for there are sounds in its atmosphere which unbelievers do not hear, there are hues in its sky which they do not see, and there are records on its stony tables which they do not read. It is therefore a part of our work, as a large body of Christians, to join them in exploring this domain—a service to the cause of truth which we can hardly render without the aid of men who have improved superior advantages for prolonged study.[117]

Hovey's point with this statement was not so much that an unbeliever cannot do exceptional work as a scientist, mathematician, historian, or linguist. Rather, he was pointing out that the personal character of a person influences conclusions. This would mean that the unbeliever, and also the believer, might twist data to their liking. The spiritual Christian could serve a helpful purpose here: "He will detect the subtle influence of personal character in shaping the conclusions of science to its will; and so he will appreciate our need of men who tried ability and ample knowledge qualify them for high intellectual service."[118]

Within the prolonged discussion surrounding the need for Christians trained at the highest academic level, the interesting conclusion that Hovey came to in regard to the relation of faith and knowledge was that full

114. Hovey, "Preparation for the Christian Ministry," 455–56.
115. Hovey, "Character Tested by Religious Inquiry," 498.
116. Hovey, "Character Tested by Religious Inquiry," 501.
117. Hovey, "Post-Graduate Fellowships," 517.
118. Hovey, "Post-Graduate Fellowships," 518.

knowledge, or at least more complete knowledge, was a spiritual test from God.[119] "Partial knowledge is all we can now obtain in regard to any subject. Partial knowledge is all we can now have in matters of religion. And it is wholesome for us to bear this in mind while we investigate doctrines of surpassing interest."[120] That we only have limited knowledge is a test from God through which Christians are to learn at least three lessons. First, Christians are to have "*reverence* towards God; for it is his works that transcend our powers; his judgments that are unsearchable; his ways that are past finding out."[121] Second, this is a lesson of *faith*. Hovey's comments here are essential to understand his view of theological education in particular and theology in general.

> For, wonderful as it seems, faith must increase with reasoned knowledge, or the Christian life will languish. This is not, perhaps, the common opinion, but it is nevertheless true. And, if you will believe it, God expects more faith in a Jew than in a Greek; in a Christian than in a Jew; and in a Christian that can reason well, than in a Christian who has little power of reflection; and he expects this, not merely because greater knowledge furnishes more nutriment to faith, but also because it reveals more difficulties for it to overcome, and lays upon it heavier burdens to bear. Brethren, permit me to say that trust in God and confidence in his revealed Word, as manifested in Jesus Christ, his Son, are not secondary matters in religious inquiry or speculation, but rather primary, essential, and vital. The whole system of Christian truth is meant for those who have put their hand in the hand of Christ, who have experienced the peace of sins forgiven, and who are not likely to be shaken from their steadfast confidence in the Lord, though they perceive that clouds and darkness are round about him. And if you refuse to walk in his fear and love, the secret of his wisdom will not be revealed to your hearts.[122]

---

119. Hovey, "Character Tested by Religious Inquiry," esp. 508–12.

120. Hovey, "Character Tested by Religious Inquiry," 508.

121. Hovey, "Character Tested by Religious Inquiry," 509 (emphasis added). Hovey also said in this regard: "At all events, it will do us good to bow our heads when we utter the name of Jehovah, and to indulge the conviction that he is worthy of profound veneration. And never, perhaps, are we in greater danger of failing in this respect than when we are called, as we believe, to get at the philosophy of God's infinite plans by the aid of the rush-light of our feeble intelligence" (Hovey, "Character Tested by Religious Inquiry," 510).

122. Hovey, "Character Tested by Religious Inquiry," 510.

Several points need to be observed here. With greater theological knowledge came more difficulties and burdens to bear. The inability of reason to give all the answers placed a premium on the Christian's trust in God and his Word. True religious conversion must be at the heart of theological study or the student will have no anchor to hold when the winds of doubt and difficulty come. Further, without a true and vital faith, theological knowledge was essentially incomplete because the depths of God's truth illuminated that faith and provided answers and understanding not found elsewhere. Hovey clearly felt that faith would be tested the more one studied their faith.

The third lesson is that of *hope*. Though there is a limitation to learning, there is hope that "the time will come when we shall no longer see through a glass darkly, but face to face, when we shall no longer know in part, but shall know even as we are known."[123] This hope was eschatological,[124] but had real benefits in the trials of the here and now. "But twilight and doubt impede our progress now, for this is our probation. We are little children, as unprepared in character as we are in mental power, to meet the blaze of fuller knowledge. Yet under the guidance of the Divine Word and Spirit we are moving in the direction of highest truth, we are slowly but surely drawing nearer and nearer to the sun."[125]

To Hovey, the study of theology brought testing from God on at least three fronts: reverence, faith, and hope. This testing needed to be understood as it was difficult. The requirement of study meant that growth in understanding was needed. The pride of knowledge had to be tempered by reverence, faith, and hope. Indeed, understanding without faith was impossible. For Hovey, this was all good news: "Take heart, then, my friends; be thankful that there are limits to your knowledge here, since those limits furnish a part of your needed discipline in virtue and piety; but fail not to be also thankful for the assurance that those limits are not fixed and ultimate."[126]

Well-rounded Baptist education, then, would need to have several parts. First, it needed an educated pastorate that could minister in a multi-faceted manner. Second, education that could produce this kind of minister had to be carried out over a lifetime, but the initial, pre-ministry preparation was best done in a post-undergraduate theological institution. Third, the need for specialists beyond the standard seminary degree was real and best modeled after the British "fellowship" scheme. Fourth, and most

---

123. Hovey, "Character Tested by Religious Inquiry," 511.

124. When it came to eschatology, Hovey held to post-millennialism, and so his language of progress should hold that idea in mind. For Hovey's treatment of eschatology and the millennium, see his published theologies as well as Hovey, *Biblical Eschatology*.

125. Hovey, "Character Tested by Religious Inquiry," 511–12.

126. Hovey, "Character Tested by Religious Inquiry," 512.

importantly, whatever mode or level of education, the character of the theological student was paramount. Faith and learning could not be divorced. At its heart, then, a well-rounded Baptist education was to produce leaders with a humble, "intelligent faith."

Conclusion: The Educational Ideal and Theological and Pastoral Authority

The opening of this chapter asked: according to Hovey, did the more theologically educated person have more theological or pastoral authority than the less (or non-) educated? He certainly did see theological education as a necessary endeavor for the pastor. They needed more understanding than their people so that they could speak with wisdom. Time at a theological school was not the only place where this understanding was gained, but it was the best place where a student could settle the cardinal doctrines and obtain the skills to continue effectively their education for the rest of their lives.

And so, according to Hovey, pastors needed more theological training, but does that mean they had more authority? He believed that the seminary-educated pastor was more useful and had more ability. This superior understanding and ability was meant to be passed on to those underneath them and was meant to be used to convince those who disagreed. Thus, Hovey did see theological education as providing more authority in certain settings. More education and more knowledge allowed one to have more usefulness and accomplish new levels of persuasion. Hovey saw more authority in their opinions on matters of doctrine and spirituality based on their increase in skill and understanding. But this added authority was only present in the person who had the proper increase simultaneously in both faith and understanding because that was where they were able to get to the deeper wisdom of God. Having a diploma was not what gave authority, it was the maturation of the whole person that brought authority. By definition this authority that came with increased understanding that needed to be tied to piety and humility, if it was genuine. Yet one could not simply assert such authority, it had to be demonstrated through argument and through example.

In the writings where Hovey discussed education, he provided an interesting glimpse of his view of theological and biblical authority. First, more understanding, which came through more education, did bring a certain level of authority both in terms of skills and theology. But second, as was shown, there was also a burden that came with more education and more understanding. It tested one's faith because it would continually probe into difficult areas. Unless there was a genuine, vibrant, and growing faith working simultaneously with the growth in understanding there would be failure. The person who could properly balance the theological life and dive into the deep things of God was also the person who could find greater wisdom and who had the responsibility to pass this on to those around them. To Hovey, the potential authority that could come when education and piety were properly mixed was not authoritarian, it was humble and wise. Yet, it was real and effective.

Hovey's educational writings give a glimpse into his understanding of authority, but these writings also raise further questions about his theological method, including themes such as sin, epistemology, soteriology, and anthropology, which the next chapter addresses.

4

Theological Method

"Weeds grow without culture, and errors flourish in the dark; but true religion claims a prepared soil, a warm light, refreshing showers, and varied culture; for it promises a perfect fruit, a living soul, large, strong, pure, complete, every faculty matured, every susceptibility refined, every stain removed. Time and culture are requisite, and the work of the spiritual husbandman is but just begun when the seed of divine truth first takes root in the regenerated heart; it must be watched and watered and kept in the sun; the weeds of error must not be suffered to take its life, nor the cares of the world to choke it."[1]

THROUGHOUT HIS THEOLOGICAL CORPUS, Hovey held certain underlying presuppositions which influenced his theological framework, organization, and content. What the presuppositions, framework, organization, and content are show his theological method.[2] This chapter will begin with a consideration of the historiographical discussions of nineteenth-century conservative theological method. It will also explore the areas where Hovey explicitly addressed the issues of biblical and theological authority and how these areas influenced the doing of theology. As such, this chapter will

---

1. Hovey, "Value of Systematic Theology to Pastors," 494.
2. For a helpful summary of theological method, see, Stiver, "Method," 510: "Whether in biblical interpretation per se or in systematic theology, method concerns both the basic rational procedure for yielding and arranging results and, importantly, the presuppositions and conceptual framework that one brings to the task."

consider several areas with direct bearing on his theological method. These include: issues of prolegomena, including the nature of theology and the limitations of the theologian; revelation, including the interpretation of the Bible; tradition, particularly its use and authority; and further areas of theology that pertain to epistemology, such as anthropology, sin, soteriology, and the relation of faith and reason. This progression of subjects closely resembles Hovey's own outline in his theology textbooks, though I am inserting a few discussions that are not discussed in his theology textbooks but are discussed at length elsewhere, the most important being theism and tradition. Hovey was known as a deliberate, comprehensive, and consistent theologian, giving time and attention to several voices and multiple sides of any issue before offering a final word. Thus, the sections on Hovey's thought ought to be considered in their sum total.

Understanding Nineteenth-Century Theological Method

Historians have recognized that American Protestantism before and during the nineteenth century gave unique solutions to the theological questions that vexed the Western world. This also shows that they were aware of the major intellectual currents in Europe. Simplistically put, following the Reformation and the so-called Wars of Religion, the Enlightenment challenged many of the reigning ideas and helped to bring in the modern world, thus producing new challenges and new opportunities to think about religion.[3] In contrast to other Western nations, and important for Hovey's situation,

---

3. The Enlightenment can be understood as "the age which brought together the humanistic spirit of the Renaissance and the scientific revolution of the seventeenth century and thereby ushered in what we call 'the modern world'" (Livingston, *Modern Christian Thought*, 5). Normally, the Enlightenment is thought of as the time between the end of the Thirty Years War (1648) and the French Revolution (1789) and is often referred to as the "Age of Reason." Famously, within this time frame, Paul Hazard has pointed to the years 1680 to 1715 as the intellectual hinge wherein the ideas of a pre-modern mindset were finally put away (Hazard, *European Mind*). Though seminal, Hazard's treatment has had its critics. For a helpful overview, see Outram, *Enlightenment*. For this general time period, see Reardon, *Religious Thought in the Nineteenth Century*; Cragg, *Church and the Age of Reason*; May, *Enlightenment in America*; Vidler, *Church in an Age of Revolution*; Hampson, *Enlightenment*; Van Kley, *Religious Origins of the French Revolution*; Byrne, *Religion and the Enlightenment*; Pearse, *Age of Reason*; Woodbridge and James, *From Pre-Reformation to the Present Day*, chapters 8–14; Brown and Tackett, *Enlightenment*.

the United States is normally considered unique in the ways it utilized the changing world and in the ways it created a new synthesis of religion.[4]

In his classic, two-volume work, *Protestant Thought in the Nineteenth Century*,[5] Claude Welch argued that one of the three major themes that occupied theologians during the century was "the question of the possibility of theology."[6] By this he meant "both the question of the inner logic or rationale of the theological enterprise and the question whether theology is possible

---

4. As was noted in the first chapter, Thomas Howard suggests that many Europeans see America as either an "erroneously religious society" or an "overly religious society" (Howard, *God and the Atlantic*). Often, the coming of the modern world meant the secularization of the nations. Owen Chadwick's brief statement summarizes the relationship of Enlightenment and secularization: "[Understanding the thinking of the ordinary person] is why the problem of secularization is not the same as the problem of enlightenment. Enlightenment was of the few. Secularization is of the many" (Chadwick, *Secularization of the European Mind*, 9). The pace of the secularization is not agreed upon. And, some historians see not a secularization or decline but rather a changing of how religion was done (Bayly, *Birth of the Modern World*, 325–65). One world history of this time period that notes the limitations of the secularization idea, particularly in respect to the United States, is Osterhammel, *Transformation of the World*, 873–901. "The trend reversal toward secularism that became unmistakable in Europe toward the end of the [nineteenth] century did not happen among either Protestants or Catholics in the United States. The American case also shows that religious vitalization—or what Enlightenment critics referred to as *Schwärmerei* (raptured enthusiasm)—did not inevitably lead back into theocracy, fanatical social controls, and irrationalism in other areas of life. The consequences of religious excitement can be contained if the distinction between private and public space has already been solidly established at an earlier stage" (Osterhammel, *Transformation of the World*, 883). When discussing the general character of nineteenth-century theology in America, Britain, and Germany, Claude Welch has argued that the immediate background "must be described by reference to at least three broad movements of thought, commonly labeled pietism, rationalism, and romanticism" (Welch, *Protestant Thought in the Nineteenth Century*, 1:22). Welch includes discussion of the American Great Awakening under his first category, the various forms of American Enlightenment under his second category, but the third category does not have an explicitly American referent. Romanticism is imbibed by nineteenth-century Americans through the German sources Welch discusses and appears later in the century in the American Transcendentalists and also in Horace Bushnell. As such, it is not a background of nineteenth-century American religious thought so much as a new stream within the century. On the inroads of the Transcendentalists and of Bushnell, see Dorrien, *Making of American Liberal Theology*, 58–178.

5. Welch, *Protestant Thought in the Nineteenth Century*.

6. Welch, *Protestant Thought in the Nineteenth Century*, 1:4. The other two were "the question of the possibility of Christology, and . . . the question of Christianity and culture." Welch saw all three of these as interweaving thematically and historically, yet he also saw them as each predominating three successive time periods: the period dominated by the repercussions of revolution (1799–1835), the period of transition surrounding the collapse of idealism (1835–1870), and the period of industrialization and urbanization (1870–1914).

at all. It is the problem of *theological method* as well as the constellation of problems that could later be summed up as the question of 'God-talk' or of the nature of religious assertions."[7] Because of the intellectual challenges of the day, when theologians rethought theological method it included a wider constellation of related ideas. Kant and Hume shared the supposition that the rationalism of the eighteenth century was empty and bankrupt. And it was Kant that shaped much of the boundary wherein theology would operate in the nineteenth century. Forms of romanticism, pietism, and evangelicalism began largely to rethink and reshape Christianity.[8]

A major reason for the fall of rationalism was the rise of historicism, or the realization that if humans are products of time and history then their understanding of truth and theology is also subject to historical conditioning.[9] This had huge significance for theological method because it forced theologians of all persuasions to study the Bible and doctrine through a historical lens. This change in method hit close to home for traditional conservative theologians. Bernard Reardon stated that, "the historical study of the Scriptures quickly suggested that traditional ideas concerning revelation and inspiration, as well as the customary style of literalist exegesis, were due for revision. If historical study could so easily discredit deist assumptions it yet pointed to consequences hardly less encouraging to the orthodox appeal to rational 'evidences.'"[10] What was revelation? How could we know God? How do we do theology? Who was Christ? These were some of the basic questions that nineteenth-century theologians were forced to answer. Paul Allen has helpfully stated that, "The methodological variety in Christian theology becomes more entrenched and self-aware by the nineteenth century."[11]

---

7. Welch, *Protestant Thought in the Nineteenth Century*, 1:5 (emphasis added). Welch continued: "Other labels calling attention to different aspects or elements might also be used, for example, the problem of the knowability of God, or reason and revelation, or the meaning of revelation, or the relation of religious knowing (or believing) to science's way(s) of knowing, or the right of theology to exist alongside other *Wissenschaften*, or the nature and authority of the Bible as an organ of revelation, or the nature of religion. This area of questioning could be said to dominate Protestant thought in the whole of the nineteenth century (or even from the Enlightenment to the present)."

8. More issues occupied nineteenth-century theologians, so this is a (still accurate) simplification that is discussed in standard overviews of nineteenth-century theology. See Mackintosh, *Types of Modern Theology*, 1–30; Reardon, *Religious Thought in the Nineteenth Century*, 1–35; Welch, *Protestant Thought in the Nineteenth Century*, 1:22–55; Livingston, *Modern Christian Thought*, 1–82. Also see Berkhof, *Two Hundred Years of Theology*; Thielicke, *Modern Faith and Thought*; Barth, *Protestant Thought in the Nineteenth Century*.

9. See Howard, *Religion and the Rise of Historicism*.

10. Reardon, *Religious Thought in the Nineteenth Century*, 4–5.

11. Allen, *Theological Method*, 143. Also see McCormack, "Introduction."

THEOLOGICAL METHOD 87

Working from within new methodological boundaries and with new concerns, mainstream nineteenth-century Protestant theologians produced a wide array of theological methods and theological systems, all applying nuance and sophistication to a plethora of topics. In contrast, and whatever the theological challenge might be (Darwinism, Biblical criticism, romanticism, etc.), theological conservatives were regularly seen as unable to cope with the need to nuance their theology. Welch, speaking of Protestantism broader than just America, offered this summary of the issue:

> In fact, it was conservatives like Charles Hodge in America and Otto Zöckler in Germany who were most attentive to Darwin's own position, which they took to be simply contrary to the biblical teaching about the origin of humanity. *One sees here orthodoxy's tendency to the all-or-nothing-view, a way of thinking operating at many levels.* These range from Newman's sophisticated commitment to "dogma" and his contention in the *Apologia pro Vita Sua* (1864) that there was no real middle-ground between Catholic truth and rationalism, to some simplistic fundamentalist objections to any "higher criticism" on the grounds that, like being only "a little pregnant," being only a little doubtful of scriptural inerrancy opened the door to scepticism [sic] and atheism.[12]

Welch, and others, contend that conservatives often tried to answer the questions by repristinating past theologies, a strategy which caused many to unwittingly build traditional conservative theology on modern foundations.[13] Conservative theology, such as Hovey's, is thus normally seen as lacking in nuance, guilty of holding to outmoded theology based on pre-modern forms of thinking, and/or guilty of holding to outmoded forms of theology wedded to modernistic assumptions.

This basic critique of conservative theology has dominated the historiographical landscape. It has also received more precision from several historians who have argued that the underlying modernistic foundation of many conservative theologians was the moral philosophy of Scottish Common Sense Realism.[14] On these issues, historians regularly point to

---

12. Welch, "Nineteenth Century," 484 (emphasis added).

13. Welch, *Protestant Thought in the Nineteenth Century*, 1:190–240. The charge that conservative theologians in the nineteenth century were looking to Scottish Common Sense Realism was not created by twentieth century historians, it was made during the nineteenth century as well. For one example, see Smyth, "Orthodox Rationalism."

14. Scottish Common Sense Realism came as a response to David Hume's skeptical philosophy as it, in turn, critiqued the philosophy of John Locke. An important summary of this transition and its significance in the historiography is found in Bozeman,

the influence of Scottish Common Sense Realist philosophy that stressed the ability of the human mind in regards to intellect and senses as well as the method of Baconianism with the scientific gathering and use of data. This supposed trust of human rational ability directly bears on theological method. Theodore Dwight Bozeman gave the following four "principal elements" of the Scottish use of Baconianism:

1. A spirited enthusiasm for natural science.
2. A scrupulous empiricism, grounded upon the confident "trust in the senses" and in the reality of the outer world supplied by the Realist doctrine of "judgment."
3. A sharp accent upon the limits of scientific method and knowledge, directed to the inductive control of generalizations by continuous reference to "facts." Abstract concepts not immediately forged from observed data have no place in scientific explanation.
4. A celebratory focus upon "Lord Bacon" as the progenitor of inductive science; a flat identification of Newtonian methods with Bacon's "induction."[15]

This understanding of the influence of Scottish Common Sense Realism upon America theology was given explanation in Sydney Ahlstrom's seminal 1955 article, "The Scottish Philosophy and American Theology."[16] Ahlstrom argued that many conservative American theologians felt the need for an apologetical philosophy that could counter the skepticism of Hume and also avoid major metaphysical heresy. Their solution was found in Scottish Common Sense Realism.[17] The problem was that the acceptance of this philosophy "accelerated the long trend toward rational theology which had

---

Protestants in an Age of Science, 3–31. For an overview of Hume and Locke, see Norton, "Hume, David"; Wolterstorff, "Locke, John."

15. Bozeman, *Protestants in an Age of Science*, 21. There are many works on this subject. Some of the most important include Ahlstrom, "Scottish Philosophy and American Theology"; May, *Enlightenment in America*; Bozeman, *Protestants in an Age of Science*; Hatch, "Sola Scriptura and Novus Ordo Seclorum"; Holifield, *Gentlemen Theologians*; Stewart, "Tethered Theology"; Marsden, "Scotland and Philadelphia," 8–12; "Everyone One's Own Interpreter?"; "Collapse of American Evangelical Academia"; Noll, "Irony of the Enlightenment"; "Common Sense Traditions."

16. Ahlstrom, "Scottish Philosophy and American Theology." Ahlstrom primarily looked at Reformed theology.

17. Ahlstrom, "Scottish Philosophy and American Theology," 267. "The Scottish Philosophy, in short, was a winning combination; and to American theologians, even if they felt the need for philosophic support only subconsciously, it was the answer to a prayer. It was, moreover, free enough from subtlety to be communicable in sermons and tracts. It came to exist in America, therefore as a vast subterranean influence, a sort of water-table nourishing dogmatics in an age of increasing doubt."

developed, especially in England, during and after the long Deistic controversy." Ahlstrom concluded that "there resulted a neo-rationalism which rendered the central Christian paradoxes into stark, logical contradictions that had either to be disguised or explained away."[18]

According to this historiography, part of the crisis of conservative theology in the nineteenth century and beyond was that the insistence on the reasonableness of Christianity had enshrined a Christianity that gave evidential arguments a superficial place of authority. The philosophical and scientific revolutions of the era supposedly revealed as much and contributed to the exodus of educated people from traditional evangelical understandings of Christianity.[19] Normally it is an insistence on biblical inerrancy or some form of "biblical rationalism" that is seen as the primary indicator of such a maverick theological method. And, the finger is often pointed at the Princetonians[20] (or sometimes the post-Reformation dogmaticians)[21] to be the progenitors or the quintessential representatives and thus the culpable party. With these epistemological tools in place, historians have argued, Protestants constructed their theology from an Enlightenment-inspired epistemological foundation.[22] As David Bebbington has succinctly stated: "Rationality, it was universally held, was what separated humanity from the animal kingdom. There must be no toying with limiting the powers of reason in the name of exalting faith. . . . Reason must not be trammeled by restrictions of any kind."[23] Reason was trusted and given no restrictions either philosophically or theologically.

---

18. Ahlstrom, "Scottish Philosophy and American Theology," 269.

19. Smith, "Religion and Science in American Philosophy." Smith argues this exodus continued in the twentieth century but expanded to be an exodus from any kind of Christianity at all.

20. Livingstone, "Princeton Apologetic"; Stewart, "Tethered Theology"; Sandeen, "Princeton Theology"; "Towards a Historical Interpretation"; *Roots of Fundamentalism*; Marsden, "Collapse of American Evangelical Academia," 238–47; *Fundamentalism and American Culture*, 109–18; Noll, "Irony of the Enlightenment"; "Common Sense Traditions."

21. Rogers and McKim, *Authority and Interpretation of the Bible*. See Marsden, *Reforming Fundamentalism*, 285. See the direct responses of Woodbridge, *Biblical Authority*; Woodbridge and Balmer, "Princetonians and Biblical Authority."

22. This idea is central to three seminal theological histories of antebellum America. See Hatch, *Democratization of American Christianity*; Noll, *America's God*; Holifield, *Theology in America*. As Daniel Walker Howe stated, "Bible-centered Protestantism, synthesized with the Enlightenment and a respect for classical learning, helped shape the culture, determine the patterns of intellectual inquiry, and define the terms of debate in the antebellum American republic" (Howe, *What Hath God Wrought*, 482).

23. Bebbington, *Dominance of Evangelicalism*, 120.

This foundation had essentially caused a split between thought/reason and experience/piety. As Mark Noll has argued, these apologetics "rested on one Enlightenment assumption and two Enlightenment procedures. The assumption was that disputants could maintain intellectual neutrality when confronting arguments of fundamental religious significance. . . . The two Enlightenment procedures which the Presbyterians worked assiduously, were scientific demonstration and common-sense intuition."[24] Though historians and philosophers have questioned how far such an explanation can go and to whom it should be properly applied, none doubt the tendency toward reasonableness in the majority of Protestant theologies.[25] But is a tendency toward reasonableness different than rationalism?

Despite this being the dominant historiographical explanation, several historians have pushed back and asserted that conservative theologians were more nuanced.[26] The argument that is gaining traction among these historians is that the presence of forms of reasonableness or evidential apologetics is not controlling but only a part within the greater theological superstructure. They argue that "presence of" does not equal "control by." As Paul Helm has argued, one could theoretically hold to a theological position such as Calvinism along with aspects of Scottish Common Sense Realism without becoming a Common Sense Realist. Helm explains that, "The propositions of Calvinism could not be *stated* if Reid's 'logical axioms' were not observed. This is not to say that Reid's arguments for the acceptance of such axioms are or ought to be convincing, much less that the axioms entail

---

24. Noll, "Irony of the Enlightenment," 148. Noll argues that this prop was destined to give way, which it did, leading to the demise of conservative theology. Other historians who have noted this irony in the Princetonians include Vender Stelt, *Philosophy and Scripture*; Marsden, *Fundamentalism and American Culture*; Loetscher, *Facing the Enlightenment and Pietism*; Reymond, *Faith's Reasons for Believing*.

25. I agree with E. Brooks Holifield when he argues that "a majority of theologians in early America shared a preoccupation with the reasonableness of Christianity that predisposed them toward such an understanding of theology" (Holifield, *Theology in America*, 4).

26. This prevailing historiography has also been challenged by some seeking to establish the historical continuity of inerrancy with the Christian tradition. Examples include Hoffecker, *Piety and the Princeton Theologians*; Muller, *Prolegomena to Theology*; Woodbridge, *Biblical Authority*; Woodbridge and Balmer, "Princetonians and Biblical Authority"; Edwards, *New Spirits*, chapter 8; Satta, *Sacred Text*; Smith, "B. B. Warfield"; Helseth, *Right Reason and the Princeton Mind*; Hoffecker, *Charles Hodge*; Aubert, *German Roots of Nineteenth-Century American Theology*. Ronald Satta makes the interesting suggestion that the tendency to blame the Princetonians with creating the doctrine of inerrancy is not only historically untenable, but also may trace its roots the heresy trial of Charles Briggs where Briggs lays blame to the Princetonians (in contrast to several other contemporaneous liberals who saw inerrancy as the historic view). See Satta, *Sacred Text*, chapter 4.

Calvinism. But they are entailed by Calvinism, at least in the sense that any intelligible and consistent set of propositions presupposes certain rules of intelligible discourse."[27] Using arguments such as Helm's, the counter-historiography argues that further theological categories, such as anthropology and soteriology, with their theological import on rationality, need to be simultaneously considered. In other words, the conservative theologians were aware of problems vexing their times and sought to reconstruct theology to speak to the issues without also capitulating to its demands. Their epistemology was more complex. This historiography allows that these conservative theologians utilized aspects of Scottish Common Sense Realism, but it was not controlling in the way the prevailing historiography has asserted. They are suggesting that historians look at the historical context afresh.[28]

Baptist historiography has also dealt somewhat with the place of theological method in the nineteenth century. Stephen Holmes has argued that Baptists basically followed the pattern of conservative Protestantism in that they tended "to affirm a commitment to biblical authority" when it came to theological methodology.[29] While some followed the turn to religious experience after the example of Schleiermacher, most remained in the traditional Baptist stream throughout the nineteenth century.[30] The turn away from more conservative theological methodology reflects the turn away from theological conservatism in general that can be observed after about 1870.[31] James Garrett noted that one major reason for the changing theological scene (not just for Baptists) was that "the older Scottish commonsense realism and the German and British idealism yielded to the newer American philosophies of evolution, personalism, and pragmatism."[32]

This change in philosophical outlooks challenged theological method. In Baptist studies, this change in method was part and parcel with changing views of the Bible. Most historians look at the influx of biblical criticism and

27. See especially Helm, "Thomas Reid," 88.

28. Another instance of someone questioning the place of Scottish Common Sense Realism in history is Carson, "Recent Developments in the Doctrine of Scripture," 1–48. Also see Woodbridge, "Is Biblical Inerrancy a Fundamentalist Doctrine?"; "Sola Scriptura."

29. Holmes, *Baptist Theology*, 83.

30. Holmes, *Baptist Theology*, 83–87. Holmes lists Nathaniel Kendrick, Augustus Strong, and E. Y. Mullins as three American examples of those who followed the turn to religious experience in their theology.

31. Most Baptist historians note this turn. See, for example, Maring, "Baptists and Changing Views of the Bible [I]"; "Baptists and Changing Views of the Bible [II]"; Garrett Jr., *Baptist Theology*, chapter 7; Bebbington, *Baptists through the Centuries*, chapters 6–7; Straub, *Making of a Battle Royal*.

32. Garrett, *Baptist Theology*, 279.

changing views of inspiration, infallibility, and inerrancy. These views form a part of theological methodology, but they also reach beyond simply issues of methodology. To the extent that they influence methodology, they will be discussed in this chapter. The following chapter will deal in more depth with critical views of the Bible, and Hovey's interaction with them.

Despite the fact that the preponderance of Baptist historiography deals more with Baptist views of the Bible, there are some works that mention methodology and the influence of Scottish Common Sense Realism in particular. The most significant is Grant Wacker in his study of Augustus Strong.[33] He argued that the majority of nineteenth-century (and earlier) Baptists were "orthodox rationalists." By this he meant they held to the normal Protestant theologies stated in standard confessions as well as "a cluster of epistemic assumptions."[34] These epistemic assumptions are those of Scottish Common Sense Realism outlined above. Wacker contends that nineteenth-century Baptists had to choose between the newer theologies and philosophies that understood the challenge of historical situatedness and the older "ahistorical" theologies.[35] Wacker admits that many conservative Baptists felt the struggle between these two worlds but still held on to the ahistorical assumption that religious knowledge was divinely revealed (through the process of inspiration) in a perfect book (thus the Bible was infallible/inerrant) and could be understood correctly (because of epistemic assumptions).[36] The theological result was orthodox rationalism.

Wacker's understanding of Baptist theological methodology in the nineteenth century (following after that of Marsden, Noll, and others on American Protestantism in general) has been widely followed.[37] But given that some are challenging the place of Scottish Common Sense Realism in non-Baptist studies, this challenge deserves to be heard in Baptist studies as well.

33. Wacker, *Augustus H. Strong*.

34. Wacker, *Augustus H. Strong*, 17.

35. Wacker's book is an exploration of how Strong felt the push against this orthodox rationalism and tried to construct a theology more sensitive to the dilemma of historical consciousness. In the end, Wacker sees Strong as a tragic figure who unsuccessfully tried to bridge this chasm.

36. Not all have been convinced by Wacker. William Brackney flatly denies Wacker's contention that the New Hampshire Confession of Faith was a bedrock of Baptist orthodox rationalism (Brackney, *Genetic History of Baptist Thought*, 40n108). Further, in his several seminal works on Baptist history and theology, Brackney does not utilize the Scottish Common Sense Realist explanation. See also his comment on Ezekiel Gilman Robinson's interest in Scottish Common Sense Realism in Brackney, *Genetic History of Baptist Thought*, 322n216.

37. See also Holifield's chapter on Baptists in Holifield, *Theology in America*, 273–75.

A related scene change for Protestants was due to the disestablishment of state supported religion. The First Amendment of 1791 stated that Congress could not establish any "law respecting an establishment of religion or prohibiting the free exercise thereof." It took until 1833 for the last state (Massachusetts) to officially accept the separation of church and state in their constitution. And, as William McLoughlin has stated, "For the most part these disestablishments collapsed not with a bang but a whimper. . . . The old established systems were whittled away bit by bit until they finally tumbled down by the weight of their own rotted timbers."[38] While it is true that the growth and vitality of Protestantism was not reliant on disestablishment, since these numbers were steadily growing before the Revolution and continued to grow in Canada and Great Britain,[39] it is also true that Protestants (evangelicals in particular) were greatly benefited by the new situation. Roger Finke gives this summation:

> The new boundaries supported a religious market where competition was not only endured, it was encouraged. With the new rules of law, upstart sects and new religions were not only given a right to exist (toleration), they were given "equal" rights; and the once privileged religious establishments lost the legislative and financial support of the state. By denying the establishment of any religion, and granting the free exercise of religion to all, the state could no longer support regulation that denied privileges to or imposed sanctions on specific religious organizations—or their members. The state was denied the privilege, and freed from the obligation, of regulating religion. The result was an unregulated religious economy.[40]

---

38. McLoughlin, *Soul Liberty*, 289. The full history and presentation of the long path to disestablishment in the various states is presented in detail in McLoughlin, *New England Dissent*. Also see the discussions in Hamburger, *Separation of Church and State*, 19–144; and Green, *Second Disestablishment*.

39. John Wolffe is correct in his statement that "neither the state churches of England and Wales, Ireland and Scotland, nor the socially privileged Congregationalism and Presbyterianism of the United States were by any means moribund. They were themselves to become important channels for the expansion of evangelicalism" (Wolffe, *Expansion of Evangelicalism*, 43). See also Noll, *Rise of Evangelicalism*, 195–202.

40. Finke, "Religious Deregulation," 609. For further discussions on the connection of evangelicalism to the political scene during this time and the ways in which upcoming denominations took advantage of the new scene, see Finke and Stark, "How the Upstart Sects Won America"; Bloch, "Religion and Ideological Change"; Howe, "Evangelical Movement and Political Culture"; *What Hath God Wrought*, 446–82; Carwardine, *Evangelicals and Politics in Antebellum America*; "Evangelicals, Politics"; Noll, "Revolution and the Rise of Evangelical Social Influence"; Rawlyk, "Total Revolution."

The payoff was a newfound deregulation open to new possibilities. In brief, "creative exploitation of institutionalized disestablishment was a significant factor in rapid evangelical growth."[41] Protestantism in nineteenth-century America is in many ways an outplaying of this situation.

As has been mentioned more than once previously in this book, democratization reshaped much of the authority structure within American Protestantism. Popular interest was shaping religion after their own concerns. Nathan Hatch has argued that, "The democratization of Christianity, then, has less to do with the specifics of polity and governance and more with the incarnation of the church into popular culture."[42] This shows in three places: the denial of the distinction between clergy and laity, the freedom to take spiritual impulses at face value rather than scrutinizing them according to established orthodoxy, and it allowed religious outsiders to feel as if they had no limitations. Hatch goes on to further argue that, by 1840, democratization had waned, but centralized authority and professional expertise had been subverted within American Protestantism. In its place, the right to think for oneself had replaced the authority of creeds, the established systems, and the established ways to read the Bible.[43] This has a bearing on methodology in terms of attitudes toward and use of tradition, in terms of the need for expertise, and in terms of Bible interpretation.

This remainder of this chapter will speak directly to the historiographical questions outlined above. The questions this chapter asks are two-fold: Does Hovey, as an undeniably conservative theologian, exemplify the historiographical descriptions of conservative theology as "orthodox rationalism?" Does Hovey, in a denomination known for its democratization, exemplify the descriptions of democratization?

Prolegomena

In his *Manual of Christian Theology* (1900), as in all his theologies, Hovey began with matters pertaining to the construction of theology. Also, several of his published essays and articles speak to his prolegomena. Further, his handwritten lecture notes provide a few glimpses of his extended thought.

---

41. Noll, *America's God*, 174.

42. Hatch, *Democratization of American Christianity*, 9.

43. Hatch, *Democratization of American Christianity*, esp. chapter 6. Hatch argues elsewhere that the explosion of religious influence meant that "the most dynamic popular movements were expressly religious" (Hatch, "Democratization of Christianity"). Also see Marsden, "Everyone One's Own Interpreter?"; Hatch, "Sola Scripura and Novus Ordo Seclorum"; Weber, "Two-Edged Sword."

Several main topics within these discussions are important and form the headings below. His theism highlights how he understood the Creator/creature distinction and how it affected knowledge of God. His understanding of the scientific nature of theology alongside his understanding of the qualifications, limitations, and benefits of the theological exercise show how he understood the nature of theology in relation to the intellectual and spiritual capabilities of the theologian. His theological organization further also shows understanding of the nature of the theological exercise.

Theism

In his 1892 publication, *Studies in Ethics and Religion*, Hovey dedicated three essays to the study of theism. These essays gave the clearest presentation of Hovey's view of theism as it pertained to his prolegomena.[44] In the first essay, "Our Knowledge of Infinites," Hovey's main assertion was that "*we have a partial knowledge of infinite objects.*"[45] Just because God is infinite does not mean that we cannot know him. It was equally true that "our partial knowledge of infinites is trustworthy, when treated as partial; but if treated as complete it is liable to mislead."[46] Furthermore, even though we cannot correlate our understanding of the infinite by any representation, we may still know it. Hovey believed that from a finite starting point the infinite could be discovered.[47] He concluded that it was a just inference to say that God is an infinite being and it was a great blunder to consider God to be finite. "In view of these considerations, we do not hesitate to infer the infinitude of God from the religious nature of man."[48]

His second essay, "The Relation of God to Nature," was a review of German philosopher Rudolf Hermann Lotze and American philosopher Jacob Schurman, both of whom argued that God was the ground but not

---

44. Hovey also discussed traditional matters of Christian theism in his theologies, but he did so after his discussion of introductory matters (prolegomena) and after his discussion of the two major sources of revelation (nature and the Bible). This major section on prolegomena will discuss theism as well as the nature, limitations, qualifications, benefits, and organization of theology. The subsequent major sections will discuss revelation, tradition, and theological epistemology.

45. Hovey, "Our Knowledge of Infinites," 2.

46. Hovey, "Our Knowledge of Infinites," 15.

47. "For we find that the soul, starting with the finite, discovers the infinite; we find that the soul, starting with temporal being, perceives the certainty of eternal being; we find that the soul, starting with a consciousness of moral and religious duty, divines the existence of a being whose power, knowledge, and goodness are infinite" (Hovey, "Our Knowledge of Infinites," 20–21).

48. Hovey, "Our Knowledge of Infinites," 22.

the Creator of nature. The philosophy of monism was a hot-button item in Baptist circles of the time, especially because the significant figure of Augustus Hopkins Strong assimilated it into his theology.[49] The issue was whether someone was to think of nature as simply dependent on God, or as dependent on *and* created by God. Hovey rejected the views of Lotze and Schurman and argued:

> According to the tradition received from our Christian fathers, nature or the world was created, that is, brought into being, by the will of God. It is eternal neither in substance nor in form. It is an effect of which God is the cause, rather than a body of which God is the soul. Moreover, every part of it is dependent on the will of God for its continuance in being, and the same is true of the sum-total of its forces, whether organic or inorganic. Still further: As nature is a cosmos, every part is related to every other part, and in a qualified sense dependent on it. . . . To affirm their dependence as a whole upon God is consistent with the hypothesis that they are linked together by invisible ties in a single system, the parts of which are truly interdependent. God works through second causes or means, and some of these second causes may do his will without choice or consciousness, while others do it voluntarily.[50]

Hovey's view was not pantheism that rejects origins, nor was it deism that rejected any kind of constant relation of God and the world. He saw it as classic Christian theism.

His final essay on "God and the Universe" argued from Romans 11:36 that all things are of God, are through him, and are unto him. Speaking about the idea that "all things are of God," Hovey made the argument not only that God is the Creator but he adds an interesting point about what can be known about the creative act: "But I hasten to say that the act which we call creation is inscrutable. What we mean by the word is evident enough, but the possibility of such an effect of energy baffles conception."[51] God is infinite reason, love, being, power, and goodness. God is undiminished in

---

49. Strong, *Christ in Creation*. The clearest statement of Strong's ethical monism appears in his final *Systematic Theology*: "Ethical Monism is that method of thought which holds to a single substance, ground, or principle of being, namely, God, but which also holds to the ethical facts of God's transcendence as well as his immanence, and of God's personality as distinct from, and as guaranteeing, the personality of man" (Strong, *Systematic Theology* [8th ed.], 105). Strong's ethical monism and Hovey's interaction with it will receive extended attention in chapter 6.

50. Hovey, "Relation of God to Nature," 51–52.

51. Hovey, "God and the Universe," 58.

any of these attributes by these attributes being present in other finite beings. And, the fact that created beings have an imperfect possession of these attributes means that there is a certain distance between God as he is and as he acts and human understanding of God and his acts. The idea that "all things are through Him" means that God controls the world's progress through providence, preservation, discipline, and improvement. As in the first point, Hovey argued that there is an element of mystery here when trying to grasp what this all means.[52] Hovey argued that science can explain much, but it only gets to the phenomena and not to the essence of things. The Christian was to believe the testimony of Scripture above that of science, philosophy, logic, or intuition because it comes from a source that knows the essence.[53] This understanding of revelation and of providence left ultimate understanding to mystery but Hovey was quick to assert, on the testimony of scripture, that God was still active in all events. The final phrase, "all things are unto God," did not mean that the world is absorbed into God in the end. It referred to the idea that all things find their ultimate fulfillment in God: "To manifest the glory or perfection of God is therefore the chief end of our existence."[54] God's relation to the universe is one of infinite Creator to created being. But this does not mean that God is aloof. "The God revealed to us by the Scriptures is more than infinite being, without character or life. He is One who knows and feels and loves, who proposes and executes, who is our father, our friend, our helper, our Saviour, and who in the fulness of time entered into human life and carried its burdens even to the cross."[55]

The debates of theism were important to Hovey as he constructed his theology.[56] He clearly believed that a finite being could attain true under-

---

52. "For God is said to 'uphold all things by the word of His power,' And before this testimony of inspired men physical science is dumb. For that science deals only with phenomena, with manifestations, with changes in the realm of nature; it does not penetrate or lay open the essence of things" (Hovey, "God and the Universe," 61).

53. "Nor can intuition or logical reasoning be said to impeach the testimony of holy Scripture as to the relation of God to the universe. We who reverence the Bible believe that all which it teaches on this subject is in profound agreement with the best results of philosophical inquiry" (Hovey, "God and the Universe," 62).

54. Hovey, "God and the Universe," 65.

55. Hovey, "God and the Universe," 68. Hovey continued: "If we wish to know him truly, and to be certain of his wisdom and love, we have but to study the fourfold Gospel till we see his mind in the face of Jesus Christ."

56. Hovey also dedicated an essay to "Christian Science and Mind-Cure." He argued that such a metaphysic was against Christian tradition and altogether incredulous. Hovey, "Christian Science and Mind Cure," (89): "Until Mrs. Eddy and her friends give up eating and drinking for the support of the body, we shall believe them to be distrustful of their own metaphysics. If hunger can be removed by food, disease may be cured

standing of the infinite, if only in a partial sense. Further, one could reason to the point of belief in an infinite God. But still, science, philosophy, and reason could not penetrate the essence of things as well as scripture. His theism showed that he had a place for reason, under scripture, in his theological method. Both the true knowability of the infinite by finite beings and the limited nature of that knowledge were consistently present in his theology. The next three sub-sections highlight various aspects of those two issues.

The Scientific Nature of Theology

Speaking of the knowability of the infinite, Hovey's works certainly reflected the nineteenth-century spirit of scientific theology.[57] Consider his definition of theology: "By Christian Theology is meant *the science of the Christian religion*, or the science which ascertains, justifies, and systematizes all attainable truth concerning God and his relation, through Jesus Christ, to the universe and especially to mankind."[58] He further explained: "The word 'science' is here used to signify knowledge correctly arranged or systematized, a knowledge of principles as well as of facts, of causes and effects as well as of events. Here the science of the Christian religion must be a well-ordered and coherent exposition of the facts and principles of that religion."[59]

This understanding of theology as scientific gave him reason to write a systematic theology. It was dependent on "Natural and Biblical Theology, for the facts and principles which it correlates and interprets," the "history of the Christian religion," and to a lesser extent on "Logic and Metaphysics."[60] Indeed, Hovey's first two main chapters (after his short prolegomena) are on "God Revealed in Nature" and "God Revealed in Scripture." Part of the reason that theology could do this was because Hovey asserted, "the normal

---

by medicine."

57. E. Brooks Holifield's major work on eighteenth- and nineteenth-century theology in America states: "The overarching theme of this book is the claim that a majority of theologians in early America shared a preoccupation with the reasonableness of Christianity that predisposed them toward such an understanding of theology" (Holifield, *Theology in America*, 4).

58. Hovey, *Manual of Christian Theology*, 3.

59. Hovey, *Manual of Christian Theology*, 3.

60. Hovey, *Manual of Christian Theology*, 4. In his lecture notes, Hovey clarifies: "[Christian Theology] depends for its facts or data upon Biblical Theology and Interpretation, and more remotely upon Natural Theology, History, Psychology, and Metaphysics" (Hovey, "Christian Theology: Introduction: Definitions and Explanations (Lecture Notes)," 3 (AHP).

action of the human mind is trustworthy."⁶¹ Further, *"men have some true knowledge of God."*⁶²

When discussing the "normal action of the mind," how it is trustworthy, and how the mind weighs evidences, Hovey made use of various arguments and tenets of Scottish Common Sense Realism. In his 1877 *Manual*, Hovey referenced William Hamilton and James McCosh for how to weigh evidence, both of whom are universally recognized for their acceptance and propagation of Scottish Common Sense Realism.⁶³ Borrowing from McCosh, Hovey accepted three kinds of evidences: "(1) That which is furnished by direct cognition, namely, axiomatic or necessary truths. (2) That which is furnished by clear perception or recollection; it being in either case indubitable. (3) That which is furnished by testimony or analogy; this kind of evidence being variable in force and often characterized as probable."⁶⁴

There is no doubt that Hovey's epistemological assumptions on this point borrowed from Scottish Common Sense Realism in that he saw the mind as normally trustworthy and he used Scottish terms to describe how the mind worked and weighed evidences. Still, it should be remembered that Hovey's theism recognized a significant difference between God and humanity, which then affected theological construction. At this location in his lecture notes, Hovey records: "It is too much to expect perfect success in exhibiting the argument and interdependence of all Christian facts and principles. Some of them are but partial revelations of an infinite being, while perfect knowledge is necessary in the constitution of a perfect system. But a measure of success may be expected in this part of our work."⁶⁵ Thus, while it is true that Hovey accepted the basic idea of the reasonableness of theology, it is not accurate to suggest that he was "ahistorical" or an "orthodox rationalist"⁶⁶ who was wholeheartedly taken by this rationality. His

61. Hovey, *Manual of Christian Theology*, 4.

62. Hovey, *Manual of Christian Theology*, 6.

63. Hovey made the same arguments in his 1900 edition, though he omitted the footnote references to Hamilton and McCosh. See Hovey, *Manual of Systematic Theology*, 12; *Manual of Christian Theology*, 4–5.

64. Hovey, *Manual of Christian Theology*, 5. The 1877 edition states it this way: "Evidence may be divided into several classes, as that which is afforded (a) by primitive beliefs, judgments, and intuitions; (b) by distinct perception or recollection; and (c) by testimony or analogy" (Hovey, *Manual of Systematic Theology*, 12).

65. Hovey, "Christian Theology: Introduction: Definitions and Explanations (Lecture Notes)," 3 (AHP).

66. Wacker, *Augustus H. Strong*, 1–19. The modern historiographical argument that Scottish Common Sense Realism is to blame for much of the rationalistic nature of nineteenth-century conservative theology has its roots in Ahlstrom, "Scottish Philosophy and American Theology." However, the notion that theologians have been

recognition of the Creator/creature distinction argues in this direction as do his hints at the limits of reason.

According to Hovey, theology as a science must be ordered, have all the facts, be coherent, and be systematically arranged.[67] This means he believed that God had made himself known and he likewise trusted the powers of the intellect to have some ability for theological construction. But Hovey explained both God's revelation and human rational ability further. Before that, however, he spent time discussing the limitations, qualifications, and benefits of the theological exercise.

Limitations, Qualifications, and Benefits of the Theological Exercise

Qualifying his belief in the trustworthiness of the mind, Hovey said: "We do not assume that it is infallible. . . . A mind's grasp of a complex problem is often less perfect than its grasp of a simple problem; but the mind is itself aware of this difference, and the positiveness of its conviction is proportioned to the clearness of its comprehension."[68] He further stated, "We know in part. All our knowledge is fragmentary, but it is not therefore untrustworthy, as far as it goes."[69] While Hovey believed in the ability to infer the infinite from the finite, he put a warning on how far one may infer. "Finite intelligence may not know how infinite intelligence will act in given circumstances. . . . For in each of these instances the inference is from cause to effect, while the cause is imperfectly known."[70] Hovey likewise warned against "giving too high a place to philosophical speculation," "yielding unconsciously to pride of opinion," and "giving place to selfishness."[71] This agrees with what was seen in the previous chapter on education. That chapter demonstrated that Hovey believed the student of theology needed to cultivate "intelligent faith" or "intelligent piety."[72] While training and the use of reason were needed, they were incomplete on their own. In order to know the things of God, the theological student needed to follow God with

---

illegitimately taken by this philosophical school reaches back to at least Smyth, "Orthodox Rationalism." Also see Briggs, *Biblical Study*; *Whither?*; *Authority of Holy Scripture*. For historical summary, see Satta, *Sacred Text*, chapter 4.

67. Hovey, *Outlines of Christian Theology*, 5.
68. Hovey, *Manual of Christian Theology*, 5.
69. Hovey, *Manual of Christian Theology*, 6.
70. Hovey, *Manual of Christian Theology*, 7.
71. Hovey, *Manual of Christian Theology*, 7–8.
72. Hovey, "Preparation for the Christian Ministry," 440; "Value of Systematic Theology to Pastors," 495.

their heart also. "The strictly religious emotions, faith, love, adoration, cannot be pure and healthful while the intuitions of moral right or the impulses of conscience are disregarded. Genuine piety and morality will flourish or languish together. The same is true of reason and faith; they cannot be divorced; and if one of them suffers, the other must suffer with it."[73] In his essay entitled, "Character Tested by Religious Inquiry," Hovey clearly laid out the limits of reason in the study of theology. These limits of reason are not to hold one back, rather they are to turn one toward God since they test the student. Reverence, faith, and hope are meant to be built up in the theological student. That there are limits to knowledge was positive to Hovey since the lesson learned from those limitations point to those things which are more important. "Take heart, then, my friends; be thankful that there are limits to your knowledge here, since those limits furnish a part of your needed discipline in virtue and piety; but fail not to be also thankful for the assurance that those limits are not fixed and ultimate."[74]

The qualifications for the study of Christian theology were mental, moral, religious, and educational.[75] He believed in each case that these qualifications were important, that they relate to one another, and that lack of any one was a detriment to all the others. Each qualification was presented as a warning for the theologian to pay attention to the limits of each. For instance, on the "moral" qualification, Hovey argued this meant "fairness of mind and deep reverence for truth. Candor, though not indifference, is attainable. Prejudice can be laid aside, and docility cultivated."[76] He then offered Augustine's explanation from *De Trinitate* on this point: "It will not grieve me to seek when I am in doubt, nor will it make me blush to learn when I am in error. Whoever reads these studies, where he is equally certain, let him go with me; where he is equally in doubt, let him inquire with me; where he discovers his own error, let him return to me; where he discovers mine, let him recall me. Thus let us walk in the way of love, tending towards Him of whom it is said, Seek ye his face always (Ps 104:4)."[77] Hovey's guiding principle through his discussion of limitations was that theological study was a continual spiritual exercise directed toward seeking the face of God.

---

73. Hovey, "Value of Systematic Theology to Pastors," 494.
74. Hovey, "Character Tested by Religious Inquiry," 512.
75. Hovey, *Manual of Christian Theology*, 8–9.
76. Hovey, *Manual of Christian Theology*, 8.
77. Augustine quoted in Hovey, *Manual of Christian Theology*, 8. The translation appears to be Hovey's own.

This meant that the "religious" qualification could be simply stated as: "We must love divine things in order to know them."[78]

"The study of theology is, throughout, a study of the relations of finite beings to an infinite Being; and therefore great caution is necessary. Better leave many blanks in the system than go beyond the warrant of facts."[79] The student could know God in truth though not in full comprehension, because humans were still finite. Further, reason was necessary and foundational, though still fallible and requiring piety to function properly. When these things were all in place, there were several benefits to studying theology. The student of theology could claim deeper realization mentally, morally, religiously, and practically of those qualities befitting a Christian.[80] This was seeking the face of God.

Organizing a Theology

After discussing theological assumptions and then cautions, Hovey discussed the arrangement of his theology.[81] He preferred his outline because it was logical in the sense of how each section presupposes what comes before.[82] In his 1900 theology, Hovey called his arrangement "synthetic,"

78. Hovey, *Manual of Christian Theology*, 9.

79. Hovey, *Manual of Systematic Theology*, 14.

80. Hovey, *Manual of Christian Theology*, 9–10.

81. Hovey, *Outlines of Christian Theology*, 12–13; *Manual of Systematic Theology*, 17–18; *Manual of Christian Theology*, 10–13.

82. Hovey listed six sections to his arrangement in his 1870 and 1900 editions and seven in the 1877 edition. The subjects of each edition actually are arranged chronologically the same, but the divisions (and the number of divisions) are placed differently in each case. In 1870 the divisions were: "I. The existence of a Supreme Being, inferred from the works of Nature. II. The Bible a supernatural Revelation from Him; involving the 'Evidences of Christianity.' III. The Doctrine of God; his Perfections and Providence. IV. The Doctrine of Man; especially, of his moral and sinful state. V. The Doctrine of Salvation: of the Savior and his work, of the Spirit and his work, etc. VI. The Doctrine of the Last Things; of natural Death, of the Middle State, of the Resurrection and Final Judgment, and of the Eternal State of Unbelievers and Believers." In 1877 the divisions were: "I. The Existence of God. II. The Bible from God. III. The Perfection of God. IV. The Doctrine of Man. V. The Doctrine of Salvation. VI. Christian Churches and Ordinances. VII. The Doctrine of the Last Things." In 1900 the divisions were: "Part First: God, in Nature and in Scripture. Part Second: Mankind, Their Nature, Character and Condition. Part Third: Jesus Christ, His Person and Work. Part Fourth: Christian Life, Its Beginning and Growth. Part Fifth: Christian Service. Part Sixth: Issues Hereafter." The 1877 edition also had a fifty-page appendix dealing with Christian Ethics. Ethics was not dealt with in the Outlines, and by 1900 Hovey had printed his 1892 book that had several essays which dealt with Ethics: Hovey, *Studies in Ethics and Religion; or, Discourses, Essays, and Reviews Pertaining to Theism, Inspiration, Christian Ethics, and Education for the Ministry* (1892).

by which he meant: "It takes the revealed facts and puts them together in logical order, so that their relations to one another are readily perceived. It avoids, as far as possible, any assumption as to the relative importance of Christian doctrines, yet on the whole, may be characterized as theocentric, starting from God and returning to God."[83] After discussing his own chosen arrangement, Hovey listed out a handful of other methods that other theologians have followed. These are Trinitarian, Christocentric, Kingdom of God, and Reconciliation.[84] Interestingly, Hovey did not have any theological reason for his arrangement, and, further, he did not find any other theologian's arguments for theological arrangement convincing. He did not offer any reason why he chose his arrangement other than it was logical and it adequately covered all the necessary topics.

Summary

Throughout his prolegomena Hovey spoke of the scientific nature and logical ordering of theology, of the trustworthiness of reason and of nature's teaching, of the central place for reason, and even the dependence of Christian theology on natural theology. Yet, he tempered all those with explicit recognitions of the limitations of human reasoning, the transcendence of God as opposed to the finitude of humanity, and the necessary spiritual qualifications of the theologian. Hovey certainly expected the reasoning person, who possessed the correct qualifications, to follow his train of thought and affirm these basic points of prolegomena. He also clearly affirmed that the furthest that human reasoning could take was still not far enough. In the end, the study of theology was a spiritual exercise undertaken by limited and sinful creatures seeking to know an infinite God. It remains to be seen more precisely how Hovey understood the nature of God's special revelation and more precisely how Hovey saw the human problem and its solution.

Revelation

This major section on God's revelation will focus on a few points that Hovey set as central in this discussion: revelation in nature, the revelation of Jesus, biblical revelation, and also the process of biblical interpretation

---

83. Hovey, *Manual of Christian Theology*, 11.

84. In his 1870 Outlines, Hovey also mentioned an inductive method that was essentially logical like his, though from a different direction. The inductive is the method "beginning with the nearest and most certain facts, ascends to the more remote, complex and difficult" (Hovey, *Outlines of Christian Theology*, 13). Hovey listed Chalmers as the example of this method.

(hermeneutics). Hermeneutics was not discussed in Hovey's theology textbooks but was discussed in several other places and was demonstrated in his published commentaries. It is helpful to discuss hermeneutics here as it is the prime window to see how Hovey believed Christians should interact with God's revelation in the Bible.

Natural Revelation

Natural theology based on natural revelation of God was the theological starting point for Hovey. It was limited in how far it could go, but yet a few things were important. First, nature is trustworthy in its teaching. By "nature" Hovey meant "the whole universe of matter and mind, with the exception of God."[85] He followed his previous pattern of affirming the ability to know the truth of something, but only in part. Nature is trustworthy, but it is "vast and mysterious." This was a problem because to know nature perfectly would require knowing it comprehensively. Since this was impossible we must "be satisfied with knowing it in part."[86] In his class notes, Hovey gave this brief explanation of what he meant by natural theology and what it may accomplish: "Nature is employed to connote everything finite and mutable; and the most important religious facts and principles taught by nature are, the existence of a Supreme Being, the Author of Nature, the personality and character of that Being, the dependence of all other beings upon Him, and the special relation of mankind to Him."[87]

Hovey distinguished his viewpoint of the content of nature as theistic from the materialistic and the idealistic. He felt that since these three were the major viewpoints of nature and that if he could make a case for the supremacy of the theistic viewpoint, then, importantly, natural theology would be fulfilling its purpose. Materialism did not worry Hovey much and received little more than a dismissal. He defined materialism as the idea that "matter is self-existent and the course of all things."[88] Hovey argued that this view was simply unable to provide a sufficient explanation for the entire universe, which is made of material and of mind.

His objections to idealism (and idealistic monism specifically)[89] occupied portions of his theologies as well as several essays in his 1892 work. Hovey goes through pains to survey various idealistic viewpoints and their

85. Hovey, *Manual of Christian Theology*, 17.
86. Hovey, *Manual of Christian Theology*, 17.
87. Hovey, "Theological Propaedeutics (Lecture Notes)," 18 (AHP).
88. Hovey, *Manual of Systematic Theology*, 27.
89. Though here, Hovey referred his readers to his 1892 essays, Hovey, *Studies in Ethics and Religion*.

major tenets, plus their major problems with the theistic viewpoint. The basic argument Hovey provided is that: "The fact of [God's] immanence in nature when divorced from the fact of his creatorship leads to far more serious difficulties than it removes."[90] After critiquing the opposing viewpoints, he provided at least ten reasons why the theistic viewpoint better answered and explained issues such as design and order. Hovey's theology demonstrated at this point that he was not opposed to the concept of evolution per se, but he was opposed to the metaphysics of materialism, or what he called "merely natural evolution."[91] Hovey was more concerned to prove the superiority of the theistic hypothesis (from the basis of natural theology) than to argue for or against evolution. Still, it is clear that Hovey accepted some form of evolution. Concerning his main point, Hovey went through pains to show that "merely natural evolution" (used either materialistically or idealistically) could not offer a sufficient explanation of nature. Particularly, he argued that the evolutionary explanation of the "genetic history of the earth" showed elements of design and order, thus arguing for a theistic origin. Further, the appearance of humanity on earth argues for the theistic view since it needed divine imposition to explain the character of humanity. "For man is a being at once *rational, moral*, and *religious*; and we must either suppose that he is the product of mere vital energies, acting without reason, or that germs of reason, moral sense, and religion were latent in animal life, and still earlier in chemical atoms, or else that a Supreme Mind was concerned in the creation of mankind."[92] In other words, Hovey makes the major argument that the makeup of humanity as rational, moral, and religious *necessitates* a supernatural imposition of God in the creation of mankind, even if one accepts an evolutionary model.[93]

90. Hovey, "Relation of God to Nature," 50.

91. Hovey, *Manual of Christian Theology*, 32. In his lecture notes, Hovey referred to this view as "simple evolution" (Hovey, "Christian Theology: Introduction: Definitions and Explanations [Lecture Notes]," 39 [AHP]).

92. Hovey, *Manual of Christian Theology*, 33.

93. See his arguments in Hovey, *Manual of Christian Theology*, 33–39. Also see Hovey, *Manual of Systematic Theology*, 35–42. Hovey's 1870 *Outlines* also give this argument, though in brief (Hovey, *Outlines of Christian Theology*, 29–30). Hovey's essay "Our Knowledge of Infinites" also argues from natural theology and from philosophy that because there is a religious nature within humanity that can conceive of an infinite being and wants to worship that infinite being that it is entirely reasonable to know and believe that there is a God who is infinite (Hovey, "Our Knowledge of Infinites"). In his argument surrounding evolution, Hovey reflects the Princeton theologians who also found a place for evolution within their theological construction (particularly God's providence, creation, and miracles) while rejecting the idea that evolution could sufficiently answer metaphysical questions that properly belonged to theology. For one view of the Princetonians on this discussion, see Gundlach, *Process and Providence*. For

This only argued that the theistic view was more reasonable. Hovey also appealed to the classic arguments for the existence of God: *a priori*, cosmological, teleological, anthropological, and Christological; but these were not "logically conclusive."[94] Altogether, the argument (based on natural revelation) for affirming theism over the other two options was that it was more reasonable. But again, these arguments for the existence of a Supreme Being—though more reasonable—are nevertheless unable to convince all.[95] "Yet most of the evidence on which [the existence of a Supreme Being] rests is probable, rather than demonstrative. It may therefore be discredited by one who is unwilling to believe in God. Some parts of it suffer from ignorance of Nature in its vast extent."[96]

In conclusion, Hovey affirmed that the "revelation of God in nature is insufficient."[97] It could lead to certain knowledge that was trustworthy and useful and convince the reasoning person of the existence of a Supreme Being. But it left many vital questions unanswered and looked for better understanding. "We are ready therefore to welcome clearer light upon the Author of our being."[98]

The Revelation of Christ and the Biblical Revelation

In his theology textbooks, Hovey moves directly from discussions of "God Revealed in Nature" to "God Revealed in Scripture." This reflected Hovey's view of the distinction between natural and special revelation. Biblical revelation was the subject that occupied more of Hovey's printed work than any other. Outside of his theology textbooks, he published additional books and several articles and essays, some popular and some technical, that dealt with the Bible, its authority, and its interpretation.[99] The focus of the next sub-

---

a contrary view, see Zaspel, *Theology of B. B. Warfield*.

94. Hovey, *Manual of Christian Theology*, 40.

95. Hovey believed that one could get to the point of belief in a divine being through natural theology. He also believed that based on the moral and religious qualities of humanity that it is reasonable to argue that this divine being is perfect since that would satisfy humanity's religious and moral needs.

96. Hovey, *Manual of Christian Theology*, 25. The 1877 edition does not make such a statement explicitly, though hints at the limitations of the claims of reason are present (Hovey, *Manual of Systematic Theology*, 27).

97. Hovey, *Manual of Christian Theology*, 41.

98. Hovey, *Manual of Christian Theology*, 41.

99. Presented chronologically, these works are: *The Miracles of Christ as Attested by the Evangelists*; "The Bible the Only Standard of Christian Doctrine and Duty"; *Outlines of Christian Theology*; *Normal Class Manual for Bible Teachers*; *Manual of Systematic Theology*; "Theories of Inspiration"; "A Symposium"; "The New Testament as a Guide

section for this chapter will be to see how he understood the Bible within his theological method. Hovey distinguished natural revelation from biblical revelation for the primary reason "that the sacred Scriptures are records of views of chosen men who were enlightened and guided in a supernatural way by the Spirit of God in doing their work as religious teachers."[100]

There is reason to insert a discussion here about the place of Christ's teaching in the scheme of biblical revelation and theological method. Though, as will be seen, the distinction between Jesus' teaching and the teaching of the New Testament is theoretical and not actual. In his 1895 book, *Christian Teaching and Life*,[101] Hovey gave a popular level explanation of what Christians taught and what the Christian principles of life were. The book provided a helpful understanding of the origins of Christian teaching

---

to the Interpretation of the Old Testament"; "A 'Symposium' on the 'Gradualness of Revelation'"; *Doctrines of the Bible*; *Origin and Interpretation of the Bible*; "The Sacred Writings Described"; "Inspiration of the Prophets and Apostles"; "Inspiration of the Scriptures"; "The New Testament as a Guide to the Interpretation of the Old Testament"; *Christian Teaching and Life*; *Manual of Christian Theology*; "The Seat of Authority in Religion"; and *The Bible*. The Alvah Hovey Papers housed at the Yale Divinity School special collections also contain over a dozen handwritten lectures on various aspects of the Bible, such as authority, inspiration, and alleged contradictions in scripture. These handwritten lectures and notes do not contradict any published material, and they often provide elongated discussions of each of the various topics. To clarify some of the chronology, Hovey's undated work, *The Bible*, was previously published in 1873 as the first half of the co-published work, *Normal Class Manual for Bible Teachers*. Hovey's part in each is an exact replica. The second-half of Hovey's part in this book includes an exposition of Bible Doctrine, which was republished verbatim in 1892 as *Doctrines of the Bible*, with the minor exception that the student questions provided as a long list at the end of *The Bible* are provided at the end of each section in *Doctrines of the Bible*. While *The Bible* does not include a date, its preface remarked that the *Normal Class Manual* (1873) preceded it. *Doctrines of the Bible* (1892) indicated in its preface that *The Bible* preceded it. Thus, *The Bible* was published between 1873 and 1892. Still, since it is an exact replica of the *Normal Class Manual*, its substance was first published in 1873.

100. Hovey, *Manual of Christian Theology*, 42. The nineteenth-century discussions surrounding biblical criticism also have a significant role in this discussion. For Hovey, the Bible clearly played the central role in his theology and method. The debates surrounding biblical criticism and Hovey's interaction with it speak to the character of the biblical revelation, especially when it comes to discussions of inerrancy, his understanding of inspiration, and how to deal with critical studies of the Bible. They are also extensive and require much more space than this section will provide. The next chapter will present a detailed look into Hovey's views on biblical criticism, his interactions with it, and if or how it affected his own views on authority. Taken together, these sections and the next chapter will present a full-orbed picture of Hovey's views on the Bible. Still, this sub-section will give a shorter but still accurate presentation of the place of the Bible within Hovey's theological method.

101. Hovey, *Christian Teaching and Life*.

in Jesus Christ, the development of this teaching by the apostles, how this teaching was formed and used in creeds and confessions, how this then applied to contemporary Christian life, and then further areas of Christian teaching and life that are being debated along with the goal of these debates. In sum, the work was a short, popular level explanation of how Hovey conceived the origin, encoding, and development of Christian doctrine.[102]

Hovey started with the teaching of Jesus, which he described as "basal."[103] He went on to say that the teaching of Jesus is found in the four gospels primarily and he defended the character and genuineness of the gospels. Hovey explained the starting point of Jesus, "We begin with the teaching of Jesus Christ, the founder of our religion. Yet not because his teaching is in our judgment more trustworthy than that of his apostles, but because the trustworthiness of their religious teaching rests, in the last analysis, upon his."[104] Hovey simply argued that Jesus commissioned the apostles to disseminate his teaching and he promised divine help to do this. "But the sufficiency of their knowledge and the truthfulness of their teaching do not render their words as original or fundamental or germinant as their Lord's (Matt 11:27; 13:37). He remains forever the Great Teacher (Matt 24:35), the fountain-head of truth concerning God and his grace (John 4:14), and to him therefore we first look for instruction."[105]

Hovey made a similar argument in his short article that he published near the end of his life (1902) in *Watchman*, "The Seat of Authority in Religion."[106] Hovey recognized that all religious people agree that God is the primary authority, but nobody has direct, undiluted access to God. The question is, rather, who is the primary derivative or proximate authority. Hovey did not see humanity's own soul as the primary seat, nor the common belief of humanity, nor the papacy. Rather, "Jesus of Nazareth is the sufficient and supreme accessible authority in religion for mankind."[107] Hovey listed seven reasons why this was so. The arguments that he gave began with the assumption that the New Testament is a trustworthy historical record, which then claims and demonstrates (through miracles, the quality

---

102. This work does not disagree with Hovey's theologies. It does, however, provide explanations of points that are not developed in his theologies. The concept of development of doctrine and the use of creeds also appeared in his class notes and his published work on church history. See Hovey, "Good Church History"; "History of Opinions (History of Dogma—Lecture Notes)" (AHP).

103. Hovey, *Christian Teaching and Life*, 13.

104. Hovey, *Christian Teaching and Life*, 13.

105. Hovey, *Christian Teaching and Life*, 13–14.

106. Hovey, "Seat of Authority in Religion."

107. Hovey, "Seat of Authority in Religion," 12.

of his teaching, the history of the church, and the fact that Christianity is hope-inspiring and soul-uplifting) this authority for Jesus and those who properly understand his teaching as recorded in the New Testament.[108] "Jesus Christ, then, is the fountain-head of true religion in its highest form, the supreme authority for it and in it; and the New Testament Scriptures are the almost fleckless mirrors by which His personality and teaching are set before our rational souls."[109]

Hovey's "Christocentrism" is important, and a few words should be said in relation to contemporaneous discussions of Christ's centrality in theology. In his searching critique of the various unhelpful uses of the term "Christocentrim," Richard Muller explains how such a term has been used to describe Irenaeus, John Calvin, and Karl Barth, among others.[110] Christocentrism may be soteriological (Calvin), teleological (Irenaeus), or principial (Barth). Calvin was Christocentric in that he insisted on the unequivocal centrality of Christ in salvation, and such Christocentrism could be found nearly everywhere. Irenaeus may be termed Christocentric because he emphasized the preeminence of Christ over the first Adam. And Barth could be called Christocentric because he saw Christ as the center point in his theology by which all other points are understood. Such a variation renders the bald descriptor "Christocentric" completely meaningless and normally misleading. In his discussion, Muller mentions various nineteenth-century theologians within the principial designation; Isaak Dorner, Gottfried Thomasius, and Emmanuel Gerhart can all be seen to hold that "the Christ-idea must be used as the interpretive key to understanding and elucidating all doctrinal topics."[111] Though this "principial" form of Christocentrism was in vogue during Hovey's time, it is not a good descriptor of his use here. Rather, Hovey was simply saying that within discussions of religious authority that is based on principal revelation, Christ's revelation is supreme, yet it is primarily found in the New Testament.[112]

To return to how Hovey understood Christ to be central and to say it another way, Hovey held that God's revelation in Jesus, particularly his

---

108. Hovey, "Seat of Authority in Religion," 12–13.
109. Hovey, "Seat of Authority in Religion," 13.
110. Muller, "Note on 'Christocentrism.'"
111. Muller, "Note on 'Christocentrism,'" 256.
112. I say "primarily" because Hovey did recognize that the revelation of Christ was most accessible in Scripture but also accessible through "spiritual presence": "And he is [the seat of authority in religion] because, through the New Testament records *and His spiritual presence*, He is now, to all who know the gospel, what He was to His first disciples, who saw in Him, 'a glory as of an only begotten from with the Father, full of grace and truth'" (Hovey, "Seat of Authority in Religion," 12 [emphasis added]).

teachings, are basic. However, these teachings are recorded in the inspired writings of the apostles (the New Testament), which inspiration Jesus promised. The biblical record of Jesus is trustworthy, which is where we can learn the life and teaching of Jesus. The apostles also give exposition of the teaching of Jesus. The New Testament is not exhaustive of Jesus' teaching, but it is an inspired record and therefore true. All put together, this shows that while Hovey held to the theoretical primacy of Jesus and his teaching, he also believed that the only current access to Jesus' teaching is in the Bible. This is why Hovey moved straight from "God revealed in nature" to "God revealed in Scripture."[113] It is also why he remarked above that Jesus teaching is basal not on the grounds of historical trustworthiness (or availability), but on the grounds that Jesus is the fountain head. We should remember that according to Hovey organizing the "facts" or "data" of Christian theology is what the theologian is to do in a systematic theology. From the perspective of "data," there is no practical distinction between Jesus' teaching and the apostle's teaching because we have no writings from Jesus. Christians have a reliable historical record of Jesus' teachings from the apostles. They also have a promise from Jesus that he would provide supernatural help to the apostles to record Jesus' teaching as well as their own teaching. In his theologies, then, Hovey followed a consistent outline for how he understood that "the sacred Scriptures are records of views of chosen men who were enlightened and guided in a supernatural way by the Spirit of God in doing their work as religious teachers."[114]

When discussing the revelation of God in Scripture and its supernatural character, Hovey made the appeal that a rational person on rational grounds may accept the Bible as supernatural revelation. He quickly dealt with *a priori* objections against the possibility of a divine special revelation and moved on the discuss why the Bible was the central source of theology. Hovey had an outline that he followed from as early as 1867 and as late as 1900 (with some modification) that gives his full understanding. Tables 1 through 4 give the various forms of his outline.[115]

---

113. This is true in Hovey's theology. Though, in *Christian Teaching and Life*, Hovey began with the teaching of Jesus (as found in the New Testament) and then moved to the teaching of the apostles.

114. Hovey, *Manual of Christian Theology*, 42.

115. In addition to the points given in each outline, Hovey also dealt extensively with objections to his views. These objections vary somewhat in each edition. The objections show the arguments that Hovey felt were difficult to answer. Several of them deal with critical studies of the Bible and will be dealt with in the next chapter.

Table 1. Hovey's Explanation of Biblical Authority in 1867 "The Bible the Only Standard of Christian Doctrine and Duty"	

1 – The Divine Authority of the Bible Demonstrated by:
  1. Christ was infallible
  2. Christ promised to give truth to the apostles
  3. The apostles were upright
	2 – The Completeness of the Bible Demonstrated by:
	  1. Christ's promise for all truth
	  2. The position and work given to the apostles
	  3. The actual contents of the Bible
	  4. The failure of all attempts to make additions

Table 2. Hovey's Argument for the Bible as a Supernatural Revelation in 1870 *Outline of Christian Theology*						
1. The NT scriptures worthy of entire confidence as historical records.	2. The NT scriptures, considered merely as trustworthy historical records, prove the infallibility of Christ.	3. These records testify that Christ promised the inspiration of the Holy Spirit to the apostles.	4. The NT scriptures were all either written or sanctioned by apostles.	5. The OT scriptures were declared by Christ and his apostles to be the Word of God.	6. That the inspiration of the apostles and prophets was different in kind from that of ordinary Christians.	7. The inspiration of the apostles and prophets made them infallible teachers of truth.

Table 3. Hovey's Argument for the Bible as a Supernatural Revelation in 1877 *Manual of Systematic Theology and Christian Ethics*					
1. The NT scriptures are worthy of full confidence as historical records.	2. These writings prove that Jesus Christ was an infallible teacher.	3. These records prove that Christ promised the inspiration of the Holy Spirit to his apostles, by whom, with some of their associates, the NT was written.	4. Both Christ and his inspired apostles indorsed the OT scriptures as from God	5. That the inspiration of the apostles and prophets was different in kind from that of ordinary Christians.	6. The inspiration of the apostles and prophets made them infallible teachers of truth.

Table 4. Hovey's Argument for the Bible as a Supernatural Revelation in 1900 *Manual of Christian Theology*			
1. The NT scriptures are trustworthy as historical records.	2. The NT scriptures, especially the gospels, prove that Jesus Christ was an infallible teacher.	3. The NT scriptures, especially the gospels, prove that Jesus Christ promised inspiration of the Holy Spirit to his apostles, by whom, with some of their associates, the NT was written.	4. Jesus Christ, together with his inspired apostles and their associates, indorsed the OT scriptures as from God.

In 1867, Hovey argued that the Bible was the only standard for doctrine. One part of this argument was the divine authority of the Bible. In this essay he first gave his outline that demonstrated how he established this authority. Hovey argued that the authority of the Bible was rooted in the truth that Christ was infallible in his teaching, who thus had the authority to promise the apostles that they would receive truth, and which reliability was proved by the upright lives of the apostles.

This basic outline was elaborated in 1870 to include the initial proposition that the New Testament Scriptures, and here Hovey primarily meant the gospels, were trustworthy historical records. This trustworthiness meant that when they present Christ as infallible, it should be accepted, which then means that Christ could promise inspiration to the apostles, much as Hovey had argued in 1867. The 1870 outline then added several further propositions that each built upon one another by which Hovey could establish the divine biblical authority of both testaments. He successively argued that the New Testament was either written by the apostles (who had received Christ's promise) or by their close associates and that the New Testament then declared the Old Testament to be God's word. The inspiration that Christ promised to the apostles and which was also present in the Old Testament was both different from any kind of inspiration that other Christians might experience and also showed the biblical writers to be infallible teachers.

The elongated 1870 outline was followed essentially in 1877 with the only difference being that the 1877 outline combined the third and fourth proposition into one. The 1900 outline was shortened to only four points. Despite the shorter outline, however, the same propositions appear in the 1900 book that were listed more formally in the previous editions.[116] The fifth and sixth propositions from 1877 have to do with nature and extent of inspiration, which Hovey clearly discusses in his 1900 edition.[117] A closer look at the four propositions from 1900 is useful.

The first proposition was the historical trustworthiness of the New Testament.[118] To prove this, Hovey asserted that "the trustworthiness of primary historical records mainly depends on the opportunities which the writers had to learn the truth; on their powers of observation, memory and expression; on their desire to learn and to report the truth; on their number and essential agreement; and on the consistency of their testimony with

---

116. The fifth proposition (from the 1877 outline) is found on pp. 64–66 (of the 1900 edition). The sixth proposition is not simply stated as such, but the idea of infallibility/inerrancy of the apostles (and the entire Bible) is found on pp. 68, 87–88, 92–101.

117. This point will be discussed at more length below.

118. Hovey, *Manual of Christian Theology*, 46–55.

experience in similar circumstances."[119] Hovey offered mere summaries of how these may be established and fuller explanations were referred to in his footnotes, but he was quite satisfied that all stipulations were met.

The second proposition was that the New Testament proved Jesus was an infallible teacher.[120] The claims of Jesus as teacher to be infallible and sinless were considered reasonable on the grounds of their coherence, Jesus' fulfilled predictions, and Jesus' miracles. Anticipating objections to miracles, Hovey offered several rebuttals.[121] He concluded that based on the number of witnesses, their abilities to remember and transmit testimony, and their trustworthiness the miracles of Jesus were to be trusted. And, if Jesus worked miracles then his teaching was true and was to be followed.

The third proposition was that the New Testament proved Jesus promised inspiration of the Holy Spirit to his apostles.[122] This then guaranteed some sort of truth would be available to all people in the apostolic writings. Inspiration was promised as the method and as the guarantee of the inerrancy of the teaching. The final proposition is that Jesus and the New Testament writers endorsed the Old Testament to be from God.[123] The inspiration of the Old Testament was considered to be fully supernatural and the same as that of the New Testament. This extended quotation nicely summarizes his argument:

> The facts which have been adduced distinguish the Holy Scriptures from all other books, and give to their teaching a unique and divine authority—an authority which, apart from errors in the text, is equal to that of oral instruction by prophets or apostles. They are not mere ordinary records of divinely guided events; *they are records of messages and events, made or adopted by men under the impulse and guidance of the Spirit of Truth.*[124]

In sum, Hovey appealed to the character and teaching of the New Testament and then to its understanding of the Old Testament. Belief in the supernatural character of scripture was acceptable to a reasonable person. Here, as elsewhere, he appealed to the suggestive limitations of such a conclusion. While it may be reasonable, it will certainly not convince all. An essential point to recognize is that Hovey believed that the Bible's inspiration was

119. Hovey, *Manual of Christian Theology*, 46.

120. Hovey, *Manual of Christian Theology*, 55–63.

121. Hovey also dealt with miracles—specifically miracles mentioned in the Gospels—in his 1864 work, Hovey, *Miracles of Christ*.

122. Hovey, *Manual of Christian Theology*, 63–68.

123. Hovey, *Manual of Christian Theology*, 68–76.

124. Hovey, *Manual of Christian Theology*, 75.

pervasive and thus evident all throughout scripture. This is why he looked at scripture's character as evidence of inspiration.

In several places Hovey described his understanding of inspiration as "dynamic."[125] He distinguished this view from "verbal" inspiration because verbal did not necessarily give enough attention to the personality of the human authors of scripture. "In other words, the inspired man thought and spoke in his own way under the influence of the Spirit but more clearly, intensely, and to the point, than he otherwise could. And the influence of God upon his inner being was so powerful and clarifying that his words, properly interpreted, were free from error. This is meant by plenary inspiration."[126] Two other theories, "religious" and "gracious,"[127] were rejected because they either saw scripture as merely human or inspired only in its spiritual teaching. "Religious" stressed that the Bible was human, and nothing can be perfect or inerrant if it is human. Thus, inspiration is only applied to religious matters. "Gracious" argued that all true servants are inspired. The more devout one is, the more inspired they are. Thus, only Jesus was inerrant, but we only have copies of his teachings.

In the strict sense, inspiration applied only to the original writings, but it generally applied in the preserved texts. Inspiration also applied to the entirety of the text. "These writings are God's word to men. They not only *contain* divine messages, but they *are* such messages, and no sentence in them is wholly useless. Every paragraph and clause contributes something to the truth revealed or to the force of that truth."[128] It was inspired to the point of an inerrant, self-consistent, progressive revelation, but it still retained a human style. The Bible described historical and scientific information from a phenomenological viewpoint and was accurate in that sense, though history and science were not necessarily the main point of scripture. "The kind of inspiration which we have endeavored to describe appears to account for the boldness and power of prophets and apostles, for the variety of style and the popular character of the Scriptures and for many things which are supposed by some to be incompatible with absolute truth and authority in matters of religion."[129]

---

125. His most extended discussions of inspiration are found in Hovey, "Sacred Writings Described"; "Inspiration of the Prophets and Apostles"; "Inspiration of the Scriptures"; "New Testament as a Guide"; *Manual of Christian Theology*, 76–106.

126. Hovey, "Inspiration of the Scriptures," 183.

127. See Hovey, "Inspiration of the Scriptures," 184–85.

128. Hovey, "Inspiration of the Scriptures," 216.

129. Hovey, "Inspiration of the Scriptures," 217.

In his 1870 and 1877 works Hovey did not use the word inerrant but instead the word infallible.[130] By his 1892 and 1900 works he used the word inerrancy for the same ideas where he had previously used the word infallibility.[131] Infallibility and inerrancy were used to describe the quality of inspiration upon the biblical writers and the product they left behind. They were also used when answering objections against supposed biblical errors of history, science, or morals. Hovey rejected that his view of the Bible necessarily leads to bibliolatry, slowed the progress of science, forced us to have inerrant copies and translations, disallowed obscure language, was undone by the supposed unsound arguments of scripture, could explain supposed poor interpretation of scripture by scripture, taught false science, taught historical error, contained contradictory statements, contained false predictions, taught bad morality, or taught bad theology.[132]

Hovey did allow for inspiration to be understood in a certain sense as religious. What he meant was that the Bible had the purpose of the religious conversion of men. Thus, inspiration was a tool used toward that end.[133] This meant that God used the best means available at the time of composition to convince the readers of the truthfulness (and inerrancy) of the Bible and its message. This could mean there is phenomenological language, which is not strictly correct, but is understandable to the person reading (such as the sun "rising").[134] In addition to phenomenological language, there are errors of transmission (which Hovey often referred to as "errors of the text")[135] and definite difficulties to be worked through. In sum, a few parts were necessary to keep in mind when discussing inspiration and inerrancy: (1) the religious purpose to Scripture, (2) the condescension of God to present the Bible in understandable language, (3) the presence of phenomenological language,

---

130. Hovey, *Outlines of Christian Theology*, 60–62; *Manual of Systematic Theology*, 83–87.

131. Hovey, "Inspiration of the Scriptures," 186; *Manual of Christian Theology*, 86–106, esp. 87–88.

132. Hovey, *Manual of Christian Theology*, 86–106. Hovey does, however, concede that "many numerical contradictions have crept into the text of the Old Testament through the oversight of copyists" (Hovey, *Manual of Christian Theology*, 102).

133. "But we must also remember, while reading them, the ends sought by revelation, ends which go far to determine its style. For the proximate ends of revelation are instruction and *impression*, with a view to the ultimate end, the restoration of men to fellowship with God. Stupid and hardened sinners must be moved, in order to be saved. Hence the feeling of a holy God must be made real to their minds" (Hovey, *Manual of Christian Theology*, 105).

134. See, for example, Hovey, *Manual of Christian Theology*, 97. Also see his explanation in Hovey and Gregory, *Normal Class Manual for Bible Teachers*, 35–36.

135. Hovey, *Manual of Christian Theology*, 87–88, 102.

(4) the apparent and not actual difficulties of the Bible, and (5) the skillful interpretation of the Bible. His clearest summary of how to understand what God was doing in biblical revelation was given in 1892:

> It is, therefore, our belief that the Sacred Scriptures, rightly interpreted from beginning to end as the record of a progressive revelation of God to man, of man to himself, and of spiritual life to all who will accept it, will lead to truth without error, and will justify that revelation, as one that gave those addressed by it, in each particular age, the religious truth most needed by them, in the best available form for reaching the heart and purifying the life. This sentence is long, but we cannot make it shorter and express the precise meaning intended.[136]

In sum, Hovey believed his view of scripture was the most reasonable and also allowed the theologian to use biblical information for theological construal with the religious purpose of conversion and sanctification. Throughout his theology Hovey noted several difficulties and believed that sufficient answers exist whereby he was able to retain his view of scripture. The Bible, based on its supernatural and inspired nature, was the supreme source for theological data. As such, the Bible could be appealed to with confidence as from God and as trustworthy. It now remains to see Hovey's principles for biblical interpretation.

Hermeneutics

Chapter 2 noted that Hovey admired the exegetical methods of Moses Stuart and Horatio Hackett. In addition to editing a commentary set and the commentaries that he wrote, Hovey wrote a handful of works explaining the basics of Bible interpretation as he saw it.[137] In his handwritten notes under the title of "Theological Propaedeutics," Hovey explained that Biblical Exegesis "has for its object to ascertain and explain the precise meaning of the Bible or any portion of it."[138] In this manuscript and in the second part of *The Normal Class Manual for Bible Teachers*, Hovey provided several points meant to be utilized in biblical interpretation and are worth presenting in list form. First, his lecture notes:

---

136. Hovey, "Inspiration of the Scriptures," 212. This paragraph is quoted verbatim in Hovey's 1900 Manual. See Hovey, *Manual of Christian Theology*, 85.

137. See Part II in Hovey and Gregory, *Normal Class Manual for Bible Teachers*; Hovey, *Commentary on the Gospel of John*; "General Introduction to the New Testament"; "New Testament as a Guide"; *Commentary on the Epistle to the Galatians*. See also his class notes, Hovey, "Theological Propaedeutics (Lecture Notes)," 85–88.

138. Hovey, "Theological Propaedeutics (Lecture Notes)," 85.

1. Ascertain by careful reading of any book in the original or in a good translation its chief purpose.
2. Note the circumstances in which it was written, particularly the position of the writer and the implied needs of the readers.
3. Note also the general style of the book, as historic, didactic, argumentative, hortatory, ethical, poetic, proverbial.
4. Notice and mark the several stages of the discussion.
5. Study the writings paragraph by paragraph, and in a didactic or argumentative book consider the logical connection of each paragraph, sentence, and clause with the context.
6. Study also the meaning of the principal verbs and nouns as determined by their use in other passages of the same writer, their use in other writings of the same period and upon the same subjects, and by their primary and derivative meanings in the language.
7. Consider the probability (or otherwise) of any particular words being employed in a figurative sense.
8. Make a thorough paraphrase of the writer's thought.[139]

In *The Normal Class Manual for Bible Teachers*, Hovey shortened the statements, though he provided longer explanations of each. He argued that "an interpreter of Scripture, then, should consider:

1. The general style of the Sacred Record.
2. The object and quality of a given book.
3. The circumstances in which a given book was written.
4. The relation of a given paragraph to the whole book.
5. The meaning of particular words and phrases.
6. Other statements of the same writer on the topic treated in a given passage."[140]

These lists were clearly meant as methodological rules to be followed. They built off the assumption that the Bible was inspired in the very words and evinced the individual writing characteristics of the human authors. They also assumed that the interpreter would have a certain level of skill (as he argued was necessary in his prolegomena) in interpretation. *The Normal Class Manual* was written for lay readers and so did not make a requirement of learning the biblical languages. But it is clear from his views of education

---

139. Hovey, "Theological Propaedeutics (Lecture Notes)," 85–86.
140. Hovey and Gregory, *Normal Class Manual for Bible Teachers*, 35–39.

and from his own writings that thorough mastery of the biblical languages was essential.

Besides the listed rules of interpretation, Hovey also dealt with a few major issues of hermeneutics. These are: the relationship of the New Testament to the Old Testament, typology, and Bible difficulties.

When discussing the use of the Old Testament in the New,[141] Hovey made a few observations and then five general points by way of conclusion. He observed that Jesus' use of the Old Testament is the most important and that the apostles' use is likewise important. This study also assumes that there is a unity across the scriptures by which the concluding general principles could be made.[142] He argued, first, that "the New Testament is not the primary source of knowledge concerning the meaning of the Old."[143] This simply means that he thought the Old Testament should be interpreted first on its own right. Second, "the New Testament affords but little assistance to the one engaged in the textual criticism of the Old Testament."[144] Third, "the New Testament affords but little aid to the so-called higher criticism of the Old."[145] Simply put, he believed that the simple testimony of Jesus and the apostles was a major hurdle to the higher critical views. Fourth, "the New Testament is exceedingly helpful to one in discovering religious principles which underlie many passages of the Old Testament."[146] Fifth, "the New Testament is of great assistance in tracing the line of Messianic prediction in the Old."[147] In other words, the New Testament, especially Hebrews, helps to make sense of the Mosaic writings in light of God's fuller revelation. Hovey's essay on the use of the Old Testament in the New shows his trust in the inspiration and unity of the Bible as well as his view of the progressive nature of biblical revelation.

Hovey wrote about "Types and Symbols."[148] He understood types primarily as a resemblance of something or someone in the future, thus it is prophetic. This can be applied to people, things, acts, or nations. Symbols,

---

141. Hovey wrote about this first in 1889 (see Hovey, "New Testament as a Guide") and then reprinted the essay under the same title in 1892.

142. Hovey, "New Testament as a Guide," 212. Hovey also gave extended time to dealing with higher critical charges against the unity of scripture, trustworthiness of the New Testament's quotations, and Old Testament dates and authors. The next chapter will return to Hovey's interactions with the higher critical views.

143. Hovey, "New Testament as a Guide," 212.

144. Hovey, "New Testament as a Guide" 212.

145. Hovey, "New Testament as a Guide," 213.

146. Hovey, "New Testament as a Guide," 213.

147. Hovey, "New Testament as a Guide," 213.

148. Hovey and Gregory, *Normal Class Manual for Bible Teachers*, 43–47.

on the other hand, are more of a reference to resemblance. They are not arbitrary and are meant to make an impression on more than the mind. Hovey urged that interpreters use caution in declaring anything to be a type or symbol and should defer to biblical declarations of such.

Bible difficulties were more problematic for the nature of the Bible than for interpretation.[149] But they also required proper interpretation to be answered well. Hovey first warned that these difficulties should not be given overdue prominence because that could lead to overexaggerating the scope of the problem. The reader should also have the attitude of Paul when he said we only understand things dimly. In other words, it is fine for the interpreter to admit they do not know an answer and still have confidence in the Bible. The final point was to make use of the best helps to interpret the Bible. These are commentaries, encyclopedias, histories, and other useful works. "The use of such helps is important, not only because they serve to assure one of the 'intense exactness' of the word of God, but also because they add greatly to the vividness of its language and the interest with which it is read."[150]

As this work has shown in many places of Hovey's method and ministry, the method and the ability to do high-quality work (in this case, biblical interpretation) were important and essential, but they were complementary to moral and spiritual qualities and they were subservient to the greater purpose of having a close relationship with God. For Hovey, there were definite rules for biblical interpretation, but they were not all that were needed. Despite the need to master these rules, the interpreter had a more fundamental need: "Fit personal qualities are more essential to the interpreter of the Scriptures than any rules to guide him in his work. These qualities are good sense, fairness of mind, ardent love of the truth, and patience in study. Without them he will never ascertain 'the mind of the Spirit,' as revealed in the Bible, though familiar with the best rules; with them he will succeed, though ignorant of these rules."[151] The Bible was to be interpreted skillfully according to correct hermeneutical principles, but the science of interpretation needed the complement of proper personal qualities.

Summary

In an essay entitled "Sacred Writings Described" Hovey assumed that revelation and truth concerning God and humanity had been preserved in the Scriptures. He thus described the Bible as fragmentary, multiform,

---

149. Hovey and Gregory, *Normal Class Manual for Bible Teachers*, 47–51.
150. Hovey and Gregory, *Normal Class Manual for Bible Teachers*, 51.
151. Hovey and Gregory, *Normal Class Manual for Bible Teachers*, 35.

progressive, and religious.[152] This was essentially affirming the ideas that Scripture was true though not exhaustive of truth, was supernatural but not insensitive to genre and historical circumstance, was geared toward the learning capabilities of humans, and had the primary focus of helping people seek the Christian way of life. Hovey ended with words of encouragement to the biblical interpreter: "Fear not, then with the love of God in your hearts and after these years of reverent study, to enter upon the work to which you are called. May the spirit and the word, invoked by prayer and examined with diligence, guide you step by step into all the truth which is necessary to qualify you still further for the ministry of Christ, in these days of questioning and of progress!"[153]

Hovey repeatedly appealed to the reasonableness of the existence of God, of the supernatural character of biblical revelation, and of the Bible's self-description as dynamically inspired and inerrant. He then put limitations on this reasonableness by saying it can only establish probability. At the end of his major section on "God Revealed in Scripture," Hovey offered this final summary that nicely summarizes how Hovey intended to construct his theology.

> The result of our investigation is *that the Bible is a trustworthy revelation of God, i.e., of his being, his character, and his relation to other beings, especially men.* It can be appealed to with the same confidence with which we appeal to the order of nature. The testimony which it bears to the personality and the moral perfection of God is particularly emphatic. And by the Scriptures alone has God given to us a clear revelation of his trinal personality, of his infinite mercy, and of his provision for the restoration of sinners to his favor and life eternal. In our further study of theism we shall therefore make free use of the Holy Scriptures.[154]

Tradition

Tradition did not occupy an explicit section in Hovey's theology textbooks in relation to theological method. When I use the word "tradition" in this section, I am referring to the history (in a broad sense) of the church that came before, whether in individual theologians or formalized confessions. Heiko Oberman's classic construct of Reformation era understandings of

---

152. Hovey, "Sacred Writings Described."
153. Hovey, "Sacred Writings Described," 107.
154. Hovey, *Manual of Christian Theology*, 105–6.

tradition and the Bible can be helpful here. Oberman presented "Tradition I" as a single-source theory whereby doctrine is based on Scripture alone and tradition is understood as the received interpretation of Scripture. "Tradition II" is a dual-source theory whereby doctrine is based on two sources: scripture and tradition.[155] Alister McGrath adds a "Tradition 0" classification and placed the entirety of the radical Reformation into what he termed "Tradition 0" because they gave "no role whatsoever to tradition."[156] The term "radical reformation" refers to the Reformation-era Anabaptists broadly and points to the classic work of George Huntston Williams: *The Radical Reformation*.[157] Even the simple recognition of Williams's three types of Radical Reformations (Spiritualists, Anabaptists, and Evangelical Rationalists) has led some scholars not only to argue for the lack of nuance of McGrath's "Tradition 0" view but also argues for the need to somewhat clarify Oberman's "Tradition I" type since the different approaches of the Anabaptists and the Magisterial Reformers (not to mention later Protestants such as Baptists) could both fit within the category.[158] Discussion of this classification scheme is helpful to formulate the question for the Baptist Hovey: Does Hovey fit within Oberman's "Tradition I," McGrath's "Tradition 0," or is more nuance required? This, in turn, will help answer the question this work asks in relation to tradition: what purpose did any appeal to the past have in Hovey's theological method and, more specifically, his understanding of theological authority?

Hovey referred to various theologians (past and contemporaneous) and church councils and creeds in various places. The only place in his theology textbooks where he discussed theologians to be referenced in the practice of theology was in the introductory section. In his 1870 *Outlines* and his 1877 *Manual*, Hovey titled this section, "Writers on Systematic Theology," and generally followed a chronological listing of theologians along with very brief critical comments.[159] In his 1900 *Manual*, Hovey titled the section, "Theological Literature," and merely listed authors and titles under

---

155. Oberman, *Harvest of Medieval Theology*, 390–93; *Dawn of the Reformation*, 269–96.

156. McGrath, *Reformation Thought*, 144.

157. Williams, *Radical Reformation*.

158. For example, see Gonzalez, "Balthasar Hubmaier," 317–22; Klager, "'Truth Is Immortal.'"

159. Hovey, *Outlines of Christian Theology*, 13–19; Hovey, *Manual of Systematic Theology*, 18–26. Prior to the lists in each edition, Hovey included this short introductory sentence: "The following contains the names of a few men who discussed particular doctrines only; but most of those mentioned treated in their works of all the doctrines which they included in theology."

four denominational headings: Baptist, Presbyterian, Congregationalist, and Lutheran.[160] The one major difference between the earlier and later listings is that the 1900 edition did not include any theologians earlier than John Calvin or any outside the four denominations listed, while the earlier lists started at Athanasius and included several other denominations as well as Roman Catholic theologians. Though again, Hovey made free use of a much wider range of theologians throughout each of his theologies than are listed in these brief sections.

Outside of his theology textbooks, Hovey addressed the issue of church history, creeds, and tradition in a few places.[161] These will provide the basic material for this section. To consider how tradition played a part in Hovey's theological method, it is helpful to consider what he considered tradition to be, how it was to be used, and what authority it carried.

What Tradition Is

Hovey understood doctrine to have developed over the course of church history.[162] This development was based on an assumption that the Holy Spirit gave special promise and ability to the apostles to record the truth. This record is the Bible, which is the Word of God. However, the promise of full understanding and truth given to the apostles was not transferred to the later eras of church history. "What the Apostles knew by virtue of a special gift must be evolved from their writings by ages of study. One after another, men of powerful intellect and great experience must be raised up to search the Scriptures, bring to light, arrange, and apply their profounder truths, and then pour them by the agency of voice or pen into the bosom of Christian society, there to spread and work, silently perhaps, but swiftly, from member to member, till the whole body feels their quickening energy and the Church springs forward in her course of light."[163] Progress of doctrine was a natural consequence of divine revelation given to one group

---

160. Hovey, *Manual of Christian Theology*, 13–14.

161. These include Hovey, "Theological Propaedeutics (Lecture Notes)"; "History of Opinions (History of Dogma—Lecture Notes)"; "Opening Address," 3–6; "Good Church History"; *Restatement of Denominational Principles*; *Christian Teaching and Life*; "Seat of Authority in Religion." "A Good Church History" was Hovey's inaugural address as professor of church history at Newton, previously published as *An Inaugural Address, Delivered before the Newton Theological Institution, June 28, 1854*. "Opening Address" was Hovey's presidential address to the Baptist Autumnal Conference in 1883. The Baptist Autumnal Conference, which began in 1882, eventually became known as the Baptist Congress and continued to meet until 1913.

162. Hovey, "Good Church History," 553–57.

163. Hovey, "Good Church History," 555.

(apostles) that would then be studied over again and again in subsequent eras of church history. The inexhaustible nature of revelation and the limitations of human understanding mean that this progress would be continual until Christ came.

In his church history lecture notes, Hovey gave some explanation to the progress of Christian understanding as he saw it. He felt that the apostles were inspired. The apostolic fathers were good theologians but not systematically inclined. The succeeding fathers were more systematically inclined but philosophically influenced. The later fathers were more systematized and set the tone for all subsequent Christian theology. The period from Augustine to Anselm showed no progress. The period from Anselm through the scholastics provides some profit, mostly by way of the great organizers of thought. The Reformation through to his day showed greater incline in theological work.[164] Progress was inevitable because limited humans have been attempting to understand a divine revelation. But, according to Hovey, progress has happened through a few reasons. First, the rational nature of humanity wants to understand the theology that describes the wonderful salvation they have received. Second, heresies from outside the church have necessitated the shoring up and development of theology. Third, heresies from within have caused the refinement of theology. And fourth, the natural improvements in the study of philosophy and the physical sciences have provided clarity to biblical descriptions and thus theological formulations.[165] "The truth is given in the divine Word; never in this world to be increased or diminished; but only to be apprehended more and more perfectly."[166]

Tradition could be understood, for Hovey, as the various attempts by the church throughout its history to correctly express the apostolic theology of the Scriptures. This obviously gives an important place to the Bible in relation to tradition. But it also raises the question of how this tradition is to be used in subsequent formulations of theology.

The Use of Tradition

In his 1895 book, *Christian Teaching and Life*, Hovey provided an interesting look at his view of doctrinal development. He understood Christ's teaching to be basic.[167] The apostles' teaching was then based on Christ's teaching

---

164. Hovey, "History of Opinions (History of Dogma—Lecture Notes)," 4–11.
165. Hovey, "History of Opinions (History of Dogma—Lecture Notes)," 11–15.
166. Hovey, "History of Opinions (History of Dogma—Lecture Notes)," 14.
167. Hovey, *Christian Teaching and Life*, 21–92.

and inspired.[168] The next question is how to understand the "Formation and Use of Creeds."[169] Hovey felt that creeds had been formed for a few reasons. First, a strong desire to see beliefs expressed orderly and clearly. Second, a desire to openly declare Christianity. Third, a desire to unite against errors at various times. And fourth, they are helpful in catechizing.[170]

Hovey admitted that "the motives which led to their formation were praiseworthy. But it must at the same time be admitted that their influence has not been always and altogether wholesome."[171] This was because, first, these were naturally incomplete statements that were later taken as more than what they were meant to be. Second, creeds could damage when they subordinated the Bible as the ultimate rule of faith. Third, creeds could be problematic when they did not allow legitimate search for new truth. And fourth, creeds have caused antagonism to Christianity because they are sometimes seen as overly harsh, especially in Roman Catholicism.[172]

Despite the admitted problems of creeds, Hovey remarked that "the good influence of a reasonably sound creed probably outweighs its bad influence, while its bad influence springs from the abuse rather than from the use of it."[173] The major problem was when people have looked at creeds as inspired or as more important than they really are. "The more distinctly, then, it is understood that a creed is made by fallible interpreters of the divine word, and that it is no more than a careful summary of what such interpreters believe to be the religious teaching of that word, the more useful it is likely to be."[174] Hovey agreed that creeds were necessary for denominations to cooperate with any sort of unity. However, as a particular kind of Baptist that was less inclined to support denominational conventions and associations,[175] Hovey felt that "every particular church may, if it prefers, construct its own articles of faith, but if these articles disagree on important points with the articles of faith in other churches of the same denomination, separation will be likely to ensue."[176]

168. Hovey, *Christian Teaching and Life*, 93–138.
169. Hovey, *Christian Teaching and Life*, 139–80.
170. Hovey, *Christian Teaching and Life*, 142–43.
171. Hovey, *Christian Teaching and Life*, 143.
172. Hovey, *Christian Teaching and Life*, 143–44.
173. Hovey, *Christian Teaching and Life*, 144.
174. Hovey, *Christian Teaching and Life*, 145.
175. Hovey discusses this somewhat in a couple works, e.g., Hovey, *Restatement of Denominational Principles*; *Christian Teaching and Life*, 174–78. Hovey recognized that for American Baptists, the Philadelphia Confession (1742) and the New Hampshire Confession (1833) were the most recognized confessions for inter-church fellowship.
176. Hovey, *Christian Teaching and Life*, 145–46.

The history of the church's creeds was organized into four sections by Hovey: the early church, the Eastern Church, the Roman Church, and the Protestant churches. The early creeds were seen slightly differently since they were early enough to lay claim to all the branches of Christianity. Still, they were subject to the Bible. "If then we accept the creeds adopted by these early councils, it is not because they were General Councils, or because their members were specially enlightened by the Holy Spirit, but because 'they may be proved by most certain warrants of Holy Scripture.'"[177] Thus, creeds could and did have a purpose for Hovey. Yet, their relative authoritative value to Scripture must always be kept in mind.

The Authority of Tradition

It is clear to this point that Hovey did not hold tradition to be as authoritative as the Bible. This is true based on the Bible's character as inspired as well as the fact that no subsequent Christian teaching or writing can claim such authority. Hovey clearly stated that "the Bible, especially the New Testament, is the ultimate standard of Christian truth and duty."[178] Hovey felt this was a point that Baptists held along with (and more consistently than) other denominations. The following quote shows not only how Hovey viewed the relation of tradition to biblical authority, but also something of the necessity of referring to tradition.

> We are glad to know that Baptists are not alone in assigning to the Scriptures a position of supreme authority in determining what is Christian truth; but we think our allegiance to this principle has been more consistent than that of other denominations. We attach less sacredness to early councils, creeds, and traditions, to church action and the *consensus* of religious thought, than do the great historic sects of Christendom, and we insist more uniformly and confidently than they upon the solitary preeminence of the canonical record, believing that it is sufficient, when properly interpreted, to guide men in the way of Christian truth and duty.[179]

Hovey saw some necessity to the use of creeds, though he strongly asserted the ability of Christians to interpret the Bible on their own. Despite this ability to interpret on one's own (he was a Baptist who asserted

---

177. Hovey, *Christian Teaching and Life*, 151. Hovey here notes that he quotes Phillip Schaff, though he does not provide the source of the quote.

178. Hovey, *Christian Teaching and Life*, 174.

179. Hovey, *Restatement of Denominational Principles*, 6.

individual, personal accountability),[180] he admitted that a few questions could raise themselves up at the point of interpretation: "How far does this interpretation differ from that of Christendom in general since the last of the apostles finished his course? Is the teaching which one now finds in the earliest and the last documents of our faith, the same which has always been found in those documents?"[181] Hovey answered that comparison to creeds was the readiest answer to such a question. Therefore, creeds played an important and necessary role in the progressive development of doctrine, which was part of showing what God has done.[182] They were regulative for the development of doctrine. Hovey stated that "it would then be proper for me to insist upon the value of our supposed history, as contributing to breadth of mind and soundness of judgment upon religious questions in those who should peruse it. . . . Such a survey is the best safeguard against those rash conclusions which men are liable to make from current events, mistaking not unfrequently the feverish and fitful energy of a dying cause for the vigorous action of health."[183] To neglect the history of the church was to neglect a necessary tool. In that sense of a necessary tool, tradition could carry relative authority. Still, Hovey was quite adamant that the history of the church could not provide a definite authority in the way the Bible could. In his article, "The Seat of Authority in Religion," one view of authority that he rejected was the "common belief of men." Hovey includes in this view any attempt to locate the received authority or unity within the church's history or tradition. In a sense, the church's history has a proximate authority (as does natural revelation), but it is incomplete. "There is danger of mistaking a part for the whole, or of forgetting that every word, or sentence, or paragraph, or chapter, in the great and coherent volume of Nature, or of History, may be qualified by other parts of that volume. . . . Hence, it is no exaggeration to say that neither nature nor history, or the two combined, are a proximate, accessible, and sufficient, authority in religion."[184]

One question that comes up in this discussion, especially for Baptists, is how the Baptist understanding of "personal accountability to God in religion"[185] meshes with any appeal to outside authority or tradition. One

---

180. Hovey also asserted that the "Personal Accountability to God in Religion" and "Religious Liberty" were central tenets of Baptist theology. See Hovey, *Restatement of Denominational Principles*, 7; *Christian Teaching and Life*, 177.

181. Hovey, *Christian Teaching and Life*, 141.

182. Hovey, "Good Church History," 547.

183. Hovey, "Good Church History," 559.

184. Hovey, "Seat of Authority in Religion," 12.

185. This phrase is Hovey's own as it appears in Hovey, *Restatement of Denominational Principles*, 7. "Individual soul liberty," "soul competency," and "priesthood of the

helpful note of explanation was given by Hovey at the Baptist Autumnal Conference in 1883.[186] This conference began in 1882, eventually became known as the Baptist Congress, and continued to meet until 1913. It was a conference designed to discuss controversial issues among Baptists.[187] In his presidential address to the 1883 Conference, Hovey asked the direct question about Baptists: "Is it not their theory that every man should stand apart in the majesty of personal worth and duty, reading for himself, thinking for himself, deciding for himself, and following without fear and alone the light of God's truth as it shines into his separate soul? Have they not adopted for their motto the words, Let every man do that which is right in his own eyes, making no use of the eyes of other men?"[188] Hovey's answer was that the Baptist idea of soul liberty does not imply "eccentric and exclusive individualism." He argued that Baptists do believe in the ability to read for themselves, but they also clearly teach the need "to seek help from others in doing this work."[189] Rather than letting their theology push them to be radical individualists, Hovey claimed that the opposite was the case:

> There are no Christians in the wide world who should cultivate more sedulously than we the habit of mutual counsel and inquiry. With no visible head, like the Pope, with no ecclesiastical court, like the General Assembly, and with no imposed creed like the Thirty-nine Articles or Westminster Confession, our unity of faith and practice may best be preserved by a frequent and personal interchange of views, wherein head and heart, knowledge and faith, reverence for the past, sympathy with the present, and zeal for the future, meet and blend.[190]

believer" are other common phrases in Baptist parlance for what Hovey refers to as "personal accountability to God in religion."

186. Hovey, "Opening Address." This was Hovey's presidential address to the Baptist Autumnal Conference in 1883. More will be said about Hovey's participation in the Baptist Congress in the next chapter. On the Baptist Congress, see Brackney, "Frontier of Free Exchange of Ideas"; Garrett, *Baptist Theology*, 327–30; Sherouse, "Toward a Twentieth-Century Baptist Identity."

187. Indeed, the published proceedings of the 1883 conference described their proceedings as those "of the Second Annual Baptist Autumnal Conference for the Discussion of Current Questions, at the First Baptist Church, Boston, MA, November 13, 14, 15, 1883." The "discussion of current questions" was a continued and explicit descriptor of the Baptist Congress going forward.

188. Hovey, "Opening Address," 4.

189. Hovey, "Opening Address," 4.

190. Hovey, "Opening Address," 5.

Thus, for Hovey, Baptists by necessity ought to utilize regular discussion of tradition and their current relation to it in order foster unity and a properly Christian theology.

Summary

Tradition was not always an explicit tool that Hovey felt should be utilized in the theological practice. Yet, a larger survey of his writings on church history and the way that Christian doctrine has developed historically reveals that he had some sense of what tradition was, how it should be used, and its relative authority. Thus, it could be said to be true, in broad terms, that Hovey affirmed the Reformation idea of *sola scripture* but not *nuda scriptura*, thus fitting Oberman's "Tradition I" category. Though the Christian tradition was a regulative tool in theology, it was always itself regulated by scripture. In other words, scripture was not inferior or equal to any other authority but was in fact the norming norm (*norma normans*); further, it was not to the exclusion of tradition, instead they were both present.[191]

Despite this place for tradition, Hovey did not operate within an explicit theological confession (such as London, Philadelphia, or New Hampshire) that guided his theological formulation. He used tradition as a tool to refine and regulate theology, and so it was universally present. It was necessary, but tradition provided no preconceived theological system from within which to work out his theology. Its necessary use, however, guarded against individualism.

Theology and Epistemology

Hovey discussed epistemology in his prolegomena in a fairly comprehensive sense. However, the remainder of his theology also provides comment on his theological epistemology, thus rounding out the discussion. The primary goal of this section is to see how Hovey understood the epistemological qualities of humanity throughout the rest of his theology.

Anthropology

In his 1900 edition of his theology, Hovey divided anthropology into three sections: the nature, character, and condition of humanity.[192] This section of

---

191. George, *Theology of the Reformers*, 81.

192. These main points were present in his 1877 and 1870 editions, though not explicitly.

his theology covered the typical topics of nineteenth-century conservative theology. Hovey affirmed the bipartite nature of humans, moral responsibility for sin, total depravity, condemnation and guilt for sin, and eternal punishment for the unconverted.[193] Nowhere did Hovey deal with the rational capabilities of human beings in a systematic sense. Yet he did bring up various aspects of human rational ability. We have already seen that he considered general human reasoning trustworthy, though not infallible, which reflects his views of how humanity was created. And, we will see, his understanding of reasoning was also given further theological explanation in what the effects of sin were and in what ways regeneration could help.

Hovey spent some time on the created character of humanity. He said that "according to the testimony of sacred history, man was created upright, with a pure heart, and by an act of his own will disobeyed the will of God."[194] Hovey then stated that "will is the cause of sin in a holy being, and wrong desire the source of sin in unholy beings."[195] Yet, for Hovey, reasoning ability and willing ability were part of humanity's larger moral makeup. "If we divide the faculties of the human soul into those of knowing and feeling, desiring and willing, all these are concerned in moral action, and perhaps in every moral action."[196] The initial created ability of humanity will become clearer in his discussion of the Fall.

Sin

For Hovey, there was a clear distinction between the pre-Fall and post-Fall capabilities of humanity. "If all men are either morally depraved or sinful at birth, it must be in consequence of the apostacy [sic] in Eden; for Christians agree in teaching that man was originally upright. As he came from the hand of his Creator, he was inclined to good rather than to evil; but, since the fall, all men are inclined to evil."[197] The fall into sin had rendered the moral abilities of humanity defect.

But Hovey also saw this defect in human intellectual capabilities. "Again, a considerable part of the ignorance of mankind is due to their sinfulness. For, however intense a desire for certain kinds of knowledge may exist in the hearts of wicked men, they have an aversion to other kinds of knowledge.... If mankind had continued upright, they would have made

193. Hovey wrote several books on eschatological topics: Hovey, *State of the Impenitent Dead*; *State of Men after Death*; *Biblical Eschatology*.
194. Hovey, *Manual of Systematic Theology*, 128.
195. Hovey, *Manual of Systematic Theology*, 129.
196. Hovey, *Manual of Christian Theology*, 149.
197. Hovey, *Manual of Systematic Theology*, 141.

far higher attainments in knowledge than they have made as sinners."[198] Importantly for Hovey, as we have seen already, the moral ability of humanity encompassed knowledge as well as other categories. After listing several passages on the "moral weakness of sinful man," Hovey asserted, "These passages assume that there is no such thing as repentance for sin, or faith in Christ, or spiritual service of God, apart from divine help. And some of them express the view that sinful men are morally weak, so weak that they cannot—because they will not—seek the Lord and make him the joy of their souls."[199] The reasoning ability of humanity was limited because it was affected by the Fall. The moral fallenness of humanity also infected the reasoning ability of humanity. But Hovey saw hope for fallenness.

Soteriology

In his discussions of the Christian life Hovey pointed to the work of the Holy Spirit in the new life of Christians in overcoming the crippling results of the Fall. Speaking on 1 Corinthians 2:13–15, Hovey commented that "Paul represents the unrenewed man as unable to receive the things of God, because they are spiritually understood; while the renewed man rightly estimates all things, he appreciates truth."[200] The "new creation" was not a full separation from what had been there, but it was new. "So the old man does not cease to live, but his life becomes a new and richer and sweeter life; with the change in his spirit all the works of God appear to be changed."[201] New life brought renewed understanding.

The change in the believer was unto a new life that was qualitatively different from the old life, but it was also progressively built upon after entering. The Christian should always look for spiritual illumination by the Spirit. Hovey explained:

> Another kind of action favorable to Christian growth is the *study of God's world and word and providence.* Prayer for spiritual light should always be accompanied by study. If we ask God for bread, we sow and reap, in order to cooperate with him in answering our own prayer. So likewise if we ask God for spiritual illumination we should search the Scriptures, his word, examine his works, and observe his providence, in order to obtain from him the instruction needed. These are fountains of knowledge

---

198. Hovey, *Manual of Systematic Theology*, 169.

199. Hovey, *Manual of Christian Theology*, 152. The passages listed by Hovey were Jer 13:23; 31:18; Ezek 36:26; Ps 5:10; Matt 7:18; John 6:44, 65; 15:5; Eph 2:10; Phil 2:13.

200. Hovey, *Manual of Christian Theology*, 329.

201. Hovey, *Manual of Christian Theology*, 303.

opened by him, and his grace will enable us to draw from them refreshing draughts.[202]

The work of the Holy Spirit in regeneration and in illumination was important and knowledge was always tied to the moral stance of the individual. In the end, "*doing his will* is prerequisite to the fullest knowledge."[203]

Summary

Hovey's view of the pre-Fall reasoning ability was that it was not only trustworthy but devoid of wrongful desire and limited capabilities. His view of the post-Fall reasoning ability was that it was full of wrong desire and inextricably tied to a sinfully corrupt morality. His view of the new life of Christians was not one of perfection but of a renewed moral ability, including reason, and a continued opportunity for growth through the work of the Holy Spirit.

Conclusion: Doing Theology

How did Hovey understand and implement theological method? He affirmed the knowability of God and the world. He affirmed the trustworthiness of human reasoning. He affirmed the necessity of systematizing theology in scientific ways. He affirmed the reasonableness of Christianity. But he also clearly insisted on the limitations of all these affirmations. These limitations, despite their softening of the claims, left a theology that was strongly centered on reason and the positive ability of humanity's reasoning powers. And, his view of the Bible was that it was inspired and inerrant in the original manuscripts. The teaching contained therein has been preserved and was sufficient for the construction of theology that was more specific than natural theology. But it should be remembered that the reasonableness of theology could still only establish probability and not certainty.

The Bible was the clearest source of truth that the theologian could access. This is because it was divinely inspired and inerrant. Proper interpretation was needed, as was an awareness of and interaction with the church's tradition. As a self-conscious Baptist who affirmed that each person was accountable to God, he felt that creeds and confessions were helpful and even necessary when considering the viability of biblical interpretation and theological viewpoints, but tradition was still submissive to the Bible.

202. Hovey, *Manual of Christian Theology*, 338.
203. Hovey, *Manual of Christian Theology*, 339.

Further, since Baptists insisted on the theological idea of individual soul liberty, Hovey felt that they had a responsibility to rigorously discuss their theology amongst one another and with an eye toward tradition. These tools helped the theologian to gather and arrange the biblical data into a systematic, theological arrangement. And they helped guard from overdue individualism.

This chapter further argues that Hovey's anthropology significantly contributes to this discussion. His understanding of anthropology and specifically the reasoning powers of humanity were important. Reasoning was always affected by morality. Thus, the sinless stance of the pre-Fall individual resulted in superior reasoning ability. Consequently, the post-Fall individual suffered from defect morality and reason while the regenerated and illuminated individual found some restoration. Clearly, the individual living on this side of the Fall was affected by their sin to the detriment of their reasoning ability. This understanding significantly helps to explain some of the self-imposed limitations in his initial theological prolegomena and bibliology.

The doing of theology (method), for Hovey, served the greater purpose of having a right relationship with God (seeking his face). The doing of theology required technical and intellectual skill at the same time as complementary moral and spiritual qualities. For Hovey, theological method was necessarily a scientific as well as spiritual exercise. Scripture was the supreme authority. But it was never studied in a vacuum by dispassionate students. Intellectual abilities (such as reason, study skills, and interaction with the tradition) along with spiritual and theological recognitions (such as the Creator/creature distinction, regeneration, sanctification, and general human limitations) were likewise necessary conditions which when balanced properly lent authority to the theologian.

A part of his theological method is his view of the Bible. His bibliology was discussed at some length in this chapter and it is clear that he held a conservative view of biblical authority and inspiration. But Hovey interacted in his writings and personal experience with challenges to biblical authority. The next chapter will look in much more depth at Hovey's lifelong interaction with the various challenges to biblical authority.

5

Biblical Criticism

ONE OF THE MAJOR challenges of the nineteenth century for conservatives was that of biblical criticism. This challenge came from many directions, but they generally shared the emphasis on the rights of reason and the new science of historical biblical criticism. The publication of David Friedrich Strauss's (1808–1874) two-volume *Das Leben Jesu* of 1835 was not the first instance where the trustworthiness of the Bible was heavily critiqued along historical-critical grounds,[1] but it was a seminal treatment.[2] Hovey was aware of not only Strauss, but other major critiques of the Bible. This chapter will survey the places where Hovey encountered and answered such critics and will demonstrate Hovey's full views on the nature and authority of the Bible.

---

1. For a discussion of Strauss's reception in America, see chapter 9 in Brown, *Rise of Biblical Criticism in America*.

2. Modern instances would perhaps begin with Baruch Spinoza (1632–1677) and Richard Simon (1638–1712) and include seminal figures such as Johann David Michaelis (1717–1791), Johann Salomo Semler (1725–1791), Gottfried Ephraim Lessing (1729–1781), Johann Gottfried Eichhorn (1752–1827), Johann Philipp Gabler (1753–1826), Heinrich Eberhard Gottlob Paulus (1761–1851), and Ferdinand Christian Bauer (1760–1826). For helpful overviews of this history, see Brown, *Rise of Biblical Criticism in America*; Frei, *Eclipse of Biblical Narrative*; Reventlow, *Authority of the Bible*; Burnett, "Historical Criticism"; Livingston et al., *Modern Christian Thought*, chapters 12–13; Muller, "Biblical Interpretation"; Sheppard and Thiselton, "Biblical Interpretation"; Thiselton, *Hermeneutics*, chapter 7; Treier, "Scripture and Hermeneutics"; Woodbridge and James, *From Pre-Reformation to the Present Day*, chapters 9–15. Also, see the essays in Hauser and Watson, *Enlightenment through the Nineteenth Century*.

Early Experiences and Formulations, 1849–1877

The theological context of Hovey has already been discussed at some length in chapter 2. In that chapter, the biblical and theological training of Hovey was shown to be generally conservative. In such a context Hovey was taught to be aware of the international Protestant theological scene. The diaries from Hovey's trip to Europe make it clear that he was aware of the theological context of each of the professors he sat under and he was especially aware of those who argued for or against the traditional understanding of the Bible as the inspired and trustworthy Word of God.

For instance, during the month and a half that he was in Berlin, Hovey commented about the many times that Professor Ernst Hengstenberg (1802–1869) defended Old Testament history as true, defended Mosaic authorship of the Pentateuch, and how he understood that the terms "Elohim" and "Yahweh" could be understood as both employed by Moses in Genesis.[3] He also noted when Professor Emil Rödiger (1801–1874) described the scholarship of F. C. Bauer and D. F. Strauss on the life of Christ as "fantastical."[4] When Hovey visited Tübingen he noted that it was the place where "Bauer elaborated his skillful assaults upon the sacred records of Christianity"[5] and he commented that it was good that an evangelical professor now occupied Bauer's place. Hovey also noted the theological positions of Franz Delitzsch (1813–1890), Gottfried Thomasius (1802–1875), Isaak August Dorner (1809–1884), Johann Peter Lange (1802–1884), Richard Rothe (1799–1867), and others. He would often make a brief commentary on whether they could be considered evangelical and if their work defended evangelical beliefs.[6] In sum, the diaries of Hovey's trip indicate that he was aware of the European theologians' stances on a variety of theological issues, though none of the entries provided extended commentary.

What is more concrete, however, is that when Hovey returned, he began to write almost immediately about issues of biblical authority and the conservative defense. These early works show Hovey's initial views on the subject as well as the enduring influences upon his thought. The year 1877 is chosen as a terminus of this early period because it is when the first edition of his systematic theology was published for public dissemination. At about that same time Hovey also became heavily involved in the instances

---

3. Hovey, "Personal Journal (1861a)," December 5, 19, 1861; January 7, 1862 (AHP).

4. Hovey, "Personal Journal (1861a)," December 5, 1862 (AHP).

5. Hovey, "Personal Journal (Europe 1861–1862)," July 21, 1862 (AHP).

6. See entries for January 31; June 20; July, 16, 21, 24, 1861, in Hovey, "Personal Journal (1861a)"; "Personal Journal (Europe 1861–1862)."

of biblical criticism in Baptist life as a seminary president, a scholar, and especially the editor of a major commentary series on the Bible.[7]

Miracles and the Radical Skeptics

Near the end of his European journey, when leaving Tübingen (July 24, 1862), Hovey remarked in his diary:

> On the whole, I have found the hearing of theological lectures in this land of universities very stimulating. Occasionally, to be sure, a feeling of discouragement possessed me as I have thought of the vast amount of work which I wish to do in order to be a good teacher of the truth as it is in Christ; but this feeling has soon given place to another, namely, the feeling that I will do with my might what my hands find to do, remembering that God often takes the weak things of the world to confound the mighty. He will accept of earnest endeavors, even though the power be as nothing.[8]

From the first, Hovey wanted to respond to the major theological issues not only in his native America but also those of Western Christian theology. His first book after returning was *The Miracles of Christ As Attested by the Evangelists* (1864) in which he strongly argued the case for the authenticity of the miracles of Jesus.[9] He provided several reasons that had been given for rejecting the testimonies for miracles and then responded to each objection (speaking mainly to David Hume). To the argument that said because some extra-biblical miracles are known to be spurious and so all miracles should be rejected, Hovey responded by granting the premise but denying the conclusion. In essence, the opposite may be the case where a genuine miracle would spur many to manufacture false miracles.[10] The next objection argued that miracles are inconsistent with the uniformity of nature in normal experience and therefore incredible. Hovey was not willing to grant that a power outside of nature could not theoretically act upon nature. Further, the theological purpose of a miracle by definition requires that it

---

7. George Hovey also noted the change of 1877 in the life of his father: "The felicitations of the semicentennial had hardly ceased when a period began in which sorrow, anxiety, and friction marred the serenity of Doctor Hovey's life" (Hovey, *Alvah Hovey*, 165).

8. Hovey, "Personal Journal (Europe 1861–1862)," July 24, 1862 (AHP).

9. Hovey, *Miracles of Christ*. Hovey defined a miracle as "an event, which, according to the principles of sound reasoning, may and must be referred to the extraordinary agency of God" (Hovey, *Miracles of Christ*, 11).

10. Hovey, *Miracles of Christ*, 13–15.

be rare (normally with the very specific purpose of validating something) and not indefinitely multiplied, thus it is by definition contrary to normal experience.[11] The third and final objection to miracles stated that because God created the laws of nature, they are therefore inviolable because God does not repudiate his own work. Hovey countered this objection by saying it wrongly assumes that human reason can determine what sort of creation is worthy of God. Also, miracles may be a part of God's plan and do not sever cause and effect because they are beside and above nature rather than against it.[12]

Essentially, he argued that to discount miracles à priori was wrong because it places a limit on God and was irreligious. "For how weak is our reason in its best estate! How dim our spiritual vision because of sin! The idea of man pronouncing an à priori judgment on plans of creation and providence is preposterous. It is enough for him to discover and adore the wisdom of God as actually manifested, without pretending to limit the action of Jehovah to particular modes and channels."[13] Hovey admitted some will simply have different presuppositions and could not accept his arguments because of that. Here he was thinking specifically about Spinoza and Strauss and their insistence on a pantheistic conception of God that could not allow the world and God to be separated.[14]

The evidence should point to the possibility of miracles and thus the student should weigh the evidence of the biblical accounts, which the majority of his book did. Hovey surveyed every miracle of Jesus in scripture and considered the views of Paulus and Strauss in each case. Hovey considered Paulus to represent a "naturalistic methodology" that assumed the impossibility of miracles and thus had to show that no miracle belongs to Christ. Hovey then considered Strauss as a representative of the "mythical methodology" that assumed the Gospel writers attribute miracles to Jesus and thus the stories were fabricated by the early Christian community.[15] Hovey concluded that the views of Paulus and Strauss were completely incredible and that the miracles were credible because the Bible was credible. "Miracles are the appropriate credentials of a messenger from God, and when properly attested they are decisive."[16] Thus, when the miracles of Jesus

---

11. Hovey, *Miracles of Christ*, 15–19.
12. Hovey, *Miracles of Christ*, 19–27.
13. Hovey, *Miracles of Christ*, 22.
14. Hovey, *Miracles of Christ*, 27.
15. Hovey, *Miracles of Christ*, 28–32.
16. Hovey, *Miracles of Christ*, 314.

were studied, they should provide much evidential value for the supernatural character of Christianity.

This was no mere academic discussion for Hovey. He drew two important points from his work on the miracles of Christ. The first had to do with the very nature of Christianity.

> The miracles which the gospels describe were connected with the teachings of Jesus. They enter many times into the substance as well as the form of his discourses. Rend them away from their place in the record and many a precious message must go with them, for the latter could never have fallen from his lips of truth without the former. But this is not all. His miracles, according to the evangelical record, were closely connected with the words and conduct of his foes. Indeed, they enter into the very warp and woof of our Saviour's history. Remove them from the gospels, and the pieces which remain can be brought together and made one by no mortal skill. One after another will be found worthless, until it becomes evident that by rejecting the miracles of Christ the whole gospel is condemned. No middle post is tenable; whoever is not for the evangelical record, miracles included, is against it; whoever does not welcome Christianity as a supernatural religion in origin and character, does not welcome it at all. The birth, the insight, the wisdom, the moral purity, and the matchless teaching of Christ, were all miraculous, no less so than his resurrection from the dead and his ascension into heaven.[17]

The second conclusion had to do with the idea that the miracles of Jesus revealed the true character, wisdom, holiness, and love of God. "Such was Christ while on earth, as the record of miracles shows; and such he is even now in glory. May all who study the record of his mighty works be drawn to him by the love and compassion which they reveal!"[18]

The book, therefore, was a firm rejection of the historical criticisms which denied the possibility of miracles or which attempted to restructure the life of Christ by considering miracles to be mythology or mere fabrications. More than that, the book shows that Hovey believed the historical records of the Gospels to decisively prove the historical veracity of the miracles of Christ. "Skepticism enforces a credulity which is truly monstrous to the sober reason of Christians; a credulity which is capable of but one explanation, namely, a resolve to dethrone reason sooner than

---

17. Hovey, *Miracles of Christ*, 308–9.
18. Hovey, *Miracles of Christ*, 318.

accept Christ."[19] Hovey wanted to keep a central place for reason, rightly understood, in the discussion of miracles. Further, miracles were necessary as the God-ordained method of verification. Historical criticism, when approached with the proper assumptions and tools, did not destroy the Bible's authority. Rather, because the quality of the historical record, it proved the veracity of Scripture and God's expressed purpose for miracles.

Based on the importance of the subject of miracles, Hovey always retained a place for this discussion in his published theologies. This discussion concerning miracles was housed within the wider discussion of the "Bible from God." More specifically, Hovey consistently argued that the miracles wrought by Jesus were part of why Jesus' teachings (as preserved in the Gospel writings) should be considered true and infallible.[20] The discussions in his theology textbooks present the same information (though sometimes reworded) that Hovey laid out in *The Miracles of Christ as Attested by the Evangelists*.

Early Formulations

Hovey's early writings on the Bible show his views on biblical authority (inspiration and infallibility) and they also show his attitudes toward the historical, scientific, supernatural, prophetic, and moral character of the Bible, all of which he understood to be under attack by various biblical critics and therefore in need of defense. Taken together (views on biblical authority and attitudes toward critical issues) these early formulations give a rounded picture of where Hovey stood on issues of biblical criticism (especially in light of contemporaneous critical studies) and in what ways that stance affected his view of biblical authority.

The previous chapter outlined the general argument that Hovey followed in his theology books to establish the supernatural authority of the Bible.[21] He began by asserting that the New Testament was trustworthy as a historical document (and he dealt with various objections briefly). These records then show that Christ's teaching was infallible (as shown through a series of proofs). Christ then promised inspiration to the apostles (and, by extension, some associates). Both Christ and the apostles say that the Old Testament has the same character of inspiration (as can also be shown through a series of proofs). After this was established then Hovey discussed inspiration and inerrancy before addressing a few typical objections. This

19. Hovey, *Miracles of Christ*, 312.
20. Hovey, *Outlines of Christian Theology*, 39–48; *Manual of Systematic Theology*, 53–67; *Manual of Christian Theology*, 55–63.
21. See especially tables 1–4 in chapter 4.

brief outline of Hovey's argument hinted at a few important places where Hovey dealt with critical studies of the Bible and it also showed that the summation of the argument was to lay out what was meant by inspiration and inerrancy.

In Hovey's 1870 *Outlines* and his 1877 *Manual* he made several references to the historical veracity and trustworthiness of the Bible. This was essential to Hovey because he saw Christianity as "a historical religion,"[22] by which he meant that it was founded on real historical events and claims that could be verified. In these early writings, Hovey was quite clear that he thought the historical events discussed in the New Testament and the Old Testament were correct. Yet he also allowed for a measure of inaccuracy in some of the details of the historical record. Speaking about "The New Testament Scriptures are Worthy of Full Confidence as Historical Records," Hovey explained that "this statement is meant to affirm the general correctness of the New Testament writings, but not the absence of all minor inaccuracies. They are perfectly credible, as compared with the best works of history, though it is not now affirmed that they are wholly free from unintentional errors."[23] How they are trustworthy and what types of errors are allowed are important points to elucidate.

In both 1870 and 1877 Hovey provided a few reasons why the New Testament was trustworthy. He argued that Christianity was founded (with the historical figure of Jesus) and the New Testament was written before the close of the first century,[24] that the New Testament books were written by apostles and their associates, and that the authors were competent and upright. Hovey went through extensive pains to explain why he can assert that Jesus was real and lived during the early first century, why the New Testament books were written before the end of the first century, and why the writers were upright and accurate.

Hovey's *Outlines* and *Manual* evidence considerable interaction with the major literature both rejecting and accepting the historical accuracy of the New Testament, though most of this is done in the notes. He lists Strauss and Bauer as the two most important modern opponents, but he also points

---

22. Hovey, *Outlines of Christian Theology*, 33–34.

23. Hovey, *Manual of Systematic Theology*, 45.

24. In 1877, Hovey had the additional point that "as a historical religion Christianity took its rise with the public ministry of Jesus Christ in Palestine near the end of the third decade of our era" (Hovey, *Manual of Systematic Theology*, 45). Thus in his 1870 book he had three points and in his 1877 book he had four points. The discrepancy can be explained by the fact that this first point was subsumed under the introduction of the 1870 edition. Thus, the same four points were made in each edition.

to several others in that school.[25] For extended responses he directs his readers to his book on the miracles of Christ and he directs them to "scholars as Neander, Ullmann, Ebrard, Schaff, Meyer, Godet, Fisher, Pressensé, Luthardt, and others, too numerous to mention."[26] Hovey concluded that, "After the severest scrutiny, the evidence will be found ample and conclusive as to *nearly all* of the New Testament writings; and were those of a *slightly* doubtful origin set aside, the theological system would itself remain unchanged. But there is no adequate reason for believing that any book of the New Testament is unworthy of its place in the canon."[27] Here it is important to notice that in 1877 Hovey felt like the general legitimacy of each book of the New Testament was well established and only rejected by radical critics.

In the end, Hovey felt confident to assert the historical trustworthiness of the New Testament. This point was important for Hovey, as he explained in some detail:

> Our examination of the New Testament records has been of this nature; and the result is plain—*a conviction of their historical trustworthiness*. They are entitled to full credence, when stating clearly matters of fact; and a discovery now and then of minor unintentional errors would not invalidate this conclusion. The result now reached may appear small, and the process of reaching it slow; but it is all-important for the investigation which is to follow.[28]

Hovey felt his conclusions on trustworthiness were those that carried the day. Though some in the Bauer or Strauss schools doubted the historical trustworthiness of the New Testament books, Hovey felt that such critics were the minority. The Old Testament books were treated in similar fashion. Hovey accepted the inspiration of the Old Testament on the grounds that Jesus and the apostles declared it so, but he also believed it could be evidenced, and one of those evidences was its trustworthiness as a historical record.[29] Hovey did not develop this point at all, he merely stated that

---

25. Hovey, *Outlines of Christian Theology*, 36; *Manual of Systematic Theology*, 49–50.

26. Hovey, *Manual of Systematic Theology*, 50.

27. Hovey, *Manual of Systematic Theology*, 50. It is also worth mentioning here, and it will be discussed further below, but Hovey eventually wrote a forty-page introduction to the New Testament that went into much more depth about the canon and the dates of the New Testament writings. Also, his commentaries on John and Galatians discussed each of those books at some length. Hovey, *Commentary on the Gospel of John*; "General Introduction to the New Testament," iii–xliii; *Commentary on the Epistle to the Galatians*.

28. Hovey, *Manual of Systematic Theology*, 53.

29. Hovey, *Outlines of Christian Theology*, 55; *Manual of Systematic Theology*, 76–77.

they were reliable. He pointed his readers to a few works by Hengstenberg and others before discussing other reasons to consider the Old Testament to be inspired.[30]

Still, his statements appear to allow some measure of error. For one example, Hovey stated that, "The conclusion which has now been reached is this—*that the sacred writers were moved and assisted by the Holy Spirit to put on record all which the Bible, apart from errors in the text, now contains*. As to the Old Testament, this is taught by the Saviour and his apostles; and, as to the New Testament, it is established by evidence previously given."[31] There is an obvious nod to the errors in the text that could be subsumed under "lower criticism" or textual criticism.[32] This plays into Hovey's answers to objections and his understanding of the quality of inspiration.

In both 1870 and 1877 Hovey ended his discussion of the inspiration of the Bible by asserting its infallibility. He gave this definition of the infallibility of the apostles and prophets: "And, by 'infallible teachers,' we mean those who set forth by voice or pen the will of God in the best manner practicable—whose teaching the reason of man has no right to modify or reject, but only to ascertain and obey. Rightly interpreted, their teaching is correct so far as it goes."[33] Hovey discussed whether the infallibility of Scripture is meant only for the religious truths taught or for the secular matters as well. He admitted that the Bible certainly has more to say about religion and the evidence for infallibility in religious matters is much stronger than for secular matters. Still, he made it abundantly clear that he believed that errors in historical matters would damage infallibility in religious matters. The following extended quote addressed this issue directly:

> Yet it is difficult to see how inaccurate representations of history can give just views of divine providence or of human character. And, therefore, upon examination, it will be almost impracticable to draw a line between secular and religious truths in the Bible. Indeed, all events that have found a place in the sacred record appear to have found it by virtue of their relation to the moral government of God.
>
> Looking, then, at the claims of the sacred writers, and at the object for which they were inspired, the argument for their

---

30. Hovey, *Outlines of Christian Theology*, 55; *Manual of Systematic Theology*, 76–77. These additional reasons are the fulfillment of prophecy, the working of miracles, and obvious divinity of the doctrines taught therein.

31. Hovey, *Manual of Systematic Theology*, 77. See also Hovey, *Outlines of Christian Theology*, 56.

32. On textual criticism, see Rodgers, "Textual Criticism."

33. Hovey, *Outlines of Christian Theology*, 58; *Manual of Systematic Theology*, 79.

> infallibility as teachers of religion is far stronger than that for infallibility in speaking of ordinary affairs; but looking at the way in which they teach—that is, by frequent reference to ordinary affairs—it is hard to see how mistakes in the latter will not vitiate the former. We are therefore left to *infer* the correctness of their references to secular matters from their divine authority in teaching religious truth.[34]

Infallibility, rightly understood, for Hovey, meant that the historical references in the Bible needed to be true if the religious references were to be believed. So, how then does one understand his previous reference to minor historical errors? Hovey answered this question in his responses to the charges that the Bible could not be infallible. Hovey argued that his understanding of infallibility did not lead to bibliolatry and did not require the infallibility of copies, translations, or interpretations. Further, he felt that the objection that the Bible had scientific or historical errors was completely false. His full explanation of both of these objections will be given here.

> *Because it teaches scientific errors.* In reply to this charge, it may be remarked that all references to matters of science in the Bible are (1) Merely incidental and auxiliary; (2) Clothed in popular language, and (3) Confirmed by consciousness, so far as they relate to the mind. Remembering these facts, we say that the Bible has not been shown to contain scientific errors.—Astronomy, geology, ethnology.
>
> *Because it teaches historical errors.* On the supposed historical errors of the Bible, we remark, (1) They relate, for the most part, to matters of chronology, genealogy, numbers, &c. (2) Transcribers are specially liable to mistakes in copying numbers, names, &c. (3) Different names for the same person, and different termini for the same period, are quite frequent. (4) Round numbers are often employed for specific. Making proper allowance for these facts, we deny that historical errors are found in the Bible.[35]

These paragraphs give light to his earlier statements that appear to allow historical errors in minor items. The scientific or historical "errors" are only apparent errors and not actual. Instances of phenomenological language, poor transmission, and lack of scientific precision when using numbers can account for most problems. Hovey accepted the infallibility of the Scriptures

---

34. Hovey, *Manual of Systematic Theology*, 80–81.

35. Hovey, *Manual of Systematic Theology*, 85. Also see Hovey, *Outlines of Christian Theology*, 61.

based on a theological understanding of Christ's promise of inspiration in religious matters (since it inferred correctness in references to secular matters), but he also accepted infallibility on a historical and scientific study of the Bible. Many disparate arguments (such as historical trustworthiness, miracles, high moral teaching, and fulfilled prophecies) when all put together render an exceptionally strong argument for the divine authority and infallibility of the Bible.[36]

This discussion of infallibility is a subset within Hovey's ideas concerning inspiration. It was after Hovey described how Jesus promised that the apostles and their associates would be inspired, and it was after Hovey described how Jesus and the apostles considered the Old Testament to be inspired that Hovey then turned to the nature of inspiration. At this point it is important to note that his discussions of inspiration in 1870 and 1877 are quite brief, especially when compared to 1892 and 1900. As a matter of fact, in 1877 Hovey merely gives the name of his theory of inspiration (dynamical)[37] and in 1870 he does not even provide that much information.[38] Despite the lack of discussion on the name of his theory, however, Hovey does provide several clear ideas behind his understanding. The first is what we have seen in regard to the promise of inspiration from Jesus that extends to the entire Bible. Second is what we have seen in regard to infallibility and that the teaching of the entire Bible is infallible.

Two further ideas are present. For the first of these it is helpful to remember tables two and three that were presented in chapter 4. Those two tables summarize Hovey's 1870 and 1877 arguments for why the Bible is a supernatural revelation from God. They both contain the proposition that "the inspiration of the apostles and prophets was different in kind from that of ordinary Christians."[39] Hovey asserted this proposition because he believed that many modern theologians argued that it was possible for certain people to have an "even higher degree of inspiration from God than the ancient prophets or apostles."[40] Here Hovey was simply asserting that the nature of inspiration that Jesus promised and that applies to the entire Bible is different in kind and quality from any other type of inspiration that one may infer. Thus, any modern notion that wants to allow modern Christians to have the same type of inspiration as the Bible is wrong. The second

---

36. Hovey, *Manual of Systematic Theology*, 86–87. See also his popular level work, Hovey and Gregory, *Normal Class Manual for Bible Teachers*, 1–29.
37. Hovey, *Manual of Systematic Theology*, 81.
38. Hovey, *Outlines of Christian Theology*, 58–60.
39. Hovey, *Outlines of Christian Theology*, 57; *Manual of Systematic Theology*, 78.
40. Hovey, *Outlines of Christian Theology*, 57.

important idea to pull out of Hovey's early discussions of inspiration is how Hovey described the "psychology, or human side, of inspiration." This is referring to how he understood both the divine and human to be interacting in inspiration. Hovey provided three points of explanation and they are worth quoting in full as they are succinct and expressed exactly the same in 1870 and 1877.

> (a) The words which they were to employ appear to have been sometimes given to the sacred writers by inspiration. Prophets and seers of visions were addressed through their spiritual senses. (b) The mental powers of the sacred writers were raised and cleared and guided, but not suspended by inspiration. The action of their bodily senses may have been arrested in cases of ecstacy [sic], but not the action of their mental and moral powers. (c) The apostles as well as the prophets received the truth by inspiration gradually and as they needed it for their work, and not all at once.[41]

This quote shows that Hovey clearly wanted to retain a place for the human authors' own style and manner of writing as well as a place for the divine agency in inspiration.

In summary, Hovey's early formulations of inspiration were based on a multifaceted argument. The biblical and theological argument said that the Bible was inspired based on Jesus' promise of inspiration to the apostles (and by extension the Old Testament prophets). The historical argument said that the New and Old Testaments were reliable historical documents. The evidential argument said that the high moral teaching and the fulfilled prophecies point to the Bible's inspiration. Hovey made allowance for transmission errors and differences of authorial style. He was aware of and dealt with the various charges concerning the reliability of its history, science, morals, and miracles. In 1870 and in 1877 (and also 1900),[42] Hovey made the following summation of the matter.

> In view of what has now been stated, we claim that our theory of inspiration accounts for all the phenomena of the Bible better than any other; for its varieties of style as well as numerous writers; for its verbal discrepancies, as well as essential harmony; for the personal feelings and tastes which are revealed by its writers; and for a thousand traces of high yet free spiritual action on

---

41. Hovey, *Outlines of Christian Theology*, 58; *Manual of Systematic Theology*, 81. In both editions Hovey went on to explain that the inspired men had four sources of knowledge: revelation, observation, experience, and study.

42. Hovey, *Manual of Christian Theology*, 85–86.

their part. How anyone can read the New Testament, the Book of Revelation excepted, and doubt whether its writers speak with conscious freedom, and also with conscious authority, passes our comprehension. The letters of Paul are intensely *natural*, and equally *supernatural*: the Word was made flesh without losing its heavenly truth and power.[43]

He believed that the Bible was divine based on its quality as inspired. It was also human in that humans wrote it and it has been historically transmitted by humans. Above all, the Bible had divine authority and divine inspiration and could thus be the basis of the Christian religion. As the dynamically inspired and infallible Word of God the Bible had supreme authority in matters of faith (theology) and practice.

These early years of Hovey's career are interesting for how he initially explained his theology and they are interesting for several budding friendships. It was in 1868 that Hovey became president of Newton Theological Institute and it was also in 1868 that he hired a young professor, who had just graduated from Newton, named Ezra Palmer Gould.[44] One year later Hovey served as the chairman of the pulpit committee that recommended William Newton Clarke to become the pastor of the First Baptist Church of Newton Centre, MA.[45] And, a few years later, in 1876, Hovey agreed to be the editor a new Baptist commentary series on the New Testament.[46] Each of these friendships and professional endeavors would force Hovey to come face to face with the changing Baptist attitudes toward critical studies of the Bible.

Controversy and Nuance, 1877–1903

American Baptists in the first two-thirds of the nineteenth century were overwhelmingly conservative in their theology and their views of the Bible.[47] Though there were some tremors that this was changing, the major

---

43. Hovey, *Outlines of Christian Theology*, 59; *Manual of Systematic Theology*, 83.
44. Hovey, *Alvah Hovey*, 128–29.
45. Hovey, *Alvah Hovey*, 155.
46. Hovey, *Alvah Hovey*, 173.
47. For specific explorations of Baptists views on the Bible at the time, see Maring, "Baptists and Changing Views of the Bible [I]"; "Baptists and Changing Views of the Bible [II]"; Garrett Jr., "Sources of Authority in Baptist Thought"; Bush and Nettles, *Baptists and the Bible*; Straub, *Making of a Battle Royal*, 45–60. Also see the entries in Garrett Jr., *Baptist Theology*, 249–330.

changes in Baptist views came in the last third of the century. Hovey's interaction with changing views were both personal and professional.

Editor, President, and Friend

Crawford Howell Toy

When discussing changing views of the Bible within Baptist circles, most historians take particular note of the case of Crawford Howell Toy (1836–1919) at the Southern Baptist Theological Seminary. Toy's case is important because, as Gregory Wills has noted, "Southern Baptist Theological Seminary was the first American school to dismiss a teacher over the emerging liberal theology."[48] Toy was an exceptionally bright scholar who began teaching Old Testament at Southern in 1869.[49] Toy's scholarship was soon recognized for its quality, and his views of the Old Testament were soon noted for their progressive character. Rumblings first appeared with his 1869 book, *The Claims of Biblical Interpretation on Baptists*.[50] It took nearly a decade, however, for Toy's shifting views to become sufficiently known before he resigned from Southern under intense pressure in May of 1879.[51]

At about the time that Toy was coming under pressure at Southern he was conscripted by Hovey to write for the New Testament commentary series that Hovey was editing. It was apparently John Broadus, Toy's mentor at Southern and the author of the Matthew commentary in the set, who suggested Toy to Hovey because he was capable and because Toy would help make the set appealing to Baptists in the South.[52] Toy originally agreed in December 1876 to write the commentary on the two epistles to the Thessalonians,[53] but then in January 1877 also added the Pastoral Epistles

---

48. Wills, *Southern Baptist Theological Seminary*, 108.

49. Toy was educated at the University of Virginia, the Southern Baptist Theological Seminary, and the University of Berlin. On Toy and the controversy at Southern, see Hurt, "Crawford Howell Toy"; Duncan, "Crawford Howell Toy"; "Crawford Howell Toy (1836–1919)"; House, "Crawford Howell Toy"; Wills, *Southern Baptist Theological Seminary*, 108–49; Straub, *Making of a Battle Royal*, 61–77.

50. Toy, *Claims of Biblical Interpretation on Baptists*.

51. Some of the details of his views were that he believed the New Testament authors incorrectly interpreted the Old Testament, that Genesis 1 and 2 had different authors, that traditional messianic prophecies did not have direct reference to Jesus Christ, and that much of the Pentateuch was pieced together over a long period of time by various editors. See Wills, *Southern Baptist Theological Seminary*, 115–22.

52. Broadus originally suggested that Toy write on Isaiah (John A. Broadus to Alvah Hovey, October 27, 1876 [AHP]).

53. Crawford H. Toy to Alvah Hovey, December 21, 1876 (AHP).

to his workload.⁵⁴ As Toy worked on these commentaries, he was coming to conclusions that he recognized were not palatable to most and so he shared these with Hovey in a letter dated June 9, 1879:

> Certain conclusions that I have reached, it may be well for me to state to you. I hold to the Pauline authorship of Thess. and in II Thess. 2d chapt. I incline to interpret the ἄνθρωπος τῆς ἀνομίας of the Emperor Nero. "Philemon" also I hold to be from Paul. But, after repeated readings and comparisons I have found it impossible to attribute the Pastoral Ep. to him. "Second Timothy" seems to me to be based on a Pauline letter, and the other to come from an author quite different from Paul, or to consist of general Pauline material worked up in a manner very different from his. I am aware that these opinions may not meet with the approbation of the Publication Soc'y, and I mention them as soon as possible to you, with whom the decision rests in order that I may know whether to continue the Comm'y. If critical freedom is allowed, it will be a pleasure to me to do the work.⁵⁵

Hovey (and the publication society) did not have Toy continue. Broadus wrote to Hovey on August 8, 1879 saying that, "I am sorry, but not surprised, that my dear friend Toy has reached such conclusions about the Pastoral Epistles. It is of a piece with the view he has adopted as to the Pentateuch."⁵⁶ Toy also wrote to Hovey expressing his understanding that Hovey and the publication society would ask his resignation.⁵⁷ Though the precise reasons given by the Society for why Toy was asked to resign were not explicitly given, it is clear from Toy's June 9 letter that he felt it necessary to make his critical views known to Hovey. After this came to light (and possibly

---

54. Crawford H. Toy to Alvah Hovey, January 27, 1877 (AHP).

55. Crawford H. Toy to Alvah Hovey, June 9, 1879 (AHP). Toy's letter also goes on to request Hovey to allow Broadus more space for his Matthew commentary, stating that restricting the space had created much additional labor for Broadus.

56. John A. Broadus to Alvah Hovey, August 8, 1879 (AHP). Broadus also communicates his thanks to Hovey and the publication committee for allowing him additional space on his Matthew commentary.

57. Crawford H. Toy to Alvah Hovey, August 15, 1879 (AHP): "Your letter expressing your opinion as General Editor of the N. T. Comm'y of the Am. Bapt. Publ. Socy that it would be better for me to withdraw from the volume originally assigned me reached me here just before I left the city. I thought it likely I should meet you at Newport at the Amer. Philology Ass. and could there speak with you. Having failed to see you I write now on my return merely to acknowledge the receipt of your communication, and to say that I accept your decision, though I greatly regret the position of affairs which seems to you to require such a decision. I heartily wish success to the enterprise, and am very truly yours, C. H. Toy."

the fact that Toy had just been asked to resign from Southern) the plug was pulled almost immediately on Toy's involvement in the commentary series. At the decision of Hovey as general editor and also of the publication society as a whole, Toy's critical views must quickly have been deemed unfit for inclusion.

Though their interactions were brief, and Toy was frustrated at his requested resignation (which resignation he agreed to), Toy remained cordial with Hovey the remainder of their lives. Toy moved to Boston the following year to teach at Harvard University, where he stayed for several decades. As a result, both Toy and Hovey resided in the same city and would see each other from time to time. As a matter of fact, within a couple years, as George Hovey relates, their acquaintance was regularly renewed: "In 1881 [Hovey] accepted an election to the Semitic Club of Cambridge, later named the Harvard Biblical Club, in which, associated with Doctors Toy and Lyons and other leading liberals of various denominations he often had occasion to stand kindly and firmly for the truth as he saw it, and he won the respect and love of his fellow club members."[58] This friendship always remained cordial. On the occasion of Hovey's fiftieth anniversary of teaching at Newton in 1899, Toy wrote a congratulatory letter to Hovey, though Toy was unable to attend.[59] And, in the last months of Hovey's life, Toy sent him a friendly postcard from Geneva merely giving greetings.[60]

Hovey's position as editor of a commentary series meant that he was at least somewhat involved in dealing with Toy's critical views, though this involvement was certainly brief and somewhat detached. Hovey's position as president of Newton Theological Institute meant that his interaction with another bright and young (and progressive) biblical scholar would be much more involved.

Ezra Palmer Gould

Ezra Palmer Gould (1841–1900) was a Newton graduate whom Hovey chose to replace Horatio Hackett in 1868 as professor of New Testament Interpretation.[61] "Of him Doctor Hovey had the highest expectations, com-

58. Hovey, *Alvah Hovey*, 151–52.
59. Crawford H. Toy to Alvah Hovey, June 6, 1899 (AHP).
60. Crawford H. Toy to Alvah Hovey, September 27, 1902 (AHP).
61. This was the same year that Hovey became president and that Gould graduated from Newton. Biographical information of Gould is extremely sparse. He graduated top of his class from Harvard in 1861, then joined the Union army, rising to the rank of Major. He went from the army into Newton in 1865. See Cathcart, *Baptist Encyclopedia*, 461; Archibald and Kinzie, *Minutes of the Vermont Baptist Anniversaries*, 82; Pierce,

paring him favorably with Doctor Hackett."[62] Gould was hailed by nearly everyone as a gifted scholar and an engaging teacher.[63] And he taught for over a decade at Newton before rumblings began.

In 1881 Gould's teaching became the subject of worry and was reported to the Executive Committee of trustees in an effort to determine what to do. Evidently, Gould's advocation of unorthodox views created concern among students and faculty. It is clear that Gould had no issue presenting critical views of the Bible as well as new theological viewpoints. What is less clear is how much of those views Gould held for himself. The specifics of why Gould was let go is somewhat debatable. The Executive Committee decided to table the issue in 1881 and take a year to gather more information. After more deliberation over the summer of 1882, Gould was formally dismissed on September 7, 1882, and there was a spirited debate among Baptists over the precise nature of the dismissal. Gould himself had written a letter to Hovey two months before the final board decision was made imploring him for a second chance on the grounds that he and Hovey simply have a difference of opinions.[64] Gould felt he had been misrepresented and needed a chance to clarify. Though a few months went by as the issue was considered, Gould's pleadings were for naught. Having taught for fourteen years at Newton, Gould's position was ended.

One of the board members, Cephas Crane, later wrote his own explanation on, "The Removal of Professor Gould" in which he related that, "For two years or more there have been suspicions and rumors that Professor Gould has diverged more or less widely from what is generally held by Baptists to be the Orthodox faith and that he has proved himself an unsafe teacher of students for the Christian ministry."[65] Crane and others sought to defend Gould from charges that his views were unorthodox or heretical.[66] Being sympathetic to Gould and to help toward these ends, *The Independent* included a brief statement from Gould immediately following Crane's article.[67] Likewise, *The National Baptist* also gave space for two articles from

---

General Catalogue, 98; Brackney, *Genetic History of Baptist Thought*, 287–88; Garrett, *Baptist Theology*, 343–47; Straub, *Making of a Battle Royal*, 78–90.

62. Hovey, *Alvah Hovey*, 129.

63. Straub, *Making of a Battle Royal*, 80.

64. Ezra Palmer Gould to Alvah Hovey, July 13, 1882 (AHP). Gould asked for a year to sift the accusations. He also admitted his own struggle to bring all the truth together and correlate it.

65. Crane, "Removal of Professor Gould," 2.

66. Also see "Editorial Notes"; "Professor Gould [October 19, 1882]," 664; "Removal of Professor Gould from Newton Seminary," 10.

67. Gould, "Prof. Gould's Statement," 3.

Gould on the subjects, "Is God Love?"[68] and "A Christocentric Theology."[69] The thought was that Gould's written views would show many that his theology was not suspect, but only that he had some questions on certain difficult subjects.[70]

Some concluded that the board did not terminate Gould on suspicion of his views and thus surmised that the deeper issue was that Gould and Hovey did not get along.[71] These suggested that Gould was commenting on issues of theology in his New Testament class, where such issues should have been left to Hovey's classes, a tact which was followed by the previous New Testament instructor, Horatio Hackett.[72] This line of thought was bolstered by the fact that in Crane's telling of the story there consistently were several members of the Board of Trustees that desired to keep Gould at Newton.[73] Evidently after the Executive Committee made the recommendation to the Board on June 13 to immediately remove Gould, the Board then elected a Special Committee of five to investigate further. This Special Committee initially sat with three in favor of reinstating Gould and two in favor of removing Gould. An issue surfaced with the committee, however, before it could render a full verdict to the Board. One of its members had to withdraw (due to being hired as full-time faculty at Newton), thus leaving the four-person Special Committee split over its decision and having to recommend it to the full board. Having heard the recommendations and reports by the Special Committee, the full board voted on September 7 to terminate Gould's employment by a margin of thirteen to nine. The motion read, "Resolved, that in the judgment of the Trustees the best interests of the Institution and fidelity to their trust, require them to make an immediate change in the instructor of Biblical Interpretation, New Testament. Resolved, that the services of E. P. Gould, who has been the instructor in

68. Gould, "Is God Love?," 641.

69. Gould, "Christocentric Theology," 644.

70. A short while later, Gould also wrote on the supernatural aspect of Christianity. See Gould, "Supernatural Element in Christianity."

71. "Professor Gould [October 15, 1882]"; "Professor Gould [October 19, 1882]"; "Removal of Professor Gould from Newton Seminary."

72. "We fear Professor Gould did not make it easy as he might for other incumbents. It was the prudent habit of Professor Hackett to avoid difficult speculative questions, when they were asked him, by saying: 'This question belongs in the department of systematic theology and should be answered there. My duty here concerns only the actual contents of Scripture.' He thus saved himself, when he pleased, much labor in questions which immediately grew out of the simple exegesis. Professor Gould has not availed himself of this easy method" ("Removal of Professor Gould from Newton Seminary," 10).

73. Crane, "Removal of Professor Gould."

the department, shall terminate at the present time, and that his salary be continued for three months."[74]

Crane's article did not name any names of the Special Committee members, other than himself. The names were given, however, in a simultaneous article also published in *The Independent*.[75] George Bosworth, Adoniram Judson Gordon, Cephas Crane, John M. English, and George Bullen were the five on the Special Committee and it was English who was called to be professor of Homiletics at Newton during the deliberation. When the names were given, it suggested that the men on the Committee who were academics by profession or who were pastors by profession were overwhelmingly in favor of keeping Gould. This again suggested that Gould was not removed because of his orthodoxy. The editor of *The Independent*, H. L. Wayland, saw it as an issue of incompatibility: "The removal was done not by the ministers, who were not afraid of him; but by the laymen, who seem to have been influenced by financial fears."[76] The editors of *The National Baptist* also saw it as an issue of faculty incompatibility: "In fact, we are confirmed in the view which we have gained from well-informed sources, that the difficulty was personal, was, in fact, based upon incompatibility between several members of the Faculty, and that Prof. Gould, being the younger Professor, had to give way."[77]

Not all, though, saw the issue as one of incompatibility. A pseudonymous author, "Hillside," who appears to have been Newton professor Heman Lincoln,[78] related further issues at hand.[79] Lincoln took issue with the suggestions of Crane, *The National Baptist*, and the *Independent* when they argued it was a matter of personal incompatibility. For one reason, Hovey was widely known for his broad sympathies. Further, Lincoln argued that Hovey, along with the Committee, were desirous of shielding Gould from incorrect charges. "The reasons were more urgent. Students made known to [Hovey] and to many others the fact that their views were unsettled on vital doctrines by the teaching in the department of New Testament interpretation. Examinations for ordination gave ample proof of these unsettled opinions, and scrupulous pastors hesitated in voting for ordination. In one

---

74. Trustee Minutes, September 7, 1882, Newton Theological Institution Records, Yale Divinity School Library.

75. See "Removal of Professor Gould from Newton Seminary."

76. "Removal of Professor Gould from Newton Seminary," 10.

77. "Professor Gould [October 19, 1882]," 664.

78. This was apparently a widely known fact and was made explicit by the editor of *The National Baptist*. See "Professor Gould [November 2, 1882]," 693.

79. This essay was originally given in *The Examiner*.

case ordination was refused."[80] Lincoln argued that these charges were widespread and shared not only with Hovey, but with other professors and board members. The editor of the *Journal and Messenger*, George Lasher, agreed with Lincoln and shared his own similar story: "We may add, in confirmation of what is said of the reports by students, that two years ago a Newton student told us, in this office, of the influence of Professor Gould, and led us then to believe that either the Professor must go, or Newton would lose its hold upon Baptists as a source of sound doctrine."[81]

George Hovey, in his biography of his father, commented on the situation and pointed to Gould's theology as well as his indiscretion in sharing controversial views. "Gradually, however, the theological views of Professor Gould came to diverge considerably from those held by the majority of the Baptist denomination, and furthermore he seemed to go out of his way to ridicule the commonly accepted views."[82] George Hovey likewise rejected the idea that it was a personal matter, and he explained that Alvah Hovey received criticism from certain conservatives for not being more assertive. "The whole incident was exceedingly painful to Doctor Hovey, but he studiously abstained from taking any active part in the matter."[83]

There may have been some incompatibility among the faculty, but it is peripheral to the fact that the views of Gould were pushing the boundaries of conservative biblical understandings. In his personal defense he responded to a few charges against him. On the Bible, he explained that he saw them as authoritative, though with a pervasive human element that could allow errors: "But the Scriptures, as a whole, are a complete and authoritative revelation of truth. There is an undoubted human element in the Scriptures; but whether this involved any inaccuracies in the details of historical statement remains yet to be decided by a careful and complete induction of the facts."[84] Gould also felt that more study was needed in regard to the person of Christ: "I also believe the statement that he became flesh, and that not sufficient attention has been given to the limitations consequent on his humanity and which alone constitute the distinctions between human and divine."[85] Gould also commented on the atonement and eschatology, again stating that his views were tentative, pending further studies. Most have recognized that Gould's views were open to critical views of the Bible,

80. Lincoln quoted in "Editorial," 4.
81. "Editorial," 4.
82. Hovey, *Alvah Hovey*, 168.
83. Hovey, *Alvah Hovey*, 169.
84. Gould, "Prof. Gould's Statement."
85. Gould, "Prof. Gould's Statement."

that he positively presented progressive views to his students despite the deleterious effects, and that he was becoming decidedly more progressive in his views as he studied more.

The relationship between Hovey and Gould was no longer one of colleagues, but it remained cordial, similarly to Hovey's relationship with Toy. By the time that rumors were swirling of Gould's suspect views in 1881 Hovey had already asked Gould to work on the Corinthians volume in the commentary set,[86] which commentary he eventually finished.[87] And a couple years after Gould left Newton he wrote to Hovey twice asking his advice over a pastoral situation he was facing in Burlington, Vermont.[88] They evidently remained acquaintances even after Gould's dismissal. George Hovey noted his father's continued relationship with Gould and suggested that "As so often occurred, Doctor Hovey was in this case a harmonizing influence between a progressive thinker and the conservatives."[89] One of the last articles that Hovey wrote was a retrospective view of Newton during the years 1875–1900.[90] By that time Gould had passed away, along with several other former professors. On Gould, Hovey left these telling remarks:

> Dr. Gould was a member of the faculty fourteen years (1868–1882). He was a scholar and teacher of marked ability, evincing uncommon skill in tracing the thought of a writer word by word and clause by clause. But his turn of mind was logical, and he sometimes found it difficult to keep within the limits of his own department, preferring to discuss questions of theology on which his views were increasingly different from those of the officer in that chair. This led at length to his removal from the Institution, though no one ever called in question his ability or his integrity, and every one rejoiced when he found congenial work in another denomination and school.[91]

This statement was made twenty years after the incident and hindsight is often more clarified than reality. Yet Hovey's statement seems to ring true. Gould's classes appear to have been a place where critical and progressive views were at least expressed, sometimes in direct conflict with the theology

86. See Gould's letter to Hovey from 1881 where he states that the commentaries were coming along. Ezra Palmer Gould to Alvah Hovey, July 31, 1881 (AHP).

87. Gould, *Commentary on the Epistles to the Corinthians*.

88. Ezra Palmer Gould to Alvah Hovey, October 8, 1884 (AHP); October 20, 1884 (AHP).

89. Hovey, *Alvah Hovey*, 169.

90. Hovey, "Newton from 1875 to 1900," 43–48. Hovey also wrote a similar reminiscence of the first fifty years of Newton. See Hovey, *Historical Address*.

91. Hovey, "Newton from 1875 to 1900," 47.

professor's (Hovey's) views, and sometimes ridiculing the older views. And Gould appears to have been slowly moving away from the more conservative views of Hovey and Newton. Gould's subsequent career continued to follow the pattern of change. By the end of the 1880s he was teaching in the Protestant Episcopal Seminary in Philadelphia, and he was ordained in that denomination in 1890. Gould continued to publish, and his later views were unequivocal in their acceptance of critical views of the New Testament.[92] Perhaps this is why Hovey could say he was pleased when Gould found work in a different sphere altogether.

Hovey was more involved in the case of Gould than he was with Toy. Though it is hard to know Hovey's full opinions on the positions of Gould, it is safe to say that Hovey was in agreement with the board when they dismissed Gould.[93] Gould's progressive views were widely known, as well as the influence he had on the students at Newton. These combined factors were part of Hovey's attitude toward Gould. Still, Hovey let Gould finish his commentary on Corinthians and he took opportunity to help with his pastoral questions.[94] Hovey was complicit in the theological purifying of Newton, though he attempted to remain a bridge to his progressive friend.

92. See Gould, *Critical and Exegetical Commentary*; *Biblical Theology of the New Testament*. See the summation of Gould's views and assessment in Garrett, *Baptist Theology*, 343–47. Garrett argues that "Gould's New Testament theology was greatly shaped and overshadowed by his historical-critical views, especially the authorship and dating of the New Testament books, and by his stress on diversity, not pressed overtly to contradiction, in place of unity of teaching. Most of Gould's Baptist successors in biblical theology during the twentieth century would find unity amid diversity in biblical theology" (Garrett, *Baptist Theology*, 347).

93. In an entry to his personal journal from 1882, Hovey was active in his discussions with several people in relation to Gould. On July 31, he notes that he met with George Bullen (one of the Special Committee members who voted against Gould) and also O. S. Stearns about what to do with Gould. Though we do not have the contents of those conversations, we do know that Bullen was decidedly not in favor of Gould and we know that Hovey was struggling to decide what to do about the entire situation (Hovey, "Personal Journal [1882]," July 31, 1882 [AHP]). On the day before the final vote of the board, Hovey was present at Brown University for a meeting of their board and had a long talk with Dr. Merrill about Gould on the train ride home. Though, again, we do not have the contents of that conversation (Hovey, "Personal Journal [1882]," September 6, 1882 [AHP]). At the point of Gould's termination, Hovey succinctly stated: "Meeting of the Trustees of Newton in Tremont Temple. Final action on the case of Prof. Gould was taken, closing his connection with the Seminary, and continuing his salary until the 1st of December. Gordon, Mills, Gow, and myself comm. to nominate a new Professor" (Hovey, "Personal Journal [1882]," September 7, 1882 [AHP]).

94. Gould did take some issue with the suggested editorial work that Hovey did on Gould's commentary. See Ezra Palmer Gould to Alvah Hovey, March 23, 1888 (AHP). Evidently, Gould did not like the changes that Hovey had made to an unnamed passage as he felt it did not represent his views. There is no record of where these edits were nor

William Newton Clarke

One further acquaintance of Hovey's deserves close attention. That is William Newton Clarke (1841–1912), the widely recognized Baptist liberal and intimate personal friend of Hovey.[95] Clarke was more than twenty years younger than Hovey but the two became good friends when Clarke was called in 1869 to be the pastor of First Baptist Church in Newton Centre.[96] George Hovey related that, "Though a graduate of another seminary and an independent thinker whose views on theological questions diverged farther and farther from those of Doctor Hovey, Doctor Clarke immediately won and held a very high place in the esteem and love of the older man."[97] Clarke had previously pastored in New Hampshire and he stayed in Newton Centre for eleven years before taking a church in Montreal. He was only in Montreal for a few years, during which he wrote the Mark volume (1881) in the commentary series that Hovey was editing, and then he began teaching in 1883 at the Baptist Theological School in Toronto. In 1888 he accepted a call to pastor the Baptist Church in Hamilton, New York, the home of Madison University (later Colgate). While in Hamilton, Clarke assumed the J. J. Joslin Professor of Christian Theology in 1890 after he was asked to replace the suddenly deceased Ebenezer Dodge. Clarke remained in his position in Hamilton for the remainder of his life. Jeffrey Straub's assessment of Clarke's life is correct: "Clarke was typical of many northern Baptists who were raised in a pious, orthodox home but drifted away from the theology of their youth in the advancing wave of theological liberalism that swept American Protestantism in the mid-nineteenth century."[98] Clarke's friendship with Hovey is interesting as it illustrates Hovey's interactions with a theologian with very different viewpoints. Through their time together in Newton Centre, the production of Clarke's commentary on Mark, and into the twilight of life Clarke made a well-documented theological pilgrimage into theological liberalism. At a couple key moments in that pilgrimage, Hovey was present.

---

of how this exchange ended. The commentary was published as Gould, *Commentary on the Epistles to the Corinthians*.

95. For biographical data, see Brown, "Theology of William Newton Clarke," 167–80; Clarke, *William Newton Clarke*; Behney, "Conservatism and Liberalism"; Cochran, "William Newton Clarke"; Howe Jr., "William Newton Clarke"; *Theology of William Newton Clarke*; Tull, *Shapers of Baptist Thought*, 153–81; Van Pelt "Examination of the Concept of the Atonement."

96. Hovey was the chairman of the Pulpit Committee that called Clarke to the church (Hovey, *Alvah Hovey*, 155).

97. Hovey, *Alvah Hovey*, 155.

98. Straub, *Making of a Battle Royal*, 98.

Later in life Clarke wrote *Sixty Years with the Bible*,[99] which was a chronicle of his evolving views toward the Bible. In this work Clarke moves through the last six decades of his life and shows how he slowly came to hold liberal views on the Bible and theology. During his chapter on the 1870s, he reminisces on his interaction with Hovey, Gould, and Gould's predecessor, Horatio Hackett.[100] Clarke said that even Hackett in his day "had been guiding and inspiring his pupils to judge for themselves what is that true meaning which is binding upon mind and heart. The practice that he encouraged is more revolutionary than any one at the time was aware. In fact, the inherited belief was doomed to be altered, when once men's godliest and most scientific endeavors were devoted to the interpretation of that book to which they acknowledged absolute allegiance."[101] Clarke argued that Hackett's biblicist method of interpretation was creating a flood of new questions that were set to undermine his very practice. Clarke came to believe that any straightforward, honest reading of the Bible simply could not remain agreeable to the old conservatism.

Hovey, to Clarke, had deep reverence and loyalty to the Bible. "To him it brought the truth and will of God, and he joyfully acknowledged its authority upon his conscience and his intelligence alike. In his work of theological construction he considered himself bound, and limited, by what the Bible contains. . . . The real meaning of a text thus handled was God's meaning, and the text was God's word."[102] Clarke admitted his own difference with Hovey, but he appreciated that Hovey never forced his views and that Hovey encouraged Clarke to take his own way. Gould, on the other hand, won unreserved praise from Clarke:

---

99. Clarke, *Sixty Years with the Bible*.

100. Clarke does not give their names explicitly, but instead refers to Hackett as "one of the pioneers of modern scholarly biblical interpretation," to Gould as "the man of my own age who was nearest to me was teacher of New Testament Interpretation," and to Hovey as "the theologian to whom I looked up almost as to a father. Older than I by more than a score of years, he received me from the first into a warm friendship, which remained unaltered to the end of his days" (Clarke, *Sixty Years with the Bible*, 72, 90, 88).

101. Clarke, *Sixty Years with the Bible*, 73. Clarke went on: "When a man is set to interpret the standard that he must obey, it means that henceforth he is to obey a standard that he has interpreted. For his own mind, he has helped to determine the duty that he is required to do. But interpretation is not final. Nothing is more certain than that it will change with new light, continued study, and personal growth. Thus as interpretation advances the standard is altered, and it becomes increasingly true that the student has had a share in making the standard to which his obedience is pledged."

102. Clarke, *Sixty Years with the Bible*, 88–89.

> He began, as I did, with the assumption that all the Christian doctrines were developed within the New Testament, and that our permanent standard of belief there lay before us, needing only to be interpreted. But as he went on he became better acquainted with the writers of the New Testament, and formed a different conception of their relation to Christian students of the present day. He came to think that the writers, instead of being final authority concerning divine truth, were fellow-interpreters of the gospel with himself and with all Christians. He was not bound by all their statements, but counted it his privilege to seek the light of Christ for himself by their help. He read the New Testament as the inestimably precious record of Christianity, not as its source, or as our final standard for defining its doctrines.... I need not tell how helpful it was to me to have so conscientious and enterprising a student for my companion in the study of the Bible. Many a single passage and many a large meaning have I worked out with him, and my permanent indebtedness to him is very great.[103]

Clarke's comparison of Hovey and Gould was meant to illustrate the way in which he himself was moving from the older, received view of the Bible toward a more intellectually satisfying view. "Of these two personal companionships, each inspiring in its own way, perhaps it may be said, though with a margin of inaccuracy, that one would hold me where the Bible had brought me, and the other would send me wherever the Bible might lead me."[104] The remainder of Clarke's book explained his slow change to the acceptance of higher critical views of the Bible, rejection of inerrancy, and acceptance of liberal theology. Beyond the prototypical influences of Hovey and Gould, Clarke also related that it was his commentary on Mark that was a major turning point.

The commentary on Mark was the first volume published in Hovey's commentary series. In *Sixty Years with the Bible* and in various letters to Hovey, Clarke related how his interpretations of Mark 13 created a conundrum in his views of the Bible.[105] Clarke had been struggling with millennial views for some time before this commentary came out. The main problem he saw was that both the premillennial and the postmillennial views could be established or defeated by appealing to certain biblical texts, thus

---

103. Clarke, *Sixty Years with the Bible*, 91–92.
104. Clarke, *Sixty Years with the Bible*, 92.
105. Clarke also related that more than just chapter 13 being problematic, his intense study of Mark's gospel left him convinced that the four gospels could not be harmonized. Clarke, *Sixty Years with the Bible*, 131–40.

undermining its claims to inerrancy and ultimate authority.[106] In his commentary, Clarke took the view that the second advent occurred at the destruction of Jerusalem. Clarke anticipated some of the criticism that would come his way when he wrote Hovey on August 1, 1881. "I suppose you received my thirteenth and fourteenth chapters, some three or four weeks ago. If you did not, the game is up. I don't know what you may think of my thirteenth chapter—if it is wrong I am very sorry, but for my life I can't see it any other way."[107] Clarke and Hovey traded several letters over the next year about the commentary.[108] Hovey asked Clarke to edit his work on several points, and Clarke did not find these requests altogether agreeable. At the end of the long exchange of letters, Clarke gave this summation:

> As for the official criticisms. I have now a copy of the commentary here, and cannot say exactly what I could do with them, not knowing exactly what they call for. Some of them I presume I could satisfy. Some are ignorant criticisms, not worthy to be regarded—unless indeed it was possible to guard against such ignorant misapprehension by some new form of statement. Some of them I could not satisfy—as when I am asked to "correct" the statement that "the Son of Man did not know." That statement can be "corrected" only by a higher authority than mine. If the Publication Society feels it necessary to dictate the conclusions to which I shall come, and to accept or reject my revisions according to agreement with the conclusions it has appointed me, then I can only say that I am a man, investigating the Word of God under responsibility to Him, for the sake of finding what it contains. If the Society thinks best to suppress my book, the Society has full right and liberty to do it, and I would make no objection. Now would I object to any fairly-worded additions to my work, made by any one whom the Society might appoint. But how can I promise that my conclusions after investigating the sense of Scripture should be identical with those of Dr. Griffith and the committee that he represents? How can any man promise that?[109]

---

106. Clarke, *Sixty Years with the Bible*, 104. "It was borne in upon me that the Bible contains material for two opposite and irreconcilable doctrines about the early return of Christ to this world. Both doctrines cannot be true: one of them at least must rest upon misjudgment. Since this is the fact, it certainly cannot be that I am required to believe all that the Bible says because the Bible says it."

107. William Newton Clarke to Alvah Hovey, August 1, 1881 (AHP).

108. William Newton Clarke to Alvah Hovey, September 17, 1881 (AHP); September 27, 1881 (AHP); October 24, 1881 (AHP).

109. William Newton Clarke to Alvah Hovey, July 27, 1882 (AHP).

Evidently the most controversial statements were edited out of the commentary,[110] but the editorial committee still had a few hesitations. Hovey added a comment at the beginning of chapter 13 which said: "It is proper to remind the reader that neither the general editor nor the Society can be responsible for the interpretation of every passage in the Commentary. See General Introduction, p. 42 (2). For there are passages whose meaning, or whose full meaning, is doubtful; and the following must be regarded as one of them."[111] It was not long until the second edition came out, which had another major edit. After chapter 13, the editors inserted "An Additional View" by John C. Long.[112] As difficult as the conversations appeared to be between Hovey and Clarke over the commentary, the two continued to be close friends.

Most of the remaining correspondence between Clarke and Hovey were merely letters between friends interested in each other's lives. Although, when Gould was released from Newton, Clarke wrote to Hovey and expressed his mixed emotions. He was upset with Gould because an article appeared in the *Boston Globe*[113] (some few weeks before Clarke's letter of July 27, 1882) that cast Hovey in a very unfavorable light as an old wooden conservative. Clarke was convinced that Gould gave an interview that was the basis of the article, and Clarke mentioned that he wrote to Gould explaining his disappointment in him. Clarke's letter was mixed, though, because he then immediately chastised Hovey for letting Gould go.

110. Years later, in his *Sixty Years with the Bible*, Clarke related one such edit: "The only paragraph in which I alluded to inspiration contained the remark, which seems to me to have been tenable, that the Bible is inspired as it is inspired, and not as we may think it ought to be inspired" (Clarke, *Sixty Years with the Bible*, 133).

111. Clarke, *Commentary on the Gospel of Mark*, 180. Hovey's quote continued: "Dr. Clarke has stated his own view ably, but has also in his concluding remarks presented the view which appears to the general editor correct. Yet the subject is so important that it may be well for those who can read the following articles: 'The Coming of Christ. Matt 24:29-31,' by Dr. Edward Robinson, Bib. Sac., First Series (1843), pp. 531-537; 'The Eschatology of Christ,' etc., by Dr. C. E. Stowe, Bib. Sac., vol. vii (1850), pp. 452-478; 'Observations on Matt 24:29-31 and parallel passages,' etc., by Prof. M. Stuart, Bib. Sac., vol. ix (1852), pp. 329-355 and 449-468."

112. Clarke, *Commentary on the Gospel of Mark*, 196-201. Clarke explained this situation thus: "After the first edition, the publishing society obtained another commentary on the chapter from an older man, embodying one of the more accepted views, and bout it into the book at the end of my chapter, under the title of 'An Additional View.' To this I had no objection whatever, and cordially gave the consent which the society courteously asked. At any rate, I had made my contribution toward a substitute for the old untenable views, and that was as much as I could hope to do" (Clarke, *Sixty Years with the Bible*, 139).

113. Though Clarke does not name the article, it is most likely "Baptist Theology: The Newton Theological Institution and Its Faculty."

> I think, as you are aware, that it is not for the good of the Institution to repel and reject the style of work in theology that Professor Gould represents: that the present hope of strengthening the hold of Christian truth on the mind of the age lies very largely in just such fresh, brave, unhampered searching of the Scriptures as he has aimed to do: that the urging of systematized theology on men is not the powerful thing with this generation that it was with the last, and that the turning of popular Christian thought to the Bible is a providential call to the leaders of Christian thought to lay the foundations of their systems in still broader study of that Word which is still so far from being fully explored. I have feared that to reject Professor Gould would be to give the Institution a reactionary turn, by which it would lose something of its power to guide the best minds of the young ministry.[114]

These were harsh words from Clarke, and no doubt they were hard for Hovey to read. The following March, Hovey received a letter from Clarke in response to an inquiry from Hovey. Hovey had evidently asked if Clarke could suggest someone as a replacement for Gould, to which Clarke had no suggestions. In order to help the friendship, Clarke related that he did not doubt Hovey's sincerity in letting Gould go, he only disagreed, and there was no loss of affection.[115]

This affection was on display in the remaining letters that Clarke wrote to Hovey over the next twenty years.[116] When Hovey turned seventy-five years old, Clarke wrote a letter saying how happy he was to see that Hovey's handwriting was still strong.[117] Clarke offered happy birthday greetings to Hovey a couple more times,[118] and he wrote twice on the eve of a new year to remind Hovey that he was happy he was still alive and that many love him.[119] When Clarke heard from Mrs. Hovey that Alvah was not doing well

---

114. William Newton Clarke to Alvah Hovey, July 27, 1882 (AHP).

115. William Newton Clarke to Alvah Hovey, March 20, 1883 (AHP).

116. N.B.: There is no Clarke archive. Evidently, Clarke destroyed all his papers before he died. He and his wife were worried that he would be misrepresented by potential subsequent biographers. And so in the Summer of 1910 they burned his papers. Clarke, *William Newton Clarke*, 127–28. "Only a few note-books, brief diaries, and such notes and typewritten work as were likely to be of use later, which were kept in the study and the closet adjoining, were retained. All of the unpublished work of the earlier years and of his middle life vanished in an hour."

117. William Newton Clarke to Alvah Hovey, April 5, 1895 (AHP).

118. William Newton Clarke to Alvah Hovey, March 3, 1900 (AHP); March 5, 1903 (AHP).

119. William Newton Clarke to Alvah Hovey, December 30, 1900 (AHP); December 31, 1902 (AHP); July 7, 1902 (AHP).

(as he neared his death), he offered sincere pastoral comfort to his older friend.[120] Clarke was also present on the Newton campus a couple times. One time it was to celebrate Hovey's fiftieth anniversary at the school in 1899.[121] The last time Clarke visited was on the occasion of Hovey's funeral, at which Clarke was one of the men who eulogized Hovey. Clarke was assigned the subject of "Dr. Hovey as a Theologian."[122] Clarke ably presented Hovey's thought and method in brief, admitted that the two of them did not agree on much of their theology, and explained how they did not talk much controversial theology for the last couple decades of Hovey's life.

There is no doubt that Hovey and Clarke remained friends their entire lives, and there is no doubt that their theology grew further and further apart. But it is not entirely true that they did not discuss theology. Hovey published a review of Clarke's widely-popular theology textbook, *An Outline of Christian Theology*.[123] Hovey praised Clarke's theology for its readability and style, but he then gave four major critiques. First, Clarke had a problematic lack of biblical reference and basis. Second, his theology showed a poor view of inspiration "which tends to reduce in some degree the proper authority of Scripture."[124] Third, an unsatisfactory "treatment of the righteousness of God in punishing sinners."[125] Fourth, Hovey found Clarke's eschatology lacking in biblical basis. Hovey clearly found several major faults, but he still considered it a useful work. Clarke's theology book

---

120. William Newton Clarke to Alvah Hovey, January 28, 1903 (AHP); August 9, 1903 (AHP).

121. Which was evidently a major affair as leading Baptists (and non-Baptists) from all over the country attended, including President William R. Harper of the University of Chicago, President Elect W. H. P. Faunce of Brown University, President Augustus Strong of Rochester Theological Seminary, President C. D. Hartranft of Hartford Theological Seminary, President B. L. Whitman of Columbia University, Professor G. D. B. Pepper of Colby College, Professor F. H. Kerfoot of Southern Baptist Theological Seminary, Professor William Newton Clark of Colgate University, Professor E. M. Kierstead of Acadia University, Professor Robert Fletcher of Dartmouth College, Professors Hallowell and Whiting of Wellesley College, George Horr of the *Watchman*, Henry Burrage of *Zion's Advocate*, Thomas Conant of the *Examiner*, and many others. This list of people comes from a newspaper clipping within the Alvah Hovey Papers.

122. The eulogies at Hovey's funeral were printed a few days after the memorial service. See Clarke, "Dr. Hovey as a Theologian"; Horr, "Dr. Hovey and Educational Work"; English, "Dr. Hovey as a Teacher"; Weston, "Dr. Hovey as an Author." Newton's student body newspaper, *The Newtonian*, also published a reminiscence a year after Hovey's death. See Crane, "Dr. Hovey with His Friends."

123. Clarke, *Outline of Christian Theology*. Hovey's review came out early the next year: Hovey, "Book Review: An Outline of Christian Theology."

124. Hovey, "Book Review: An Outline of Christian Theology," 204.

125. Hovey, "Book Review: An Outline of Christian Theology," 205.

quickly became the manifesto for the liberal New Theology, and it was not long after its publication that Hovey passed away and new leadership at Newton followed the way of Clarke more than Hovey.[126]

And so, Clarke and Hovey differed greatly theologically, yet remained affectionate friends. Something similar could be said about Gould and Toy, except that neither Gould nor Toy had anything like the personal friendship with Hovey that Clarke had. Hovey clearly had theological problems with the positions of Toy, Gould, and Clarke. With each person, Hovey stepped in to the situation and either did not allow their work to continue or he significantly edited the work, and these interventions all surrounded biblical criticism. As such, these interactions are all instructive. Clarke is especially instructive as both men recognized the major difference between one another was their view of the Bible and their theological method. Clarke (like Toy and Gould) was convinced by the results of biblical criticism and felt that he must reconstruct his theology with that in mind. Hovey was well aware of biblical criticism, but he did not find it overly convincing. The next section will present Hovey's later theological work where he specifically addresses biblical criticism and will determine if Hovey's later views are consistent with his earlier views.

Later Formulations

The last twenty-five years of Hovey's life were highly productive years. As was mentioned, in Hovey's 1877 theology he did not discuss inspiration in significant depth. However, beginning with an 1884 essay, Hovey would publish several treatises that deal directly with different views and how to sort them out. Hovey also dealt directly with biblical criticism in a few spots during these years. The interactions with biblical criticism will be explored first and then his explanations of inspiration.

One place that Hovey dealt directly with biblical criticism was at what became known as the Baptist Congress. The Baptist Congress (originally called the Baptist Autumnal Conference) was an annual meeting from 1881–1913 where academics, pastors, and laypeople would come together and discuss questions of importance to Baptists.[127] In this venue Hovey had opportunity to address biblical criticism on a couple occasions. The first was in 1883 when Hovey served as President of the meeting. One of the topics that would be discussed over the three-day meeting was biblical criticism.

---

126. Straub, *Making of a Battle Royal*, 237–40.

127. Historical treatments are scarce. See Brackney, "Frontier of Free Exchange of Ideas"; Garrett, *Baptist Theology*, 327–30; Sherouse, "Toward a Twentieth-Century Baptist Identity."

When Hovey delivered the opening, presidential address he spoke directly to the subject. He asserted that there was still much to learn in the entire subject and that textual criticism would "not serious affect the teaching of our Lord or of his apostles as to any central truth preserved in the New Testament."[128] Criticism of the Old Testament, however, was "of a more disturbing character; for in this field the new criticism cannot prevail without destroying root and branch our confidence in the writings of that volume as a revelation of the Lord's will."[129] Still, Hovey felt the study must continue and the results need to be known. He warned, though, that Baptists would be slow to accept any theory that "tends to shake our confidence in the Scriptures as speaking with unique and ultimate authority to men."[130] Hovey was certainly aware of the threat to biblical authority that the new criticism posed: "Hence modern criticism must not take it amiss if it meets with sturdy resistance when it lifts up its axe against the pillars on which rest inspiration and authority of the Old Testament."[131] The primary reason was that the obvious meaning of Jesus' words was that the Old Testament was a revelation from God, and he was reticent to say that a modern-day interpreter would know more about the subject than Jesus. And so, Hovey welcomed critical studies but insisted that they be "cautious, modest, reverent, patient and mindful of the veins and arteries which connect the Old Testament with the New."[132]

The second time that Hovey spoke to the Baptist Congress was in 1895. His major presentation was on the "Relation of Monism to Theology,"[133] but he also gave a quick response to the subject of the "Books of the New Testament in Light of Modern Research."[134] Hovey's main assertion was that he had been "convinced for many years that the habit of speaking of types of doctrine in the New Testament is a mistake. Not that there are not different and partial presentations by the different writers, but we have not the data for saying that there were fundamental differences in them in respect to any

---

128. Hovey, "Opening Address," 5.

129. Hovey, "Opening Address," 5. Hovey also once contributed (1888) to a symposium in *The Old Testament Student* on "Shall the Analyzed Pentateuch be Published in the Old Testament Student." He felt this was a mistake as it would perplex the unprepared, was built merely on conjecture and not established, would have different scholarship in ten years, and needed more time and wisdom. Hovey et al., "Symposium," 316.

130. Hovey, "Opening Address," 5.

131. Hovey, "Opening Address," 5.

132. Hovey, "Opening Address," 5.

133. Hovey, "Relation of Monism to Theology."

134. Hovey, "Books of the New Testament."

one great truth which we find in the teaching of Christ or of the apostles."[135] Hovey found it greatly mistaken to see the various New Testament authors as fundamentally contradictory. This is because the data of most authors is quite small and because the authors did not have the same purposes or audiences. The major mistake of New Testament critics was to disregard the unity of the New Testament.

Hovey's archives also contain a forty-page handwritten manuscript on "The Baptist Ministry and the Higher Criticism,"[136] which has the inscription that it was delivered on February 15, 1897 at the Baptist Ministers Meeting, Boston. Hovey again assumed that the study was important, that the motives of the scholars were honorable, and that their scholarship was exemplary. But he still had several critiques to offer. The first was on miracles: "We cannot deny the occurrence of miracles, without displacing the cornerstone of apostolic faith, namely, the resurrection of Jesus Christ."[137] Another problem is the lack of place for prophecy and the ability to predict the future. He felt this was a "tendency to naturalize the revelation of religious truth to mankind."[138] Likewise, on the dating of Old Testament books, Hovey was incredulous toward those who claimed to know more about when a book ought to have been written than those who lived very close to the composition. Hovey likewise rejected the methodology that neatly compartmentalized what aspects of Israelite history could be present during certain times of history, and thus redefined the dates of composition. Hovey gave a few long examples of this type of work and questioned the necessity of the conclusions reached by higher critics.[139] In sum, he felt that higher critics introduced more problems than they provided answers. Still, Hovey was impressed by their scholarship, thankful for certain conclusions, unconvinced by others, and had no problem letting this study continue. But he believed that "their scientific principles and methods do scant justice to the freedom of God's Spirit in the sphere or revelation."[140] Hovey appreciated the work of higher critics but felt that the normal pastor could not do their pastoral work and also be an expert on it at the same time. His suggestion

---

135. Hovey, "Books of the New Testament," 102.

136. Hovey, "Baptist Ministry and the Higher Criticism," February 15, 1897 (AHP).

137. Hovey, "Baptist Ministry and the Higher Criticism," February 15, 1897, 13 (AHP).

138. Hovey, "Baptist Ministry and the Higher Criticism," February 15, 1897, 18 (AHP).

139. Hovey, "Baptist Ministry and the Higher Criticism," February 15, 1897, 19-39 (AHP).

140. Hovey, "Baptist Ministry and the Higher Criticism," February 15, 1897, 40 (AHP).

was that it is better to take the critical views that Jesus and Paul held over those of modern-day scholars.

Hovey's few direct discussions of biblical criticism were pretty similar. He did not feel that such criticism was worthless, but he often felt that it overstepped its boundaries in its methodologies and conclusions. He did not find anything overwhelmingly convincing that would cause him to accept critical views of the Bible or to abandon a high view of biblical authority. The question is whether Hovey modified his earlier views of inspiration and infallibility based on a growing understanding of biblical criticism, as is suggested by a few Baptist historians. These historians suggest that Hovey "felt the pressures toward change,"[141] as a result of being conversant with biblical criticism. They argue that this pressure toward change can be seen in his explanation of inspiration.[142] The remainder of this section will present Hovey's later conceptions of inspiration and so will speak to this discussion.

As was mentioned above, Hovey did not discuss views of inspiration at length in his 1870 and 1877 theologies. In his later work he devoted much space to discussing various views of inspiration, the issues involved, and where he fell himself.[143] Note that in the later writings, as in the earlier writings, Hovey asserted historical trustworthiness of both the New and Old Testaments and provided extended discussion of the areas often assailed by biblical criticism.[144]

When he spoke on the various theories of inspiration, he would present them on a sliding scale.[145] On one end of the spectrum was the view that considered inspiration to be the spiritual genius that makes the best religious teachers great, which he normally referred to as "gracious inspiration." On the other end of the spectrum was the view of complete verbal dictation, which he normally referred to as "verbal inspiration." Hovey normally saw two mediating positions. One was closer to the "gracious" view and saw that since the Bible was a human book (and nothing human is perfect) then only the religious matters of the Bible could be inspired,

141. Maring, "Baptists and Changing Views of the Bible (II)," 38.

142. Brackney suggests that Hovey "struggled with the doctrine of Scripture" since he lived close to Andover and Harvard and eventually "he moved away from claiming too much for Scripture" (Brackney, *Genetic History of Baptist Thought*, 285). Also see Hudson, "Shifting Patterns of Church Order in the Twentieth Century," 325–26.

143. Hovey, "Theories of Inspiration"; "Sacred Writings Described"; "Inspiration of the Prophets and Apostles"; "Inspiration of the Scriptures"; *Manual of Christian Theology*, 76–106.

144. Hovey, *Manual of Christian Theology*, 46–55, 72–76; "Inspiration of the Prophets and Apostles," esp. 180–81.

145. Hovey, "Theories of Inspiration," 27; "Inspiration of the Scriptures," 182–86; *Manual of Christian Theology*, 76.

which he normally called "religious inspiration." The last view was akin to "verbal" but emphasized the mental action of the human authors thus making the entire work both divine and human, a view which he normally called "dynamic inspiration."[146] Hovey himself preferred the "dynamical" view, but he always had a few extra caveats and explanations accompanying his acceptance. These caveats and explanations are not always the clearest and can lead one to wonder if Hovey had moved to accept the "religious" position. Some explanation will be helpful.

Beyond just the four ideal categories, Hovey recognized the issues that separated the viewpoints.[147] First of importance was what the Bible says about inspiration. The Bible, according to Hovey, taught (1) that inspiration was of the writers or their words, (2) that the purpose of inspiration was to provide special qualification for the writers to convey truth, and (3) this quality of inspiration was neither universal nor proportioned to the amount of grace of the writer.[148] Hovey also felt it important that a correct view of inspiration retain divine authority, particularly in religious matters, and recognize that the expressed object of the Bible is to form humans into holy Christians not just factually correct theologians.[149] Another important characteristic of a good view was that it recognize the various ways in which teaching was delivered throughout the progressive revelation of Scripture.[150] Fourth, a good view of inspiration should allow the consistency and coherency of the Bible.[151]

Beyond these four points are a handful of important clarification points, which were discussed above in the earlier section of Hovey's life, but which also appear in the later writings. He believed that the entire Bible was inspired. He believed that inspiration applied fully to the original documents and only derivatively to the copies and versions. He believed that the religious teaching was certainly inerrant. He also believed that the non-religious matters were likewise correct, though more explanation is needed here.

---

146. Hovey's first printed discussion of inspiration theories had more views on his sliding scale, but his 1892 and 1900 discussions had the same four typical views. All three discussions were meant to be seen as ideal-type categories and so various mediating positions could be held along the spectrum.

147. Hovey discussed "four lights" in his 1892 book that helped to delimit what the correct view was. He also discussed other important ideas which will be part of this discussion.

148. Hovey, "Inspiration of the Scriptures," 187–95.

149. Hovey, "Inspiration of the Scriptures," 195–200.

150. Hovey, "Inspiration of the Scriptures," 200–203.

151. Hovey, "Inspiration of the Scriptures," 203–7.

Hovey stated the biblical teaching clearly negated the "gracious inspiration" choice. He felt that the recognition of the Bible as a divine-human book (concursive inspiration) made the idea of dictation within the "verbal inspiration" view impossible. It was the two remaining views ("dynamical" and "religious") that Hovey struggled between. He agreed both that the purpose of Scripture was religious and that the method of how the Bible was inspired was dynamical. The clearest statement of his view was given in 1892 and then quoted verbatim in 1900:

> It is, therefore, our belief that the Sacred Scriptures, rightly interpreted from beginning to end as the record of a progressive revelation of God to man, of man to himself, and of spiritual life to all who will accept it, will lead to truth without error, and will justify that revelation, as one that gave those addressed by it, in each particular age, the religious truth most needed by them, in the best available form for reaching the heart and purifying the life. This sentence is long, but we cannot make it shorter and express the precise meaning intended.[152]

This statement shows that he accepted the dynamical idea that God so influenced the writers that their writing was divine and free from error, but still utilized human style and ability to write. Hovey was very aware of the charges surrounding the supposed historical and scientific errors of the Bible. And he was slow to say that the Bible was inerrant in scientific and historical matters, particularly as he argued strongly that the purpose of the Bible was primarily religious. That was the focus of his view of inspiration and his view of inerrancy. He stated that, "In view of what has been stated, we claim that the *dynamic* theory of inspiration within the sphere of religious teaching accounts for all the phenomena of the Bible better than any other."[153] Again, Hovey's succinct statements of his view of inspiration were primarily related to the religious teaching of the Bible. As such, these are not clear statements on his views of the historical or scientific statements of the Bible. After stating these views, however, he did provide several answers to objections that speak to those historical and scientific statements. Similar to his 1877 edition, though expanded, Hovey again stated that the alleged historical and scientific errors were more apparent than actual. In other words, understanding the progressive nature of revelation, the phenomenological nature of some references, the lack of scientific precision, and the need for

---

152. Hovey, "Inspiration of the Scriptures," 212. This paragraph is quoted verbatim in Hovey, *Manual of Christian Theology*, 85.

153. Hovey, *Manual of Christian Theology*, 85.

patient, continued study of the alleged errors would eventually vindicate the presentation of Scripture.[154]

Consistent with his earlier writings, Hovey's later writings clearly accepted a conservative view of the inspiration of the Bible (though he still rejected a dictation theory) and likewise argued that the Bible's presentation of history and science were also accurate when understood properly. In his 1900 edition, Hovey did provide longer discussions of specific issues, such as the alleged contradiction between Genesis 1 and 2, the use of non-scientific language, the problem of a universal flood, numerical exaggerations, anachronisms, and genealogical imperfections.[155] Hovey clearly saw some validity in the charges against the inerrancy of Scripture but he consistently argued that a patient and generous interpretation of each problem could be found that would vindicate the Bible's trustworthiness. Thus, despite the challenge of critical studies, Hovey's views of biblical inspiration and authority were remarkably consistent over the years. They became more refined and contained responses to new issues as time went on, but they were consistent. If anything, he perhaps became somewhat hesitant to declare historical and scientific matters free from problems and would only do so after much extended discussion of the purpose of inspiration and the nature of alleged problems.[156]

Conclusion: Holding to Biblical Authority

This chapter has shown that Hovey was aware of biblical criticism in a variety of forms throughout the length of his career. Further, Hovey interacted with biblical criticism on the theoretical and the practical level. As an editor and a president of a seminary, he was required on a few occasions to step in and stem the teaching of critical views, and the theology built off them, which Hovey was willing to do. The majority of Hovey's personal interactions with biblical criticism was in the later years of his career. Hovey's later writings evidence an increased volume of careful, comprehensive interaction with critical views. Hovey felt that critical studies had their place, but they were not as convincing to him as they were to others. As a result, there is a remarkable similarity of viewpoints between his early and later theology.

Brackney's comment that Hovey "moved away from claiming too much for Scripture" could be used to mean that Hovey did not accept the dictation theory and so did not claim that for Scripture, but it's still true that Hovey

---

154. Also see Hovey, "Inspiration of the Prophets and Apostles."
155. Hovey, *Manual of Christian Theology*, 94–101.
156. Hovey, "Inspiration of the Prophets and Apostles," esp. 180–81.

was definitely on the conservative end of the spectrum.[157] Likewise, Maring's contention that Hovey's later theology "reveals a broadening of views with respect to inspiration, although the general approach and position remain the same,"[158] could be explained to mean that Hovey deliberated longer in 1900 than in 1870 and added clarification and nuance, but held essentially the same theological viewpoint. Both Maring and Brackney are correct, however, when they argue that despite Hovey's conservatism, his attitude of openness toward new views and his equipping of students to study new views both helped significantly contribute to the eventual change of Newton after Hovey's death.[159] On the whole, it is quite clear that Hovey held to a consistently conservative view of biblical inspiration and authority,[160] even if he also remained somewhat open and welcoming to new formulations. And it is correct to say that throughout his life Hovey himself saw the Bible as the dynamically inspired and inerrant Word of God that had supreme authority, when properly interpreted, in faith and practice.

---

157. Brackney, *Genetic History of Baptist Thought*, 285.

158. Maring, "Baptists and Changing Views of the Bible (II)," 38.

159. Maring, "Baptists and Changing Views of the Bible (I)," 58; Brackney, *Genetic History of Baptist Thought*, 287–88; *Congregation and Campus*, 261, 293.

160. Garrett, *Baptist Theology*, 280–81. Garrett labels Hovey as a conservative theologian as compared to liberal or mediating. On Hovey's conservative view of the Bible, also see Priestley, "From Theological Polemic to Nonpolemical Theology," 154–57; Bush and Nettles, *Baptists and the Bible*, 248–56; Satta, *Sacred Text*, 7–8; Straub, *Making of a Battle Royal*, 45–48. Though, the works of Satta and Bush and Nettles look primarily at Hovey's 1877 work.

6

Practical Questions of Authority

BAPTIST LIFE IN THE late nineteenth century experienced a plethora of controversies. Hovey was often asked to give his opinion on pressing issues, which he regularly did. This chapter will select a handful of the issues about which Hovey decided to write. The point of surveying these writings is to observe how Hovey put his theological understanding into practice, particularly what authority he appealed to as he addressed these practical issues.[1]

Divorce

In 1866 Hovey published a short book titled *The Scriptural Law of Divorce*. The book originated after a request for counsel from a Baptist church in Grafton, Massachusetts. Evidently the church had a situation where a man married a woman who was previously divorced due to her first husband's "unkind treatment" and the church wanted to know the correct way to respond to the situation.[2] Hovey was part of the five-person committee who offered their opinion, though it was Hovey whose name is listed as the sole author of the book. The results of the study were published because the council believed that "it will prove useful to persons who are desirous of ascertaining the will of Christ on a question of vital concern to Christian

---

1. Because Hovey spoke to well over a dozen different theological issues this chapter is selective. What has been chosen will be presented in chronological order from when Hovey wrote about it. For a short treatment of some of these and other controversies, see Hovey, *Alvah Hovey*, 172–93.

2. Hovey, *Scriptural Law of Divorce*, iii–iv. Hovey provided a shortened version of this work in his 1892 collection of essays. The shortened essay does not differ from the book, except in length. See Hovey, "Divorce According to the New Testament."

morality, and in the belief that a serious effort should be made, by setting forth the teaching of Christ, to check that disregard of the Scriptural Law of Divorce which seems to be rapidly increasing in our land."[3]

The book began by asserting the supreme authority of the Bible, so long as it was properly interpreted. And the layout of the book was quite simple. Hovey worked through statements of Christ and of the Apostle Paul on the issue of divorce. Throughout the book Hovey assumed the unity and inspiration of biblical teaching. And he concluded that the sum total of Christ's teaching on divorce could be summarized in a few points: "1. That husband and wife are one flesh. 2. That marriage is a divine institution. 3. That God authorizes divorce in case of adultery. 4. God has permitted divorce in other cases."[4] On the fourth point it is important to note that Hovey said "permitted." What he argued here is that Jesus understood that Moses allowed divorce in certain cases outside of adultery not because it was good or even acceptable but only because it could not be restrained. Thus, Moses was not condoning divorce in situations outside of adultery but only restraining the already capricious practice of his fellow people. Hovey found this to be a recurring principle, that the civil government may allow more permissiveness than the Bible did, which was only allowed because the primary function of the civil government was one of restraint.[5]

Looking then at the instances where Paul addressed divorce, Hovey argued that there was unity with the teaching of Christ. He felt that 1 Corinthians 7 allowed for the reality of separation when one member of the marriage deserts or compromises the safety of the other member. He concluded, however, that this did not permit remarriage.[6] Paul talked about further instances where separation could be helpful or useful, though Hovey did not understand the allowance of separation to simultaneously grant the permissibility of remarriage. Thus, Hovey argued that the biblical teaching was that there was only one ground for divorce and that churches should recognize no other ground.

This controversy had the express purpose of providing the biblical teaching concerning the practice of divorce. As such, the Bible was the clear authority. And it was assumed that the Bible was unified. Still, Hovey knew that it was the interpretation of the Bible that was the issue. The book is essentially a study in exegesis through the pertinent passages. He merely explained the text as he understood it and then organized the results. The

3. Hovey, *Scriptural Law of Divorce*, iv.
4. Hovey, *Scriptural Law of Divorce*, 18–29.
5. Hovey, *Scriptural Law of Divorce*, 71–82.
6. Hovey, *Scriptural Law of Divorce*, 34–60.

authority was the Bible. Interpretation was necessary, which was made without appeals to extra-biblical sources and only to Hovey's explanation of the text.

Horace Bushnell and the Atonement

A more formidable theological challenge came Hovey's way a few years later in the form of a response to a well-known contemporaneous theologian. In 1872, Hovey published *God With Us: Or, The Person and Work of Christ, with an Examination of "The Vicarious Sacrifice" of Dr. Bushnell*. As the subtitle suggests, Hovey provided a ninety-page review of Horace Bushnell's (1802–1876) famous book of 1866 (and republished in 1871).[7] Anticipating those who may charge him with a lack of charity, Hovey provided an apology for his response to Bushnell. Hovey saw his response not as a desire to stir up religious controversy, nor as demeaning criticism against a distinguished author, but as an issue of truth. In Hovey's mind, "both the precept and the example of Paul authorize the servants of Christ to contend earnestly for the faith once delivered to the saints."[8]

As was usual for Hovey, he began his review with several positives within Bushnell's book, mostly commending his boldness and earnestness, though Hovey felt that Bushnell could have used more logic in his presentation rather than passion and boldness.[9] Beyond the tone of the writing Hovey structured his critique on three theological areas he found problematic as well as Bushnell's interpretation of the language of Scripture. The first theological issue was that Bushnell had an improper understanding of the nature of the moral law. Bushnell equated God's righteousness and God's love. This, to Hovey, created a deficiency in how he dealt with other aspects of God's righteousness, such as wrath. Hovey's utilized simple ethical illustrations as well as Bible passages to show that righteousness and love could not be equated.[10] The second theological issue was God's relation to the moral law. Hovey accused Bushnell of believing that he understood the mind of God perfectly without the help of Scripture. The result being that Bushnell created theological tensions in his understanding of how God relates to what is right. In other words, Bushnell's system created more problems than it

---

7. Bushnell, *Vicarious Sacrifice*.
8. Hovey, *God With Us*, viii.
9. Hovey, *God With Us*, 187. "The thought has more than once been suggested, that the writer is not always borne along by the deep current and flow of logical conviction, but is sometimes moving heaven and earth to carry a point with his reader."
10. Hovey, *God With Us*, 196–99.

solved. Plus, Bushnell's view simply did not accord with Scripture.[11] The third theological problem was Bushnell's view of the penalty of sin. Hovey regarded it as purely speculative and incompatible with conscience or Scripture.[12] In sum, the theological arguments that Hovey marshalled against Bushnell were focused on the logical coherence and consistency (or lack thereof) of his system, its incompatibility with the common understanding of ethics and conscience, and its lack of a biblical basis.

The last major section of Hovey's critique looked at Bushnell's interpretation of the language of scripture. Hovey was not interacting with Bushnell's famous "Preliminary Dissertation on the Nature of Language as Related to Thought and Spirit."[13] Hovey was simply reviewing Bushnell's use of "vicarious," "intercession," "forgiveness," "justification," and "propitiation."[14] Hovey tested Bushnell's atonement theory by looking at biblical terms and seeing how well they agreed with the theory. Hovey surveyed Bushnell's supposed understanding of each word and then he used commentaries, dictionaries, and lexicons to judge their accuracy. Hovey argued that Bushnell consistently missed the plain meaning of scripture and of each word in his effort to carry a point. He used words how he intended to use them rather than how they are normally, and biblically, used. Thus, rendering his theory weak. By doing this, Bushnell had made the atonement all about the human-ward aim and had missed the God-ward aim.[15] "'The Vicarious Sacrifice' emphasizes but a part of the redemptive work of Christ, while it treats with bitterness another part just as clearly taught in the Scriptures."[16]

Bushnell's work failed in a couple essential points. It equated God's righteousness with God's love, it made the atonement consist only in righting the sinner, it ran counter to the clear ethical notions of conscience, and

11. Hovey, *God With Us*, 200–210.

12. Hovey, *God With Us*, 210–21.

13. This was a long essay at the beginning of Bushnell's 1849 work, *God in Christ*, as well as his 1851 work, *Christ in Theology*. In these works, Bushnell worked out a general theory of language as well as a view of language in religious and moral thought. Bushnell pondered whether language had the power to adequately convey spiritual truth. "I do not propose, in the dissertation that follows, to undertake a full investigation of language. I freely acknowledge my incompetence to any such undertaking. What I design is, principally, to speak of language as regards its significancy, of the power and capacity of its words, taken as vehicles of thought and of spiritual truth" (Bushnell, *God in Christ*, 12). For the significance of this "preliminary dissertation," see Ahlstrom, *Theology in America*, 58–64, 317–70.

14. Hovey, *God With Us*, 222–71.

15. Hovey, *God With Us*, 222.

16. Hovey, *God With Us*, 270.

it made biblical terms mean something other than their obvious and normal meaning. These were not small errors because it produced a theological defect in an important subject matter. "The teaching of 'The Vicarious Sacrifice,' if defective, as I think, by denying any reaction of the Atonement upon the mind of God, is profoundly erroneous, and its influence must be even more hurtful, in many respects, than it would be if it embraced less truth and uttered it with less power."[17]

In addressing Bushnell, Hovey's view of authority certainly came into play. He appealed to multiple authorities that he felt Bushnell violated including logical consistency/coherence, ethical viability, the normal use of words, and the biblical use of words. In doing so, Hovey appealed to biblical commentators, lexicons, rules of logic, as well as the unity of the Bible. Hovey centered his critique on the authority of the Bible, but he was certainly willing to appeal to rational sources of authority, as he expected Bushnell's work to follow each of these.

Religion and the State

The subject of how Christians should relate to government was one in which Hovey took much interest. One of the first books he wrote was a biography of Isaac Backus wherein Hovey dwelt much on the relation of the state to religion.[18] Fifteen years after that book, Hovey published an extended study on the relation of religion to the state.[19] Hovey's Baptist views of the issue are on full display. He makes a few biblical and theological arguments and then applies these conclusions to a few particular situations.

The first argument marshalled by Hovey was concerning the kingdom of Christ. Hovey argued that the apostles themselves at first thought that Jesus' kingdom would be political, when it was in fact primarily spiritual.[20]

17. Hovey, *God With Us*, viii.

18. Hovey, *Memoir of the Life and Times*.

19. Hovey, *Religion and the State*. Hovey shortened this work and included it in his 1892 collection of essays. The shortened form does not differ from the book, except in length. Hovey, "State and Religion," 246–70.

20. Hovey, *Religion and the State*, 13–14. "And his Apostles came at last to understand this. By the death, the resurrection, and the ascension of Christ; by the outpouring of the Spirit on the day of Pentecost, and the light of inspiration added to that of providence, they were made to know that their Lord's dominion was not civil and national, but spiritual and universal; not of this world and sustained by force, but from above, and supported by grace; and to comprehend the new and great fact that, though engaged in a fearful conflict, the weapons of their warfare were not carnal, but mighty through God to casting down strongholds, and bringing every thought into captivity to the obedience of Christ."

The result is that the kingdom of Christ is not of this world and independent of the state. The purpose of the state is to be found elsewhere. Hovey considered the state to be established by God and he argued that, "That form of government is best for any nation which accomplished best the ends which it ought to seek."[21] He presented three basic conceptions of the state. The Roman model saw the state as its own end and used people for its own purposes. The Paternal model treated people like children that were to be controlled. And the Protective model guarded the natural rights of the people.[22] Hovey then looked at Romans 13; 1 Peter 2; and Titus 3 to see how the Bible described the relationship between religion and the state. He concluded that the New Testament did not completely describe the limits of what the state can do, but it did give a few helpful principles that provide clues.[23] First, the Bible entrusts the individual with responsibility to act for itself in matters of religion.[24] Second, Christians are supposed to follow the commands of Christ above that of the state when they are in conflict with each other. Third, "it does provide, without the agency of the State, for the spread of the gospel and the orderly existence of churches—for regular contributions to the poor, and every good work suggested by intelligent love."[25]

With these principles, Hovey then said that, "it is safe to affirm that the New Testament teaches nothing incompatible with the hypothesis that the single and great end of human government should be the protection of men in the exercise of their natural rights, and the encouragement thereby of all good conduct in earthly affairs."[26] Religious responsibilities are above that of the state, but the state does have the right enforce means to accomplish its purpose, such as taxation, education, and law enforcement. The state has the clear charge to protect the lives of all its citizens, unless they have forfeited it through crime,[27] and they have the clear charge protect the liberty of its citizens.[28] This means that the government does not give any sort of legal immunity to the clergy, it is supposed to provide the liberty to worship freely so long as it respects the liberty of others, and the state is to leave religious responsibilities to God's ordained means.

21. Hovey, *Religion and the State*, 21.
22. Hovey, *Religion and the State*, 21–24.
23. Hovey, *Religion and the State*, 32–34.
24. Also see Hovey, *Restatement of Denominational Principles*, 7–10.
25. Hovey, *Religion and the State*, 32.
26. Hovey, *Religion and the State*, 32–33.
27. Hovey, *Religion and the State*, 35–46.
28. Hovey, *Religion and the State*, 47–59.

Hovey then addressed a handful of controversial questions. The first was whether the state should implement a Lord's Day where they require state-run workplaces to let their people off work to attend worship and to rest.[29] Hovey argued that it was not the state's place to implement religious requests. A government requirement for a day of rest, to Hovey, should be made on secular and not religious grounds.[30] A day of rest is good, but it cannot be forced. However, Christians, as well as Jews, could insist that their religious practices be protected by the state and thus they should get Sunday, or Saturday, off of work. The second issue was that of the Bible in state-funded schools.[31] Hovey argued that since these schools are funded by tax money, then they could not require Bible reading or religious teaching. It could be allowed voluntarily and apart from the regular educational instruction, but it would be wrong to use tax funds to implement religious ends.

The most controversial subject that Hovey discussed was the issue of taxation on churches. He took the position that it would be best for churches to be taxed. He felt that Baptists had proved themselves to be helpful activists when it came to religious liberty, but they were inconsistent when they applied religious liberty to the taxation of churches. He felt it was an indirect benefit that was paid to the church through the agency of the government. Baptists had "protested, even to imprisonment, against direct taxation for the support of religion, but [have] winked at indirect taxation for the same purpose. It is charitable to believe that this inconsistency has not commonly been perceived; but it is now manifest to all, and the only proper course is to bring our practice as soon as possible into agreement with our theory."[32] Hovey felt this was a logical conclusion to the Baptist principle that the government should not support any religion financially, and that idea was built on the Baptist idea of individual soul liberty, which he considered to be clearly taught in the New Testament. Hovey also discussed charitable establishments and argued that it would be best if the government would only protect the liberty of religious organizations to provide this service rather than provide financial support.[33] The argument was the same as that of taxation on churches though from a different direction. Hovey agreed that charitable organizations can often perform deeds that would be considered non-religious and thus theoretically be performed by religious organizations with state funding. However, Hovey felt this would

---

29. Hovey discussed this particular issue at more length in Hovey, "Lord's Day."
30. Hovey, *Religion and the State*, 67.
31. Hovey, *Religion and the State*, 80–92.
32. Hovey, *Religion and the State*, 138–39.
33. Hovey, *Religion and the State*, 111–26.

be difficult to do consistently and could be easily manipulated to provide state funds for religious organizations. Thus, he preferred to stay away from the potential pitfalls.

In all, Hovey made a few biblical and theological arguments to determine guiding principles that could be applied to particular situations. The place that Hovey sourced authority in this book was in the biblical passages and principles concerning individual soul liberty, religious freedom, and the relationship of the church to the state. Using these principles, Hovey was able to theologically reason about how to act in various situations. Further, he regularly argued that certain actions of the state had to be defended on secular/moral grounds and not on explicitly religious grounds. The Bible provided the authority, but theological and moral reasoning was needed to apply biblical principles to situations not specifically described by scripture.

Bible Wine

Temperance was a pressing issue in Hovey's day, particularly in the north. George Hovey, in his biography of his father, related that in the 1880s there was much stir over a book published by the National Temperance Society on the meaning of wine in the Bible.[34] The short title of the book was *The Divine Law as to Wines*, by George Whitefield Samson.[35] Samson defended the idea that wine in the Bible sometimes referred to fermented juice and sometimes unfermented juice, and the Bible always condemned the fermented kind.[36] This "two-wine theory" was not new with Samson, but it did create a significant stir after its publication in 1880. Samson made many references to Greek, Hebrew, and Latin words to defend his view, along with appeals to many early church fathers. The problem with the book was that many people had trouble hunting down the references that Samson made. The criticism was loud enough that by 1883 the National Temperance Society sought advice from outside sources on the quality of the book. The chairman of their Executive Committee, Halsey Moore, wrote to Hovey on December 12, 1883 asking him to review the book for the Society.

> Dr. Lawson sent me your letter to him in reference to Dr. Samson's book, "The Divine Law as to Wines." Will you allow me to say that the Committee are unanimous in their opinion that you

34. Hovey, *Alvah Hovey*, 182–84.
35. Samson, *Divine Law as to Wines*.
36. Samson's book also went to great lengths to argue that there were not only exegetical reasons for practicing total abstinence but also universal laws that argued for total abstinence. On this, see Tait, *Poisoned Chalice*, 93–94.

are the man to do the work, and will not turn to another until they learn that it is absolutely impossible for you to put them under obligation to you. Rev. Dr. Sabine, of this [New York City] city, a member of the Committee, on hearing of your letter to Dr. Lawson wrote me: "I do hope Dr. Hovey will accept. It is very important that the work be done by some widely known, and of acknowledged scholarship."[37]

Moore then suggested that Hovey conscript help from someone to verify quotes (and send the bill to the Society), but they wanted Hovey to put his stamp of approval on everything. "You can furnish the workman, or workmen—we want you to stamp the work when it is done; your seal is what we are after."[38] George Hovey related that his father performed this work and sent his report to the Society in 1884. And as a result, "The Society suppressed the book. Doctor Hovey's letter was not published."[39] Though Hovey's report was not published, he did publish several articles on the subject.[40] Hovey's arguments in these articles are instructive in that he was seeking to make a biblical argument but he knew that he had to appeal to extra-biblical sources in order to make his argument and refute that of the two-wine view.

In his article on "The Meaning of Yayin and Oinos in Scripture" Hovey walked through every use of these words in the Bible. The point of doing this was to see if they ever decisively mean anything other than fermented wine when used alone without any further denotation. Hovey appealed to linguistic authorities such as Gesenius, Liddell and Scott, and Buxtorf to argue that the evidence simply does not provide any instance where these two words, when used without any qualification, clearly mean unfermented wine. Despite this conclusion Hovey ended his essay with a few arguments for why he still practiced and suggested abstinence in regard to alcohol. He believed that the protests in the Bible against drunkenness, the requirements to deny our own luxuries for the sake of another, and the requirement to love our neighbor all gave adequate argumentation to be a teetotaler. This is important to remember because Hovey was a lifelong temperance advocate. His critique of the two-wine view was born out of his conviction that, "bad

---

37. Halsey Moore to Alvah Hovey, December 12, 1883 (AHP).
38. Halsey Moore to Alvah Hovey, December 12, 1883 (AHP).
39. Hovey, *Alvah Hovey*, 183.
40. Hovey, "Shekhar and Leaven in Mosaic Offerings"; "Bible Wine"; "What Was the 'Fruit of the Vine'?"; "Patristic Testimonies as to Wine." The second and third of these articles were also published separately as pamphlets.

arguments injure even a good cause, and there is some reason to fear this saying will be proved true in the history of temperance reform."[41]

Hovey wrote further articles on "Shekhar and Leaven in Mosaic Offerings" and "What Was the 'Fruit of the Vine' which Jesus Gave His Disciples at the Institution of the Supper?"[42] Both these articles followed suit in arguing that the normal biblical usage of the word wine refers to fermented drinks. Further, Hovey felt like the wine used at the Last Supper was probably fermented wine mixed with water. Hovey made these arguments based on lexical studies, rabbinic studies, and logical connections between passages. Hovey also wrote in regard to the use of early church fathers in the debate.[43] He looked at Clement of Alexandria, Irenaeus, Origen, Tertullian, Cyprian, Jerome, Augustine, and also Thomas Aquinas. Hovey's conclusion is clear, and consistent with his other writings:

> My reason for associating the exposition of this subject by Aquinas with passages from the Christian Fathers of the first five centuries is the circumstance that inaccurate representations of his teaching have been published in the interest of the two-wine theory. And it is almost needless to add that I have been unable to discover any sure traces of that theory in the early history of the Church. The Fathers meant by the term wine the fermented juice of grapes, and held that this, mixed with water, was the proper material for the Lord's supper.[44]

While Hovey found no reason to advocate for the two-wine view, it is again important to recognize that he continued to be a strong advocate for temperance. In these articles he consistently argued for temperance and that temperance should have solid argumentation. His problem with the two-wine view was that it was not built on strong linguistic, biblical, and historical-theological grounds. As a result, these articles present a candid look at Hovey's understanding of authority. He again found the Bible to be the most important authority and that was where the majority of his argumentation remained, except for his article on patristic sources. However, because the debate was over the correct interpretation of Scripture, he made appeal to extra-biblical adjudicators, such as lexicons, rabbinic authorities, and historical theology. Hovey felt that each of these lent authority to his own views and vindicated his interpretation of Scripture.

41. Hovey, "Bible Wine," 151.
42. Hovey, "Shekhar and Leaven in Mosaic Offerings"; "What Was the 'Fruit of the Vine'?"
43. Hovey, "Patristic Testimonies as to Wine."
44. Hovey, "Patristic Testimonies as to Wine," 91.

Augustus Hopkins Strong and Ethical Monism

Of all the controversies that Hovey entered, the one that provides the widest display of his view of authority was his interaction with Augustus Hopkins Strong (1836–1921) on theism. This controversy was distinct from the others already looked at because Hovey and Strong both wrote much over several years on this issue and interacted with each other. The argumentations were complex and multifaceted. As such, they give a great window into Hovey's practical understanding of biblical and theological authority. Because of the extensive interaction and due to the complexity of the issue, space will be given to Strong's viewpoints before turning to Hovey's interactions.

Within the panorama of theological changes of the nineteenth century, one of the more intriguing cases involves the Baptist theologian Augustus Hopkins Strong and his idea of ethical monism. Strong felt that theologians needed to pay close attention to what philosophers were doing. And in his mind all the leading philosophers were arguing for a monistic conception of reality. Monism can refer to philosophical views which argue there is a unity of all things in their origin, substance, and/or essence.[45] It was an unusual philosophical notion to utilize for Christian theology because it is regularly thought to teach a pantheistic view of God that blurs the distinction between Creator and creation which Scripture seems to clearly teach (which could then lead to modified notions of Christ's deity, human sin, and salvation, among others). Monism also seems to make God much more immanent at the expense of God's transcendence. Strong understood that it was controversial for reasons that will be explained below. Thus, he sought to adjust his monism with the modifier "ethical." By ethical monism, Strong meant philosophical/ontological monism along with a psychological/personal dualism. The clearest statement of Strong's ethical monism appeared in his final *Systematic Theology*: "Ethical Monism is that method of thought

---

45. For a brief presentation of monism, see McLaughlin, "Philosophy of Mind." "Many philosophers reject Descartes's bifurcation of reality into mental and physical substances. Spinoza held a *dual-attribute theory*—also called the *dual-aspect theory*—according to which the mental and the physical are distinct modes of a single substance. Many philosophers opted for a thoroughgoing *monism*, according to which all of reality is really of one kind. Materialism, idealism, and neutral monism are three brands of monism. Hobbes, a contemporary of Descartes, espoused *materialism*, the brand of monism according to which everything is material or physical. Berkeley is associated with *idealism*, the brand of monism according to which everything is mental. He held that both mental and physical phenomena are perceptions in the mind of God. For Hegel's idealism, everything is part of the World Spirit. The early twentieth-century British philosophers Bradley and McTaggart also held a version of idealism. *Neutral monism* is the doctrine that all of reality is ultimately of one kind, which is neither mental nor physical" (McLaughlin, "Philosophy of Mind," 686).

which holds to a single substance, ground, or principle of being, namely, God, but which also holds to the ethical facts of God's transcendence as well as his immanence, and of God's personality as distinct from, and as guaranteeing, the personality of man."[46]

He controversially accepted ethical monism in the mid-1890s and subsequently reworked much of his theology to accommodate this change. Strong is generally considered a gifted and conservative theologian who was conscious of the history of theology and his place in it. Yet, he pioneered a controversial theism that flew in the face of classical conceptions.[47] Strong was the President and Davies Professor of Biblical Theology at Rochester Theological Seminary in Rochester, New York from 1872–1912. Prior to this he was educated at Yale University (A.B., 1857) and Rochester Theological Seminary (graduate, 1859), pastored the First Baptist Church of Haverhill, Massachusetts (1861–1865), and then pastored the First Baptist Church of Cleveland, Ohio (1865–1872).

Strong's unique theism did not come directly from any one source nor was it present throughout his entire theological career. It was in 1876 that Strong first organized his theology, which can be found in his *Lectures in Theology*. These lectures were printed for the use of his students and not made available to the wider public. The public version of his theology was first published in 1886 as *Systematic Theology: A Compendium and Commonplace Book Designed for the Use of Theological Students*. The *Systematic Theology* eventually saw seven further "revised and enlarged" editions, the final being in 1907.[48] Strong published a series of articles in 1892 and then in 1894 (jointly published in 1899, along with other essays, as *Christ in Creation and Ethical Monism*) that first gave wind of his ethical monism.[49]

---

46. Strong, *Systematic Theology* [8th ed.], 105.

47. Many have written on Strong's ethical monism and his place in Northern Baptist life in the late nineteenth and early twentieth century. A couple helpful shorter studies include: Richardson, "Augustus Hopkins Strong"; Thornbury, "Augustus Hopkins Strong"; Nettles, *Baptists*, 3:93–115; Garrett Jr., *Baptist Theology*, 294–303. The more extended studies include: Henry, *Personal Idealism and Strong's Theology*; Moore Jr., "Rise of Religious Liberalism"; Christian, "Theology of Augustus Hopkins Strong"; Wacker, *Augustus H. Strong*; Houghton, "Examination and Evaluation of A. H. Strong's Doctrine"; Priestley, "From Theological Polemic to Nonpolemical Theology"; Van Pelt "Examination of the Concept of the Atonement"; Massey, "Solidarity in Sin"; Thornbury, "Legacy of Natural Theology"; Aloisi, "Augustus Hopkins Strong."

48. Strong, *Systematic Theology*: 1st ed. (1886); 2nd ed. (1889); 3rd ed. (1890); 4th ed. (1893); 5th ed. (1896); 6th ed. (1899); 7th ed. (1902); 8th ed. (1907).

49. Strong, *Christ in Creation and Ethical Monism*. Three essays are of particular importance: "Christ in Creation" (1–15); "Ethical Monism" (16–50); and "Ethical Monism Once More" (51–86). All page references to these essays will refer to this collected work.

Thus, when considering his *Systematic Theology*, his fifth edition (1896) and the subsequent editions reveal his ethical monism as well as the progressive development of it and its significance in Strong's theology.

During the nineteenth century there were many theologies that stressed the immanence of God.[50] The German idealism of Fichte, Schelling, and Hegel all had the same assumption that in order to avoid the dualism of Kant's system you had to have a monistic basis to adequately do so. Strong eventually agreed with this assumption though he thought that sin and moral culpability were the major hurdles for a Christian theologian.[51] And, it was only after a long period of struggle that Strong eventually accepted a monistic view.

Throughout his works Strong gave several hints at why he accepted monism and the one that appears in several places is simply the idea that monism was becoming the dominant model of reality. "The tendency of modern thought in all its departments, whether physics, literature, theology, or philosophy, is to monism."[52] Strong gave examples of each of these departments to show the influence of monism. The following extended quote is extremely helpful in pinpointing Strong's reasons for accepting monism, his awareness of problems with monism, and his suggestion for how Christian theology can programmatically use monism.

> It is of great importance, both to the preacher and to the Christian, to hold the right attitude toward the ruling idea of our time. This universal tendency toward monism, is it a wave of unbelief set agoing by an evil intelligence in order to overwhelm and swamp the religion of Christ? Or is it a mighty movement of the Spirit of God, giving to thoughtful men, all unconsciously to themselves, a deeper understanding of truth and preparing the way for the reconciliation of diverse creeds and parties by disclosing their hidden ground of unity? I confess that I have come to believe the latter alternative to be possibly, and even probably, the correct one, and I am inclined to welcome the new philosophy as a most valuable helper in interpreting the word and works of God. Monism is, without much doubt, the philosophy of the future, and the only question would seem to be whether it shall be an ethical and Christian, or a non-ethical and anti-Christian monism.
>
> If we refuse to recognize this new movement of thought and to capture it for Christ, we may find that materialism and

---

50. McGiffert, *Rise of Modern Religious Ideas*, 189.
51. Aloisi, "Augustus Hopkins Strong," 73.
52. Strong, *Christ in Creation and Ethical Monism*, 16.

> pantheism perversely launch their craft upon the tide and compel it to further their progress. Let us tentatively accept the monistic principle and give to it a Christian interpretation. Let us not be found fighting against God. Let us use the new light that is given us, as a means of penetrating more deeply into the meaning of Scripture. Let us see in this forward march of thought a sign that Christ and his kingdom are conquering and to conquer.[53]

One can see that Strong was clearly aware that monism tended toward pantheism and materialism, which he thought did not accord with Christianity. Therefore, Strong wanted to let certain Christian ideas modify his conception of monism. In his *Systematic Theology*, Strong spoke about materialism and offered this brief summary: "The element of truth in materialism is the reality of the external world. Its error is in regarding the external world as having original and independent existence, and in regarding mind as its product."[54] Likewise about pantheism, Strong remarked: "The elements of truth in pantheism are the intelligence and voluntariness of God, and his immanence in the universe; its error lies in denying God's personality and transcendence."[55] So, in his conception of monism, Strong wanted to retain a place for the ethical interests of God and humanity. Primarily, Strong wanted to allow for God's transcendence and immanence, as well as humanity's sin and responsibility for sin.

With ethical monism Strong felt he could use the leading model of reality of the time and let traditional Christianity adequately modify this model.[56] He accepted the monistic idea that let him see God as thoroughly immanent in reality and it allowed humanity to have some sort of ontological unity. He also retained the traditional Christian ideas of transcendence and personality of God as well as the sin, responsibility, and personality of humans.

Strong felt that his ethical qualifications helped him avoid the errors of other monistic theories and retain the essentials of Christianity for several reasons. First, "Metaphysical Monism, or the doctrine of one substance, ground, or principle of being, is qualified by Psychological Dualism, or the doctrine that the soul is personally distinct from matter on the one hand,

---

53. Strong, *Christ in Creation and Ethical Monism*, 22.
54. Strong, *Systematic Theology* [8th ed.], 90.
55. Strong, *Systematic Theology* [8th ed.], 100.
56. This, and whether or not Strong was successful, is essentially the discussion of Aloisi's dissertation. Aloisi argues that Strong tried to appeal to both moderns and conservatives by his blended model, but was ultimately unable to satisfy either. See Aloisi, "Augustus Hopkins Strong."

and from God on the other."⁵⁷ Second, "Ethical Monism holds that the universe, instead of being one with God and coterminous with God, is but a finite, partial and progressive manifestation of the divine Life: Matter being God's self-limitation under the law of Necessity; Humanity being God's self-limitation under the law of Freedom; Incarnation and Atonement being God's self-limitations under the law of Grace."⁵⁸ Third, "The immanence of God, as the one substance, ground and principle of being, does not destroy, but rather guarantees, the individuality and rights of each portion of the universe, so that there is variety of rank and endowment. In the case of moral beings, worth is determined by the degree of their voluntary recognition and appropriation of the divine."⁵⁹ Fourth, "Since Christ is the Logos of God, the immanent God, God revealed in Nature, in Humanity, in Redemption, Ethical Monism recognizes the universe as created, upheld, and governed by the same Being who in the course of history was manifest in human form and who made atonement for human sin by his death on Calvary."⁶⁰

In summary, both terms in Strong's "Ethical Monism" prove vital to understand. Strong accepted monism because he believed that there was one metaphysical or philosophical substance of all reality, which is God. He adamantly held that "substance" should not be taken materialistically. Strong pointed to his idea that God is eternally self-existent and all else is not and everything outside of God relies on God's substance for their being. This is how "there is but one substance, one underlying reality, the infinite and eternal Spirit of God, who contains within his own being the ground and principle of all other being."⁶¹ The odd thing about Strong's monism is that it is a dualistic sort of monism. He recognized this, but he felt it was unavoidable if one wanted to hold to the ethical interests of God and humanity. He believed in a dualism of mind and matter because they were inconvertible. And he believed in the dualism of God and humanity because they are different persons. "These two sorts of dualism, since they postulate a soul, distinct from matter on the one hand and from God on the other, are only aspects of one truth, and I name that truth psychological dualism."⁶²

---

57. Strong, *Systematic Theology* [8th ed.], 106.
58. Strong, *Systematic Theology* [8th ed.], 107.
59. Strong, *Systematic Theology* [8th ed.], 108.
60. Strong, *Systematic Theology* [8th ed.], 109.
61. Strong, *Christ in Creation and Ethical Monism*, 65. "Ethical Monism is a monism which maintains both the freedom of man and the transcendence of God" (Strong, *Christ in Creation and Ethical Monism*, 25).
62. Strong, *Christ in Creation and Ethical Monism*, 54.

Strong's ethical monism was not simply one small part of his theology of God. By his own admission, it was "the key to theology."[63] Strong said, "While I still hold to the old doctrines, I interpret them differently and expound them more clearly, because I seem to myself to have reached a fundamental truth which throws new light upon them all."[64] The theology of Strong prior to his acceptance of ethical monism was decidedly conservative. Several theologians and historians have noted that Strong's ethical monism influenced several parts of this conservative theology, though some have argued that Strong did not let ethical monism run its logical course throughout the entirety of his theology.[65] And, most felt that Strong's ethical monism carried within itself several self-contradictory ideas. For the purposes of this chapter, I am interested to see how Strong let ethical monism influence his view of God's nature, God's work, creation, evolution, sin, and salvation.[66]

On God's nature, within his idea of ethical monism, Strong wanted to distinguish the personality of humanity from that of God. Strong made a curious argument that just as there are three consciousnesses and wills within the one divine (Triune) substance which we do not conceive to be divided, so also there may be "the possibility of multitudinous finite personalities within the bounds of God's being."[67]

---

63. Strong, *Systematic Theology* [8th ed.], vii.

64. Strong, *Systematic Theology* [8th ed.], vii.

65. Some of the more liberal theologians of Strong's day, such as William Adams Brown, thought that Strong did not let the logical consequences of his acceptance of God's immanence run its course through his theology (Brown, "Review of *Systematic Theology*"). Some of the more conservative theologians, such as Benjamin Breckinridge Warfield and Carl Henry, were happy that Strong did not let ethical monism influence more of his theology, at least initially, and Warfield was hopeful Strong would reconsider his acceptance of it. Warfield, "Review of *Systematic Theology*"; Henry, *Personal Idealism and Strong's Theology*.

66. Several historians have looked at places where Strong's ethical monism influenced his theology. The most extended and helpful surveys are found in Carl Henry's published dissertation and the more recent dissertation of John Aloisi. Henry discusses how Strong's new philosophical view influences his epistemology, nature of God, works of God, anthropology, Christology, Soteriology, and Eschatology. Aloisi looks at Strong's changing views of Scripture and experience, evolution and miracles, and sin and atonement. I agree with these authors that these are the general areas where Strong's modified theism shows up, for the purposes of this chapter I am focusing on Strong's theology of God. On epistemology in Strong's thought, the most important work is Grant Wacker's *Augustus H. Strong and the Dilemma of Historical Consciousness*.

67. Strong, *Christ in Creation and Ethical Monism*, 62. Strong sees this merely as illustrative. He goes on to say: "I claim only that in the Trinity we have plural self-consciousnesses, though the essence of the Godhead is one; while in man's single nature we have consciousnesses and volitions that are not only independent but abnormal. While

On the doctrine of creation and evolution, Strong's views changed over time. Before he accepted ethical monism, he held to an evolutionary viewpoint, and that did not change when he accepted ethical monism. However, prior to accepting ethical monism Strong held a classical theism that distinguished itself from deism and monistic idealism. Once he accepted ethical monism, Strong identified his old view of immanence as no real immanence but as a species of deism. On evolution, Strong felt that his ethical concerns provided the perfect addition to Darwin's ideas. Strong saw the immanent Christ at work, thus explaining how evolution worked. "Christ, the wisdom and the power of God, is the principle of evolution, as he is the principle of gravitation and of induction."[68] Likewise, miracles were no longer the supernatural work of God from outside of nature. Rather they were the immanent God working within natural laws.[69]

On the doctrine of sin, Strong felt the concept of imputation was very important. He believed that all humanity was united together ontologically. Prior to accepting ethical monism, Strong moved away from federalism and accepted natural headship and believed that by virtue of ontological realism and the traducian theory of the soul's procreation that sin was passed to all humanity, and Strong accepted this on exegetical grounds. Once he accepted ethical monism, he felt like he had the philosophical grounding for the ontological realism that he already held.[70] Reminiscing on this, and showing clearly his monism, Strong remarked: "My federalism was succeeded by *realistic theology. Imputation is grounded in union*, not union in imputation. Because I am one with Christ, and Christ's life has become my life, God can attribute to me whatever Christ is, and whatever Christ has done. The relation is *biological*, rather than forensic."[71]

On the doctrine of salvation, Strong struggled mightily with how Christ could adequately bear the sin of humanity in a just manner. Ethical

---

we are monists as to substance, therefore, we may still be dualists as to personality, and may be as far from pantheism as heaven is from earth" (Strong, *Christ in Creation and Ethical Monism*, 62–63). Unsurprisingly, many have questioned whether Strong's clarifications sufficiently guarded against the critiques.

68. Strong, *Christ in Creation and Ethical Monism*, 20.

69. See the discussion in Aloisi, "Augustus Hopkins Strong," 151–62.

70. Houghton, "Examination and Evaluation of A. H. Strong's Doctrine," 57; Aloisi, "Augustus Hopkins Strong," 166. Thornbury is certainly correct when he remarks, "Since Strong preferred neither the Old School nor the New School accounts of the doctrine of imputation, as a creative theologian formed one of his own, drawn from his principle of ethical monism and union with Christ" (Thornbury, "Augustus Hopkins Strong," 155).

71. Strong, *What Shall I Believe?*, 91.

monism provided Strong with a completely new view of the atonement.⁷² Strong felt that one of the greatest conundrums of theology was how God could impute the sins of the entire race of humanity to Christ if Christ was not guilty of them. With ethical monism, Strong felt he could answer this. He said that the incarnation shows that Christ was so united to humanity that he bore guilt that was not foreign but rather truly his own. This unity did not start at the incarnation (though it was clearly shown there), it started before the human race began. "But since these things are sin's penalty and Christ is the life of the sinful race, it must needs be that Christ should suffer. There is nothing arbitrary in the laying upon him of the iniquities of us all."⁷³ As with imputation of Adam's sin to all humanity and of Christ's righteousness to the believer, Strong felt the "Old School" federal theologies inadequately explained these as a "legal fiction" which seemed "to reduce divine justice to book-keeping, to ignore all truth and reality in God";⁷⁴ whereas the "New School" atomistic theologies incorrectly "regards men merely as individuals, and which ignores the organic unity of mankind on the one hand, and its connection with God on the other."⁷⁵

Strong's close connection of humanity to God through his monism led him to some unorthodox ideas, the most significant being possible inclusivism. Because of the doctrine of union with Christ that Strong saw on a cosmic scale,⁷⁶ he held a form of inclusivism wherein implicit faith based on general revelation may be sufficient.⁷⁷

---

72. James Garrett calls Strong's view of the atonement *sui generis* (Garrett, *Baptist Theology*, 301). This is in contrast to Peter Stephen Van Pelt who argues that strong was close to universalism (Van Pelt, "Examination of the Concept of the Atonement").

73. Strong, *Christ in Creation and Ethical Monism*, 172.

74. Strong, *What Shall I Believe?*, 85–86. This historical tendency is often discussed under the categories of "New School" and "Old School" understandings of imputation and the atonement. On this discussion, see Ahlstrom, "Theology in America," 41–48; Marsden, *Evangelical Mind*; Hatch, *Democratization of American Christianity*, 162–89; Noll, *America's God*, 253–329; Holifield, *Theology in America*, 127–56, 341–94.

75. Strong, *Christ in Creation and Ethical Monism*, 151.

76. For a full presentation of this idea, see Strong, *Union With Christ*. "We have seen that Christ's union with humanity, at the incarnation, involved him in all the legal liabilities of the race to which he united himself, and enabled him so to assume the penalty of its sin as to make for all men a full satisfaction of the divine justice, and to remove all external obstacles to man's return to God" (Strong, *Christ in Creation and Ethical Monism*, 52).

77. Strong, *Systematic Theology* [8th ed.], 843. "Since Christ is the Word of God and the Truth of God, he may be received even by those who have not heard of his manifestation in the flesh.... We have, therefore, the hope that even among the heathen there may be some, like Socrates, who under the guidance of the Holy Spirit working through the truth of nature and conscience, have found the way of life and salvation."

The notion of ethical monism runs deep through Strong's theology, influencing key doctrines in surprising ways, which have consistently concerned evangelical theologians. While Strong's major essays on ethical monism first appeared in 1894, Hovey published a series of essays in 1892 that dealt directly with theism (and monism).[78] Then, after Strong published his essays, Hovey wrote a brief three-part article series in December 1894 reviewing "Dr. Strong's Ethical Monism" in the widely circulated Baptist periodical, the *Watchman*.[79] A year later Hovey presented a paper on the "Relation of Monism to Theology,"[80] which did not directly speak to Strong but addressed the important issues of monism.[81]

What is also interesting is Strong's letter writing to Hovey during the last fifteen years of the century, which provide added depth to their written theological work. The first instance Strong wrote to Hovey on the issue was in 1886, at the release of the first volume of Strong's theology. Without giving particulars, Strong asked Hovey to review his positive view of the atonement. Evidently Strong had included a section that he was struggling through and wanted Hovey's opinion on if it were a permissible view.[82]

---

78. Hovey, *Studies in Ethics and Religion*. There were four essays on Theism: "Our Knowledge of Infinites" (1–22); "Relation of God to Nature: A Review" (23–56); "God and the Universe" (57–70); and "Christian Science and Mind Cure" (71–89).

79. Hovey, "Dr. Strong's Ethical Monism [December 13, 1894]," 10–11; "Dr. Strong's Ethical Monism [December 20, 1894]," 10–11; "Dr. Strong's Ethical Monism [December 27, 1894]," 11–12. In subsequent notes I will refer to each of the three articles as "Dr. Strong's Ethical Monism, Part 1," "Dr. Strong's Ethical Monism, Part 2," and "Dr. Strong's Ethical Monism, Part 3," respectively.

80. Hovey, "Relation of Monism to Theology," 10–21.

81. Augustus Hopkins Strong to Alvah Hovey, January 15, 1886 (AHP).

82. In his letter Strong referred Hovey to pages 596–98 (in a manuscript that he had sent Hovey) as the part that he had previously taught and pages 599–607 as an added part that he had never taught before, which discusses "Christ's relation to humanity." These page numbers do not correspond with the printed edition of the 1886 edition. Strong's discussion of the atonement begins on page 390 of the printed version and Strong's positive view of the atonement begins on page 409 with "The Ethical Theory of the Atonement." It is unclear if Hovey wrote back to Strong in time before his first edition was published. Strong urged Hovey to write to him within a week if at all possible because he was under pressure from the publisher to submit the final manuscript. In the end, Strong included a longer discussion on "The Atonement as related to Humanity in Christ" (Strong, *Systematic Theology* [1st ed.], 412–16). In this section, Strong argued that the organic unity of the human race meant that all are born with depravity, guilt, and penalty. Christ's unity with humanity through the virgin birth meant he did not have the depravity but had the guilt and penalty. This was not the guilt of personal sin or inherited depravity but the guilt of Adam's sin. The chief reason for taking this view was to answer how Christ could take guilt and penalty on himself without it being a legal fiction. As was mentioned above, Strong struggled with how to satisfy this tension and he ultimately found his own personal satisfaction with the implementation of

Again, the letter does not get into specifics, but it does show that Strong had a high opinion of Hovey's views and that Strong was already struggling with atonement views, and how God relates to humanity, even in the mid-1880s. In 1890, Strong wrote again to Hovey asking him to give his opinion more specifically on monism as it was presented by Professor Jacob Schurman of Cornell University.[83] Strong explained:

> I want to call your attention to a book by Prof. Schurman of Cornell, entitled "Belief in God." It is a series of lectures delivered at Andover Theological Seminary. Prof. S is nominally a Baptist, and has been spoken of prominently for important positions in Baptist Institutions. He is a bold advocate of the Lotzean monism and of almost unqualified Evolutionism, as applied to religious history. He seems to me that he brushes away every Christian doctrine—sin, Christ's deity, atonement, retribution. Now I want to ask you, whether we old fashioned theologians ought to let this part of teaching go without protest or whether we ought to fight it? I confess I am distressed by it, and am at a loss to know what my duty is. Please advise me, and oblige, Yours faithfully, A. H. Strong.[84]

In his 1870 and 1877 theology textbooks, Hovey presented a traditional theism that was careful to distinguish itself from pantheism and deism, but it was not concerned to present a sustained review of monism of any kind.[85] By the 1890s, with the changing theological landscape, and probably partially due to Strong's requests to know Hovey's views on the issue, Hovey began to publish on the issue. Hovey's 1892 work, *Studies in Ethics and Religion*, recognized that basic conceptions of theism were being questioned. Out of these essays, the second essay is important for this

---

ethical monism. Yet, in 1886, as his letter to Hovey shows, Strong was struggling with how Christ could theologically assume the penalty and guilt of sin. He refused to accept federalism (and creationism) because "Arbitrary imputation and legal fiction do not help us here. We need such an actual union of Christ with humanity, and such a derivation of the substance of his being, by natural generation from Adam, as will make him not simply the constructive heir, but the natural heir, of the guilt of the race" (Strong, *Systematic Theology* [1st ed.], 413). Strong felt his view could satisfy God's righteousness by both showing how the guilty could be pardoned and showing how the innocent (Christ) could justly take punishment (via a natural union with humanity).

83. Jacob Gould Schurman (1854–1942) taught at Acadia College, Dalhousie College, and Cornell University. He was variously president of Cornell University, US Ambassador to Greece, Minister to China, and Ambassador to Germany.

84. Augustus Hopkins Strong to Alvah Hovey, October 6, 1890 (AHP).

85. Hovey, *Manual of Systematic Theology*, 88–104.

discussion.[86] Hovey's second essay "The Relation of God to Nature: Review of Lotze and Schurman"[87] directly showed his awareness and attitude toward monism. Hovey approached the subject by considering a basic question: "Are we to think of God as the Ground or as the Creator of nature? In other words: Are we to think of nature as simply dependent on God, or as created and dependent on Him?"[88] Hovey argued that many accept the first (and takes Lotze and Schurman as prime examples) view, but he argued for the second. He presented what he considered to be the three main points of the philosophies of Lotze and Schurman, critiqued them along the way, and then provided a short summary of his own view.

The first main point that Hovey took issue with was: "They teach that God is the Ground, but not the Creator, of nature or the world."[89] They make this argument, Hovey said, because they believe that creation is unthinkable and incomprehensible. Hovey's basic argument was that they unduly limit what God is able to do.[90] Hovey said they then argue that there is no evidence that the world ever had a beginning and therefore matter must be eternal due to the law of conservation of force. Again, Hovey rejected these as cases of special pleading.

The second main point that Hovey rejected was, "They teach that all real being is spirit or mind, while matter is but modes of divine action in finite minds."[91] To Hovey, this was idealism, which means that our normal senses are completely untrustworthy thus making God a liar. Further,

---

86. The first essay, "Our Knowledge of Infinites," explored what may be known about the Divine given that we live in a post-Kantian world that tends to focus on the phenomena only. Hovey's basic argument is that "we have a partial knowledge of infinites" (Hovey, *Studies in Ethics and Religion*, 2). This knowledge is not complete, but it is still true. Hovey argues from natural revelation and philosophy that because there is a religious nature of humanity that conceives of an infinite being and desires to worship an infinite being that it is entirely reasonable to know and believe that there is a God who is infinite. The third essay, "God and the Universe," was also important. It is a re-printing of a Baccalaureate address delivered May 4, 1890 on Romans 9:36, "Of him, and through him, and unto him are all things." Simply put, Hovey argues that all things are bound to God by their origin, their control, and their destination and find their ultimate purpose. "God is the first cause of their being, God is the power by which they are preserved and controlled, and God is the chief end of their existence. In so far as they are endowed with moral power they are made 'to glorify God and enjoy Him forever'" (Hovey, *Studies in Ethics and Religion*, 57).

87. Rudolph Herman Lotze (1817–1881) was professor at Leipzig and Göttingen.

88. Hovey, *Studies in Ethics and Religion*, 23.

89. Hovey, *Studies in Ethics and Religion*, 24.

90. "We hold that no *a priori* judgment of ours can determine what effects can be produced by infinite power" (Hovey, *Studies in Ethics and Religion*, 27).

91. Hovey, *Studies in Ethics and Religion*, 31.

Hovey argued that two possible corollaries of this view are absurd: that any person can really only be sure of their existence and God's existence; or, all things including atoms and rocks have some amount of self-hood.[92]

The third main point occupied the main of Hovey's response: "They teach that God is immanent in nature, and nature in God."[93] Hovey was quick to recognize that he too accepted this notion, but not in the manner in which Lotze and Schurman did, basically because the Bible presents God as transcendent as well as immanent. Hovey offered a few quick responses and then some more substantive answers. He said that it is too rash to assert that spirit must externalize itself and it is a misunderstanding of creation to say all things are independent of each other. Hovey rejected this third assertion because it was an inadequate religious position. Hovey charged that monism has no adequate explanation for sin and evil other than it is part of the divine life or it is a mere illusion. In sum, "The fact of his immanence in nature when divorced from the fact of his creatorship leads to far more serious difficulties than it removes."[94] And, while there are some Scriptures that, when taken in isolation, seem to favor the views of Lotze and Schurman, they in fact ignore much of the biblical witness.[95]

In contrast to these views, Hovey argued that the Bible and the majority of Christian tradition has held that:

> [N]ature or the world was created, that is brought into being, by the will of God. It is eternal neither in substance nor in form. It is an effect of which God is the cause, rather than a body of which God is the soul. Moreover, every part of it is dependent on the will of God for its continuance in being, and the same is true of the sum-total of its forces whether organic or inorganic. Still further: As nature is a cosmos, every part is related to every other part, and in a qualified sense dependent on it. . . . To affirm their dependence as a while upon God is consistent with the hypothesis that they are linked together by invisible ties in a single system, the parts of which are truly interdependent. God works through second causes or means, and some of these

---

92. Hovey, *Studies in Ethics and Religion*, 31–37. "Let not the miner who bored deep into the solid rock, that he may rend and convulse it by the force of dynamite, shrink from his task through fear of lacerating one living being by the death-struggles of another. The dynamite and rock are insensible to pain" (Hovey, *Studies in Ethics and Religion*, 37).

93. Hovey, *Studies in Ethics and Religion*, 37.

94. Hovey, *Studies in Ethics and Religion*, 50.

95. "But the Scriptures also teach the existence of a world of things, animate and inanimate, in distinction from God" (Hovey, *Studies in Ethics and Religion*, 51).

second causes may do his will without choice or consciousness, while others do it voluntarily.⁹⁶

Hovey rejected pantheism or materialism since it rejected origins and he rejects deism since it rejected God's constant relation to the world.

After these essays were published, a noticeably struggling Strong wrote to Hovey to thank him for the work, but also to admit his own deep struggles with the monism that Hovey had clearly rejected. The body of the letter reads:

> Dear Dr. Hovey, I thank you heartily for the copy of your new book of "Studies in Ethics and Religion." I congratulate you on its handsome appearance. I am under special obligations for the second essay, which I have read with unusual interest. The subject of the relation of God to nature has been and upon which I have had very anxious thought. Your treatment of it is very helpful and suggestive. I am trying to work my way through it and still come out an orthodox believer, but I see much to attract in the doctrine of Lotze and Schurman. It seems to me more and more that this doctrine, in its philosophical and theological aspects, is the great speculative question with which we shall have to deal with for the next twenty years. I find all the recent philosophers ranged on one side. Prof. James of Harvard, Prof. Bowen of Boston, Prof. Ladd of Yale, all stand with Prof. Schurman of Cornell, and it will be a great wonder if Prof. Schurman does not appear at the head of the philosophical department at Chicago. I find Dr. Lyman Abbott declaring the "divinity of man," and Dr. C. H. Parkhurst comparing the relation between man and God to the relation between the waves and the ocean. If we wish to be popular, I am afraid we shall have to be Monists. Ah, if it were not for sin, and for the Holy Spirit who convinces us of sin, I almost think we might be! I wish I could talk this matter over with you. With revered thanks, I am, ever faithfully yours. A. H. Strong.⁹⁷

Strong had clearly struggled with monistic views for a few years by this time and was thankful for Hovey's presentation on how they relate to traditional Baptist views. Schurman also wrote to Hovey thanking him for the copy of the book and for his fair representation of his views.⁹⁸ Despite Strong's thanks for Hovey's works, it was only two short years before Strong made

---

96. Hovey, *Studies in Ethics and Religion*, 52.
97. Augustus Hopkins Strong to Alvah Hovey, February 7, 1892 (AHP).
98. Jacob Gould Schurman to Alvah Hovey, March 10, 1892 (AHP).

public his views concerning ethical monism. Thus, despite the overtures of Hovey, Strong was ultimately not convinced of the dangers of monism that Hovey highlighted.

In the wake of Strong's articles on ethical monism, Hovey penned three brief articles providing four difficulties with Strong's monism. Hovey's first difficulty "is with the notion of God, implied in this philosophy. It is wanting in unity, simplicity, consistency. It is the notion of being infinitely complex, and internally discordant."[99] The way in which God has been identified with nature in ethical monism has rendered God infinitely complex and discordant rather than simple and unified, as classical theism suggests. Further, Hovey worried that the non-philosopher would use this monism as an excuse for idolatry.

The second difficulty was closely related to the first in that "it does not make Jesus Christ 'the complete and perfect expression of God.' It is rather the eternal Word, the immediate source of all things, the Maker, Upholder and Saviour of mankind, who is regarded by Dr. Strong as the complete expression of God."[100] Again, if monism sees all things as part of God, then the "complete" and "perfect" expression of God must encompass all things. Thus, this biblical expression should point to the eternal Word and not the incarnate Word, a notion that Hovey found to be wanting in biblical support.

The third difficulty "arises from his definition of 'finite spirits' as 'circumscriptions of the divine substance,' and as 'having in them the divine life.'"[101] If all finite things are part of the divine substance and they are able to act freely then it also means they act wickedly. The problem being that this "brings strife and sin into the life of God."[102] On the whole, Hovey found monism to be less than helpful and highly confusing. More to the point, he argued that it takes human responsibility for sin away and gives it to God since God is the only real being, regardless of the caveats and pleas to the contrary that Strong makes.[103]

---

99. Hovey, "Dr. Strong's Ethical Monism, Part 1," 10.

100. Hovey, "Dr. Strong's Ethical Monism, Part 1," 10. To illustrate why Hovey would say this, consider these remarks of Strong: "This living God whom we see in nature is none other than Christ. Nature is *not* his body, in the sense that he is *confined* to nature. Nature *is* his body, in the sense that in nature we see him who is *above* nature, and in whom, at the same time, all things consist" (Strong, *Christ in Creation and Ethical Monism*, 14). Strong clearly insisted that this charge did not stick (Strong, *Christ in Creation and Ethical Monism*, 45), but Hovey was not convinced.

101. Hovey, "Dr. Strong's Ethical Monism, Part 2," 10.

102. Hovey, "Dr. Strong's Ethical Monism, Part 2," 10.

103. "Yet the tendency of a philosophy may be stronger that the caveats and qualifications with which that tendency is impeded. And we cannot easily suppress a fear that the logical tendency of monism is to deny human responsibility by referring it to God,

Fourth, Hovey did not think that ethical monism stacked up biblically in Strong's main appeals to scripture (John 1:3–4; 15:5–6; Col 1:17). Hovey argued that ethical monism required Strong to perform exegetical gymnastics to find a defense, which are ultimately unconvincing. "It is enough to say that no single passage of the Bible appears to us really favorable to monism, while there are hundreds that discountenance it. We read, and feel that to the sacred writers the difference between God and nature is the difference between the Infinite and the finite, the Original and the originated, the Creator and the creature."[104]

Essentially, Hovey was unconvinced that the best of science and philosophy demanded a monistic unity of all things and he did not think that the Bible and theology comport well with ethical monism. "We do not criticise [sic] his purpose, though we are unable to share his expectation of success. For metaphysical speculation has done very little in the past for the cause of true religion. Men have not found in it a resting place for the soles of their feet, but have been compelled to seek for religious satisfaction in the knowledge of Christ as revealed in the Gospels."[105] Hovey questioned whether Strong had asserted the monistic idea of the oneness of reality without slipping into pantheism.

In 1895, Hovey was invited to present a paper at the Baptist Congress on the topic of the "Relation of Monism to Theology."[106] Interestingly, the president of the Baptist Congress for the year, Walter Rauschenbusch, wrote to Hovey about his topic. Hovey had evidently agreed that the matter was up in the air and wondered what Strong's views were now that he had received significant pushback. Rauschenbusch wrote back to Hovey: "I can well understand your feelings in regard to the discussion of Monism, but you are doubtless right in saying that the matter is in the air now and will have to be worked over until the air is clear of it again. Dr. Strong, by the way, has not spiked his guns, but is only waiting for a good opportunity to open fire again."[107]

In his paper, Hovey did not address Strong by name nor did he directly address ethical monism. Instead, Hovey discussed three major kinds of monism and how they are appealing to theologians. The three kinds are materialistic, idealistic, and absolute. Hovey rejected the materialistic because it repudiated the idea of a personal God, which was biblically and religiously

---

the only real being" (Hovey, "Dr. Strong's Ethical Monism, Part 2," 10).

104. Hovey, "Dr. Strong's Ethical Monism, Part 3," 12.
105. Hovey, "Dr. Strong's Ethical Monism, Part 1," 10.
106. Hovey, "Relation of Monism to Theology."
107. Walter Rauschenbusch to Alvah Hovey, June 1, 1895 (AHP).

incomprehensible.¹⁰⁸ He rejected the idealistic because it allows God to be domesticated by nature, which Hovey said, "seems to me far inferior to that which has been commonly held among Christians."¹⁰⁹ He rejected the absolute because it was philosophically untenable and unsatisfying.¹¹⁰

The paper ended by Hovey giving four potential positives of monism to theology, along with responses to each. The first potential positive was that "it brings the causal agency of God into line with that of man, and thus renders it more credible, if not more comprehensible."¹¹¹ The problem still present was that despite its supposed ability to provide a comprehensive system it would lose its ability to worship God as someone divine. "It would tend to restfulness and self-satisfaction rather than to worship and aspiration."¹¹² Second, monism "satisfies the logical craving for unity which dominates certain minds."¹¹³ But the problem was that there are other desires of the human mind and we lose the differentness and majesty of God. Third, monism supposedly brings God and humanity nearer to one another. While Hovey agreed this may be theoretically so, there is too much lost when the difference between God and humanity is merely one of degree.¹¹⁴ Finally, monism supposedly helps explain better the incarnation and death of Christ. Hovey completely rejected this conclusion. He believed that monism introduced too many new problems into the incarnation rather than clarifying. And, he felt that monism created a major problem in the death of Christ because somehow God becomes responsible for sin if all of humanity (the Logos included) is essentially one being, thus lessening humanity's fault in sin.¹¹⁵ In sum, this article did not say much that was new, but it did seek to show through philosophical and theological arguments, rather than through biblical, that monism was unsatisfying.

As Aloisi has said, Strong never responded to Hovey in print, but he did deliver an interesting address at Hovey's fiftieth anniversary of teaching at Newton in 1899.¹¹⁶ Strong's address was published as "Fifty Years of Theology" in his 1899 book, *Christ in Creation and Ethical Monism*.¹¹⁷ Strong

---

108. Hovey, "Relation of Monism to Theology," 12–13.
109. Hovey, "Relation of Monism to Theology," 16.
110. Hovey, "Relation of Monism to Theology," 17–18.
111. Hovey, "Relation of Monism to Theology," 18.
112. Hovey, "Relation of Monism to Theology," 18.
113. Hovey, "Relation of Monism to Theology," 19.
114. Hovey, "Relation of Monism to Theology," 19–20.
115. Hovey, "Relation of Monism to Theology," 20–21.
116. Aloisi, "Augustus Hopkins Strong," 123–24.
117. Strong, *Christ in Creation and Ethical Monism*, 181–208.

clearly felt his view had won the day and he asserted his pleasure that more recent theology had begun to implement the truth of God's immanence in the world. There is no doubt that it was an odd occasion for Strong to assert such a conclusion. Though Hovey still did not seem too taken by Strong's assertion. Evidently, sometime after the memorial, Hovey wrote to Strong once again expressing his objections to monism, to which Strong replied:

> I think that your objections to my doctrine would in part disappear, if you took my idealistic point of view. My conception of immanence is derived from my relation to my own thought and volitions. I am not my thoughts and volitions, nor am I measured by them. I am immanent in them, yet transcendent, as not exhausted by them but as having in myself the spring and source of every future thought and volitions.
>
> You may recall that I said God's relation to nature was that of simple immanence. Nature is the thought of God made objective by his will. But man is more. In him the objective becomes relatively independent, so that which he lived moved and has his being is God, he still is capable of resisting God and of resisting him forever. In other words, man is free, responsible, capable of sin, capable of morally separating himself from his Creator, while yet he is dependent upon his Creator for every breath.
>
> I expect you to say that this is but a formulation of contradictions. Perhaps so—but I think not. It is true, I do not see fully the nexus between the two sets of truths. But I believe both are given us in reason and in Scripture.
>
> Some day, not so far off, we shall enter the ABC class of the heavenly Seminary. I anticipate the course with great joy, and I expect to have you for—not a classmate, for you will be too high up for that—but a fellow student. Meantime I congratulate you again on the things you have already attained and so nobly taught.[118]

Evidently, Hovey and Strong continued to disagree in private discussions, though it appears that both had earned the respect and admiration of the other. After Strong's collected essays on *Christ in Creation and Ethical Monism* appeared in 1899, Hovey wrote to congratulate Strong, and Strong wrote back in gratitude. Strong remarked that "Your kind letter about my book is very gratifying to me. I hardly dared to hope that you could find so much to agree with. . . . I owe a great deal to your counsel and example, and I join with all our people in wishing you continued life and blessing."[119]

---

118. Augustus Hopkins Strong to Alvah Hovey, June 14, 1899 (AHP).
119. Augustus Hopkins Strong to Alvah Hovey, January 11, 1900 (AHP).

PRACTICAL QUESTIONS OF AUTHORITY 197

Again, both men had come to understand the position of the other, disagreed strongly with one another, but remained cordial and appreciative friends.

Hovey's final discussion of monism was in the 1900 edition of his theology. Hovey simply repeated his earlier detailed critiques: he rejected that human reason wants all things resolved into one, he rejected that creation is needless or incomprehensible, rejected that all reciprocal action between beings or things is always intelligible, he rejected that biological science favors this view, he rejected that Scripture favors this view, he argued that spirit is not convertible into physical energy, he argued that monism is incompatible with human causality or freedom, and, he argued that monism refutes itself by rejecting the testimony of consciousness.[120]

One final interesting point about the 1900 edition is that Strong, as was by now the custom between the two authors, wrote a letter to Hovey after its publication to give praise and to say a few words about its content. Strong commented not on Hovey's critique of his monism, but on his view of the imputation of sin: "As to imputation of sin, it has always seemed to me that Paul intended to teach Augustinianism, and that has made me an Augustinian. If I cannot trust all Paul's methods of reasoning, can I trust him in Romans 5:12–19? Your resting the responsibility for inborn depravity on our sympathy with Adam's Sin seems to me a decided verging toward the New School view. But when I read of your imputing to Christ the sins of men because of Christ's natural union with the race I go with you wholly."[121] Though it is beyond the scope of this book to fully explore, Hovey did have hesitations about accepting ontological realism and certainly appears to hold to what Strong accused him,[122] and as we have seen, Strong felt his monism was a helpful corrective to Hovey's philosophical views.

---

120. Hovey, *Manual of Christian Theology*, 20–28.

121. Augustus Hopkins Strong to Alvah Hovey, October 15, 1900 (AHP). Interestingly, Strong also said to Hovey: "I wish you could have given more space to the review of the higher criticism. I think we must grant that some of Paul's reasoning was invalid and some of his interpretations of the Old Testament precarious, as in the case of Hagar and Sinai. But I still hold that in all the main truths that he meant to teach we can safely take his view as divinely inspired. And yet I find it hard to draw the line between the incidental and the essential, without implying that the seat of authority after all is in the Christian consciousness rather than in the Eternal Word."

122. Note the interesting comment in Hovey's second article critiquing Strong, wherein Hovey notes that, within the realm of reason, ontological realism is a chimera: "Our conception of the personality of the human race, in distinction from the personality of every individual composing it, is too shadowy to serve any purpose in reasoning. When we try to grasp it mentally, we find nothing real in our possession" (Hovey, "Dr. Strong's Ethical Monism, Part 2," 11). Though it should be mentioned that in his published theologies, Hovey admits that, within the realm of biblical statements, there is a difference between inherited guilt and inherited sinfulness (Hovey, *Manual of*

These two heavyweights of nineteenth-century Baptist theology did not shy away from discussing the major issues of the day. Both dedicated considerable efforts to discussing theism, monism, and related doctrines. A few points are worth pointing out in conclusion. The modern emphasis on the immanence of God was too overwhelming for Strong to ignore and he felt that traditional Christian theology could be adequately modified to appease the modern mind and also retain a proper amount of the Christian tradition. Hovey did not feel the same pull from the dominant philosophy of the day. Further, Hovey felt that Strong's theism failed to fundamentally satisfy issues of traditional orthodox theology. Hovey believed that Strong's theism created serious problems that Strong's explanations simply did not satisfy.

Most importantly, Hovey felt that Strong's theism failed in its appeal to Scripture. While Hovey still considered Strong's theology to be basically orthodox, he thought that all appeals to Scripture in support of ethical monism were tenuous at best. This can be seen in the ways that Strong modified his theology after he accepted ethical monism.

Finally, Strong had a decided issue with the longstanding American understanding of imputation, especially in the light of the widespread rejection of any sort of ontological realism.[123] And, Strong felt that ethical monism provided the clear philosophical underpinning to the Augustinianism that he already held. On the other hand, Hovey rejected the ontological realism inherent in Augustinianism and seems to have assumed a decidedly "New School" view,[124] which did not believe that all humanity was guilty for Adam's sin but rather humanity inherited the sinful tendency. In sum, both Strong and Hovey felt the need to accord their understanding of imputation of sin with contemporaneous philosophical ideas. Both modified their theologies to fit their acceptance of dominant philosophies of the day rather than through classical theological and philosophical categories. In this issue, both men found philosophical views to be authoritative.

To summarize this long section, Hovey's interaction with Strong on monism highlights his commitment to the supreme authority of the Bible, and his interpretation of it. He also appealed to extra-biblical requirements, such as philosophical and theological consistency and warrant. Indeed,

---

Systematic Theology, 151; *Manual of Christian Theology*, 175). See also the discussion of Hovey's view of imputation in Garrett, *Baptist Theology*, 281–82.

123. "And yet I accept Ethical Monism because of the light which it throws upon the atonement rather than for the sake of its Christian explanation of evolution" (Strong, *Christ in Creation and Ethical Monism*, 78).

124. See Henry's discussion of this and the "Old School" view of the Princeton theologians in Henry, *Personal Idealism and Strong's Theology*, 220–25, esp. 222n155.

what cannot be lost in this debate is that Hovey's philosophical reluctance to accept ontological realism limited what he viewed to be acceptable interpretations of Scripture. There was also Hovey's appeal in a few places to the received tradition of the church (classical theism) as having authority in terms of limiting the scope of acceptable theological views and acceptable interpretations of Scripture, thereby eliminating Strong's ethical monism. Thus, while clearly asserting the superiority of the Bible, Hovey allowed extra-biblical requirements, even philosophy, to restrict what the Bible could be saying.

Conclusion: Authority in Disputes

This chapter has surveyed several places where Hovey's understanding of authority can be seen in practical matters. Where was authority sourced? Are there extra-biblical sources of authority? Where does interpretation come in? What can be appealed to as an authoritative adjudicator in interpretation? These questions all find answers in this chapter by the way in which Hovey addressed the issues.

Hovey appealed in several cases to philosophical, logical, and ethical arguments for his positions. And these arguments were often made outside of appeals to Scripture. However, the normal place where these appeared was as a refutation of another viewpoint, such as his discussions with Strong. In other words, Hovey required other viewpoints to have philosophical as well as logical consistency/coherence and ethical viability. But this does not take away from the fact that in every debate he appealed to the Bible as the supreme authority. He clearly felt that the burden in each debate was to make clear what the Bible said, which would then become the foundation for action, but it seems that Hovey let a philosophical position limit what the Bible could be saying on one issue. His understanding of biblical authority also had a regular place for extra-biblical sources to act as adjudicating authorities within biblical interpretation. He appealed to philosophical and ethical consistency/coherence, ethical viability, the normal use of words, lexicons, bible commentators, rabbinic sources, dictionaries and encyclopedias, and church history and tradition. In his debate over religion and the state he also used biblical principles to then reason theologically and morally. Clearly, Hovey held that the Bible, rightly interpreted, was the highest authority. And, he normally appealed to extra-biblical authorities outside of himself to bolster his interpretation.

7

Conclusion

"No one can be familiar with modern discussions about the possibility of knowing God or about the immanence of God—in a word, about thoroughgoing agnosticism, monism, or idealism—without seeing that these discussions reach to the very heart of religion and morality, or without desiring to contribute something, if possible, to a clear understanding of the truth by thoughtful Christians."[1]

THE RELIGIOUS CLIMATE OF nineteenth-century America could be characterized by rapid growth and the multiplication of theological viewpoints. Much of this was due to the new religious climate created by revivals, disestablishment, and the significant population growth of America. Protestants, Baptists included, grew at an astonishing rate in this time period. Baptist growth was so great that it was only outpaced by the Methodists.[2] And, like many other denominations, they experienced an explosion of theological viewpoints. With growth came the establishment of Baptist schools, associations, and other organizations. Due to their growth and their organizing, Baptists went from cultural and theological outsiders to insiders. Despite these factors, Baptist studies in the nineteenth century are underrepresented

---

1. Hovey, *Studies in Ethics and Religion*, iii.

2. By 1850 Baptists were the second most numerous of Protestant denominations in America at 750,000 adherents, a number which increased to 4.5 million by 1900. Methodists were the largest at 1.25 million in 1850 and 5.5 million in 1900 (Gaustad and Barlow, *New Historical Atlas of Religion in America*, 374).

in American religious historiography, and this is particularly true of Northern Baptists.[3] There is a gaping hole in the historiography between studies of some early nineteenth-century figures, such as Isaac Backus and Francis Wayland, and some later nineteenth-century figures, such as Augustus Strong and Walter Rauschenbusch. For one example, what about the early Northern Baptist seminaries founded in the North and the theology produced there? Very little scholarly attention has been given in this direction. This book has been an attempt to begin to fill this hole.[4]

Though there are few studies of Northern Baptists during this time period, there have been a healthy number of studies conducted into American Protestantism in the nineteenth century. These studies have looked at several different themes and issues in order to understand better the times. This work has chosen to look at the concept of authority, and more specifically, biblical and theological authority. Authority in nineteenth-century American Protestant historiography has been studied at length and that historiography has provided focus to this book. Nathan Hatch's democratization thesis, E. Brooks Holifield's assertion that the desire to be reasonable was ubiquitous, as well as the assertion that conservative theologians were "orthodox rationalists" (who heavily utilized Scottish Common Sense Realism and Baconian Methods) were the main historiographical discussions to which this work sought to relate.[5]

Two historical truths drive the study from here. First, with the growth of Baptist numbers there were a number of Baptist organizations, seminaries in particular, that were established in the early to mid-nineteenth century, which in turn produced the first of the American Baptist academic theology. Second, in the mid- to later nineteenth century Baptists faced new challenges toward authority, primarily biblical criticism and liberal theology, that put these conceptions of biblical and theological authority to a new test. This book has sought to understand better how the early Baptist seminarians, who were trained and lived in a time period which had its own

---

3. "The history of the Baptists in the eighteenth and nineteenth centuries is a subject as scandalously neglected as had been, until very recently, the history of early American Methodism" (Noll, *America's God*, 149).

4. A few other studies explore these seminarians as well. See Maring, "Baptists and Changing Views of the Bible [I]"; "Baptists and Changing Views of the Bible [II]"; Garrett Jr., "Sources of Authority in Baptist Thought"; Priestley, "From Theological Polemic to Nonpolemical Theology"; Thornbury, "Legacy of Natural Theology."

5. Hatch, *Democratization of American Christianity*; Noll, *America's God*; Holifield, *Theology in America*. For orthodox rationalism, see Smyth, "Orthodox Rationalism"; Ahlstrom, "Scottish Philosophy and American Theology"; Bozeman, *Protestants in an Age of Science*; Marsden, "Scotland and Philadelphia"; "Everyone One's Own Interpreter?"; Noll, "Irony of the Enlightenment"; *America's God*; Welch, "Nineteenth Century."

unique challenges to authority, constructed their biblical and theological authority, and in what ways this construction was able to handle the new challenges to authority that surfaced in the later century. Alvah Hovey was chosen as a prime figure to consider because his personal timeline helpfully overlapped with many of the major themes to be considered, because his position as a widely-respected theologian was and is universally recognized, and because his written corpus is extensive and lends itself to the main queries of the book.

This study began by asking several research questions. The central question was: Granted that Hovey lived in a time of significant theological upheaval wherein theological and biblical authority were changing and contested concepts, in what ways did he, an early Baptist seminary theologian, understand, construct, and utilize theological and biblical authority? Subsidiary questions included: Did democratization and/or reasonableness drive Baptist thinking during the early nineteenth century and in what ways? In what ways did Hovey understand his place of authority especially as a pioneering seminary theologian in his tradition? What sources did Hovey find authoritative? What was the theological method of Hovey, particularly related to epistemology and confessionalism? What did Hovey understand the authority of the Bible to be? In what ways did Hovey address biblical criticism, especially as it pertains to biblical authority? How did Hovey's understanding of authority work out in practice?

Hovey's personal narrative and historical context, published writings, papers and letters, and some of the theological controversies that he entered provided the materials and situations that the book explored. The second chapter looked at Hovey's theological context. He was reared in a Christian home that stressed the need for conversion, a strong work ethic, and a solid education. At Dartmouth, Hovey received a good liberal arts education as well as some theological education. Hovey's theological preparation at Dartmouth may have included training in the New England Theology as well as a self-aware theological method that gave a high place to preconceived theological systems. At Newton, he was immersed in an atmosphere of high academic standards, free inquiry, no confessional standard, biblicist theological reasoning,[6] an emphasis on education, as well as Baptist theology. The close geographical proximity of Andover, and the fact that some of his Newton professors attended Andover, influenced Hovey. This was primarily through Moses Stuart's process of biblical interpretation and through Edwards Park's

---

6. Again, I have used the phrase "biblicist theological reasoning" to refer to the tendency to (1) utilize a scientific approach to Scripture, to (2) resist allowing any theological system or statement to influence biblical interpretation, to (3) utilize any source of truth, and to (4) build a positive theology from this basis.

vital connection of learning and faith as well as the more explicit exposure to the New England Theology. Hovey's trip to Europe and his continuing efforts at self-education reinforced the requirement for deep scholarship and also the importance of faith for the theologian. Throughout the rest of Hovey's life, he remained well read and highly involved in Baptist life.

With an understanding of the theological context, theological training, and major personal influences on Hovey, the remaining chapters addressed specific topics that reveal Hovey's own attitudes and positions on biblical and theological authority. Chapter 3 explored Hovey's understanding of theological education within a Baptist context. The purpose of the chapter was to understand how Hovey understood theological education to affect the authority of the student. Baptists had long debated the need and methods of theological education prior to Hovey's time. When you consider his own education and his vocation, it is no surprise that Hovey argued that ministerial candidates needed extensive theological training. He felt that the needs of the pastorate were many but one of the main needs was the ability to speak with wisdom above that of their people. Training at a theological school was a prime place where the student could gain solid theological, exegetical, and practical training. The question is if more theological training gave more authority. The trained pastor had more ability and was more useful because they could persuade more effectively. This does provide more authority in argumentation. Yet it was also shown that Hovey believed that along with an increase in learning and ability there needed to be an increase in piety and humility. Thus, whatever added authority that could come through additional education was not based on gaining a diploma but on the maturation of the whole person. Still, there was an added authority that came through theological education, primarily in terms of how persuasive one's biblical interpretation or theological positions were.

The most explicit place that Hovey dealt with the issues of biblical and theological authority was in his theological method, which was explored in chapter 4. Hovey affirmed the knowability of God, the trustworthiness of human reasoning, and the necessity of scientifically systematizing theology. That being said Hovey still believed that each of these had their limitations. The Bible was the supreme authority and source of truth based on its inspiration, so long as it was correctly interpreted. As a Baptist, he felt that each person was responsible before God and had the ability to make spiritual decisions for themselves. Still, to rightly interpret the Bible and build theology meant that one should consider the church's tradition. Hovey went further and asserted that because Baptists insisted on individual soul liberty, and needed to guard against undue individualism, they needed rigorous theological discussion and interaction with the tradition. Hovey's theology also discussed how pre- and post-Fall human reasoning differed, and how the regenerated and illuminated Christian could have some restoration. This theological reasoning, along with Hovey's strong distinction between Creator and creature, helps to understand the many places he inserted limitations on the theological enterprise. Doing theology was an important exercise, but it served the greater purpose of seeking the face of God. It was a scientific and spiritual exercise whose supreme authority was Scripture. As was stated before, intellectual abilities (such as reason, study skills, and interaction with the tradition) along with spiritual and theological recognitions (such as the Creator/creature distinction, regeneration, sanctification, and general human limitations) were likewise necessary conditions which when balanced properly lent authority to the theologian.

Hovey's theological method was the clearest explanation of how he understood biblical and theological authority. But how he interacted with biblical criticism and how this influenced his views is also important. Hovey engaged with biblical criticism both theoretically and practically. As a theologian he interacted with a variety of viewpoints that challenged the veracity of miracles, the consistency of Scripture, the inspiration of Scripture, the inerrancy of Scripture, the authorship of Scripture, and the received conservative theology. As an editor and president of a seminary he was required to confront critical views of the Bible as well as the theology that came with them. As his career progressed Hovey's writings demonstrate careful and sustained engagement with critical views. Still he was not convinced by their claims and as a result his views of biblical authority remained largely the same across his career. This is despite the claim from some that Hovey's views changed as his career progressed.[7] On the whole, it is quite clear that Hovey held to a consistently conservative view of biblical inspiration and authority, even if he also remained somewhat open and welcoming to new formulations. And it is correct to say that throughout his life Hovey himself saw the Bible as the dynamically inspired and inerrant Word of God that had supreme authority, when properly interpreted, in faith and practice.

Chapter 6 chose five test cases where Hovey weighed in on matters of controversy. These each provided glimpses into how he practically applied and understood biblical and theological authority. Hovey expected his and opposing viewpoints to have philosophical as well as logical consistency. These requirements were not at the expense of biblical authority, however. Within every debate he appealed to the supreme authority of Scripture. When there was significant debate surrounding biblical interpretation, he

---

7. Maring, "Baptists and Changing Views of the Bible [I]," 58; "Baptists and Changing Views of the Bible [II]," 38; Brackney, *Genetic History of Baptist Thought*, 285–88; *Congregation and Campus*, 261, 293.

regularly appealed to extra-biblical sources to adjudicate the correct meaning. Chapter 6 concluded that Hovey appealed to philosophical and ethical consistency/coherence, ethical viability, the normal use of words, lexicons, bible commentators, rabbinic sources, dictionaries and encyclopedias, and church history and tradition. In his debate over religion and the state he also used biblical principles to reason theologically and morally. Clearly, Hovey held that the Bible, rightly interpreted, was the highest authority. And, he normally appealed to extra-biblical authorities outside of himself to bolster his interpretation.

To state the overall argument, this book has argued that Hovey engaged critical views of the Bible yet clearly accepted the authority of the Bible based on its supernatural character as the dynamically inspired and inerrant Word of God. Hovey held to the reasonableness of Christianity and the scientific interpretation of the Bible. Human reasoning, however, had its limitations based on the problems of finitude and sinfulness. The Bible, rightly interpreted, was the supreme authority in all theological endeavors. Wherever theological issues were raised, and the Bible's authority was appealed to, Hovey resisted letting theological systems determine biblical interpretation. Yet, to adjudicate interpretive disagreements Hovey appealed to authoritative voices outside of the individual biblical interpreter, such as professional exegetes, professional theologians, and the orthodox tradition of the church in general. In sum, Hovey was in some ways a product of the nineteenth century's tendency toward democratization and reasonableness, particularly in his theological heritage, his exegesis, his theological method, and his baptistic views of confessions and individual soul liberty. Yet Hovey was not simply an "orthodox rationalist" or "democratized" for at least four reasons: (1) he advocated heavily for theological and exegetical education that would be the backbone of biblical and theological work, an education which was not only technical but also spiritual and which modified to what extent and how well anyone could simply read the Bible; (2) as a Baptist he had theological as opposed to merely philosophical/rational reasons for trusting human intellect and allowing individual decision making, yet he was quick to guard against individualism; (3) he regularly looked to authorities outside of the individual's reasoning ability, specifically in his appeals to exegetes and theologians and to the orthodox tradition of the church in general; and (4), most importantly, Hovey limited human rational ability, as evidenced in his epistemology, his understanding of the Creator/creature distinction, and his consistent requirement that the exegete and theologian understand and evidence the spiritual requirements of those disciplines.

The second chapter showed that Hovey's theological inheritance was somewhat democratized in that his teachers did not want confessions or the tradition to dictate what Bible interpretation was to find. This evidences Nathan Hatch's claim that one of the prongs of democratization was to give a lesser place to established orthodoxy. Yet it is also true that by the time that Hovey was writing and teaching, he regularly appealed to the orthodox tradition and felt some responsibility to it, though not in a confessional sense. His theological method also showed the effects of democratization in that it also explicitly did not want confessions or the tradition to dictate what theology should be. However, the extent of democratization was held in check in Hovey's method because he insisted upon proper training and skill in both biblical interpretation and theologizing. Further, while he did not want tradition to dictate interpretation or theology, he was not traditionless. An individual's personal understanding had limitations to it and necessary training and secondary authorities were required. As a Baptist who accepted individual soul liberty and limited the place of confessions, he felt that Baptists were under greater obligation to interact with each other and the tradition in general. This, then, does not agree with Hatch's description of democratization that rejects any distinction between clergy and laity, that takes spiritual impulses at face value without scrutinizing them according to established orthodoxy, or that allows religious outsiders to feel as if they had no limitations. Democratization is a helpful description of much of Hovey's Northern Baptist inheritance, but does not go far in describing his own method. It needs to be remembered that Hatch argued that his democratization thesis is meant to be applied to the early nineteenth century. He recognized that as the century progressed, democratization waned as the previously marginalized gained increased status within American religion.[8] But Hatch also argued that concentrated authority and professional expertise had been subverted, which does not seem to fit Hovey. Thus, by Hovey's time much of Baptist theology had organized and systematized enough that they had moved away some of the characteristics of democratization.

Hovey is a prime example of the impulse to insist upon the reasonableness of theology in nineteenth-century evangelicalism and the Baptists' tendency to put Scripture at the center of their method.[9] But it also seems quite clear that this reasonableness fell well short of rationalism or empiricism despite the insistence on divine inspiration, the inerrancy of scripture, the scientific nature of theology, and the trustworthiness of the normal action of the human mind. Thus, the denotation of Hovey as an "orthodox rationalist"

---

8. See Hatch, *Democratization of American Christianity*, 6. Though his last chapter also argued that there is a recurring populist impulse in American Christianity.

9. This agrees with Holifield's thesis that many early American theologians "shared a preoccupation with the reasonableness of Christianity that predisposed them toward such an understanding of theology" (Holifield, *Theology in America*, 4).

does not fit. This counters those studies that assume nineteenth-century conservative theology was necessarily overly influenced by certain modern epistemologies. A new historiography that allows the presence of some aspects of modern (or Enlightenment) epistemologies without concluding that they are the controlling aspect of their epistemology (and their theology as a whole) is needed.[10] One could hold to a scientific and reasonable approach to theology, the trustworthiness of human thinking, the theological position that religious knowledge has been divinely revealed through inspiration, the idea that inspiration also entails inerrancy, and simultaneously avoid being a rationalist or empiricist.[11] Hovey was a child of his time, and very much desired to be reasonable, but he was not an orthodox rationalist. The substance, historical awareness, and self-imposed limitations of his theology were more complex. The orthodox rationalist idea misses much by way of epistemology and also the greater theological superstructure.

Alvah Hovey desired to produce a theology that was based on the supreme authority of God's revelation in Scripture, that was based on thorough training, that would appeal to human reasoning yet was restrained in its claims for human reasoning and was restrained in its conclusions, that interacted with the best scholarship of the day and of the church's history, and that served the ultimate purpose of seeking the face of God. This is what he understood as thoughtful Christianity.

A further point should be made about Hovey's significance. Much has already been said about how he does not fit the normal historiographical description in regard to authority. His understanding of biblical and theological authority was simply more complex and robust than is normally thought of for a nineteenth-century conservative. It is also true that this is the first lengthy study of Hovey completed since his son's biography in 1928. The significance of this study, I believe, is magnified by Hovey's personal significance.

More than just plugging a historiographical hole is the fact that Hovey is highly representative of Baptist thought in the nineteenth century. Other Baptists such as William Newton Clarke, Augustus Hopkins Strong, Walter Rauschenbusch, and Harry Emerson Fosdick are the typical representatives within late nineteenth- and early twentieth-century Northern Baptist histories. The argument can be made that Hovey's theology was more representative of Northern Baptist thought than these other men for the simple reason

10. This agrees with Helm, "Thomas Reid," 15–18.

11. This runs counter to Wacker's discussion of Baptist "orthodox rationalism." See Garrett Jr., *Baptist Theology*, 279, 294. Wacker's book has been republished (2018) by Baylor University Press with an updated preface, but the text of the book remains exactly the same.

that Hovey was a prototypical conservative. Conservative theology was the dominant theology, especially in the nineteenth century. Fosdick, Clarke, and Rauschenbusch were a part of the liberal New Theology. Strong is normally seen as occupying a mediating position as opposed to a conservative or liberal. Which, as this and other works have shown, was due to Strong's acceptance of ethical monism.[12] This may help to explain the gap in the historiography. The nineteenth century is perhaps the least studied century within American religious studies. Baptists are understudied compared to other denominations. The North is less studied than the South. And, within this narrow field of nineteenth-century Northern Baptist studies, conservatives are generally overlooked in favor of mediating (Strong) and liberal (Clarke, Rauschenbusch, Fosdick) theologians.

Not only was Hovey conservative, he was prominent within Northern Baptist life. He taught at the premiere Northern Baptist seminary for half a century and saw over a thousand future pastors, professors, and leaders come through its halls. He was the president of the seminary for three decades. He was a prolific contributor to Baptist theology through his published theology texts, his topical publications, his journal essays, and his book reviews. He was also the editor of the major Baptist commentary set of his time, a fact which pleased other Baptist conservatives, including Henry Weston and John Broadus. One reason that Hovey did as much and wrote as much as he did is because he was often asked to do so. He was recognized for his scholarship and his conservative theology and thus he was highly trusted by many.

Nineteenth-century Conservative Northern Baptist theology had erudition, they had ability, they were well-read in both contemporary (synchronic) theology and the history of the church (diachronic), they evidenced theological nuance, and they showed humility. The paradigm that sees conservative theology as rational, ahistorical, and lacking nuance needs to be put to rest. A careful survey of Hovey's theological corpus reveals as much. Just as significantly, as a conservative in a time when conservatism led the day, Hovey is perhaps the best representative of the representative theology of late nineteenth-century Northern Baptists. As such, he should draw

12. William Brackney comments, "In general, Alvah Hovey lived in the theological consciousness of the nineteenth century, even more than his contemporary, Augustus Strong" (Brackney, *Genetic History of Baptist Thought*, 287). Brackney says elsewhere that, "Through the administrations of Alvah Hovey and Nathan Wood, and with the ardent support of Boston pastors like A. J. Gordon, Newton remained in the conservative stream through the 1890s" (Brackney, *Congregation and Campus*, 261). Likewise, James Garrett notes that Hovey was "foremost" among the conservatives in his time period, and he puts Strong among the mediating theologians (Garrett, *Baptist Theology*, 279, 294).

the attention of historians looking to understand what the typical Northern Baptist theology of the time period looked like. Such attention is sorely needed precisely because the reigning historical paradigm is inadequate.

This attention would also be welcome because there are many areas of potential further study, to which this book has only been able to hint. Additional studies into the primary sources of Hovey and his fellow conservatives can only add more understanding to this woefully understudied era.

Bibliography

Various Works of Alvah Hovey

Hovey, Alvah. Alvah Hovey Papers (AHP). Yale Divinity School Library, New Haven, CT.

———. "The Ark of the Covenant." *Christian Review* 17 (1852) 572–93.

———. *Barnas Sears, a Christian Educator: His Making and Work.* New York: Silver, Burdett, 1902.

———. *The Bible.* Philadelphia: Griffith and Rowland, n.d.

———. "The Bible the Only Standard of Christian Doctrine and Duty." In *The Madison Avenue Lectures*, 7–34. Philadelphia: American Baptist Publication Society, 1867.

———. "Bible Wine: The Meaning of Yayin and Oinos in Scripture." *Baptist Quarterly Review* 9 (1887) 151–80.

———. *Bible Wine: The Non-Intoxicating Wine Theory Examined: Meaning of Oinos and Yayin in the Scriptures.* Cincinnati: Baptist Quarterly Review, 1888.

———. *Biblical Eschatology.* Philadelphia: American Baptist Publication Society, 1888.

———. "Book Review: Essai d'une Introduction à la Dogmatique Protestante. Par P. Lobstein." *The American Journal of Theology* 2 (1898) 442–45.

———. "Book Review: La Création et la Providence devant la Science Moderne. Par Eugène Maillet." *The American Journal of Theology* 3 (1899) 138–41.

———. "Book Review: Life and Letters of John Albert Broadus." *The American Journal of Theology* 1 (1897) 228–37.

———. "Book Review: A New Natural Theology Based upon the Doctrine of Evolution." *The American Journal of Theology* 5 (1901) 598–99.

———. "Book Review: An Outline of Christian Theology." *The American Journal of Theology* 3 (1899) 203–6.

———. "Books of the New Testament in Light of Modern Research." In *Thirteenth Annual Session of the Baptist Congress for the Discussion of Current Questions, Held in the Central Baptist Church, Providence, RI, November 12, 13, and 14, 1895*, 102–3. New York: Baptist Congress, 1896.

———. "Character Tested by Religious Inquiry." In *Studies in Ethics and Religion: Or, Discourses, Essays, and Reviews Pertaining to Theism, Inspiration, Christian Ethics, and Education for the Ministry*, 497–512. Boston: Silver, Burdett, 1892.

———. "Christian Missions and Education." *Baptist Missionary Magazine* 55 (1875) 395–99.

———. *The Christian Pastor His Work and the Needful Preparation: A Discourse in Favor of Theological Education*. Boston: Gould and Lincoln, 1857.

———. "Christian Science and Mind Cure." In *Studies in Ethics and Religion: Or, Discourses, Essays, and Reviews Pertaining to Theism, Inspiration, Christian Ethics, and Education for the Ministry*, 71–89. Boston: Silver, Burdett, 1892.

———. *Christian Teaching and Life*. Philadelphia: American Baptist Publication Society, 1895.

———. "Church Polity." *The Baptist Quarterly* 4 (1870) 225–33.

———. *Close Communion*. Philadelphia: American Baptist, 1860.

———. *Commentary on the Epistle to the Galatians*. American Commentary on the New Testament. Philadelphia: American Baptist Publication Society, 1890.

———. *Commentary on the Gospel of John*. American Commentary on the New Testament. Philadelphia: American Baptist, 1885.

———. "Divorce According to the New Testament." In *Studies in Ethics and Religion: Or, Discourses, Essays, and Reviews Pertaining to Theism, Inspiration, Christian Ethics, and Education for the Ministry*, 321–43. Boston: Silver, Burdett, 1892.

———. "Doctrinal Theology for Christian Pastors." *The Christian Review* 28 (1863) 646–69.

———. "Doctrine of the Higher Christian Life Examined." In *Studies in Ethics and Religion: Or, Discourses, Essays, and Reviews Pertaining to Theism, Inspiration, Christian Ethics, and Education for the Ministry*, 344–428. Boston: Silver, Burdett, 1892.

———. *The Doctrine of the Higher Christian Life Compared with the Teaching of the Holy Scriptures*. Boston: Henry A. Young, 1876.

———. *Doctrines of the Bible*. Philadelphia: American Baptist Publication Society, 1892.

———. "Dr. Hackett at Newton." In *Memorials of Horatio Balch Hackett*, edited by George H. Whittemore, 227–38. Rochester: E. R. Andrews, 1876.

———. "Dr. Strong's Ethical Monism." *Watchman*, December 13, 1894. 10–11.

———. "Dr. Strong's Ethical Monism." *Watchman*, December 20, 1894. 10–11.

———. "Dr. Strong's Ethical Monism." *Watchman*, December 27, 1894. 11–12.

———. "The Duty of Christian Women in Public Meetings." *Christian Era* 27 (1873) 1.

———. *Election*. Philadelphia: American Baptist Publication Society, n.d.

———. *Evils of Infant Baptism*. Philadelphia: American Baptist Publication Society, 1880.

———. "Fellowships." In *Proceedings of the National Baptist Educational Convention: Held in the Pierrepont Street Baptist Church, Brooklyn, April 19–21, 1870*, edited by Sewall S. Cutting and Lucius E. Smith, 56–65. Brooklyn, NY: Brooklyn Baptist Social Union, 1870.

———. *Future Punishment*. Philadelphia: American Baptist Publication Society, n.d.

———. "General Introduction to the New Testament." In *Commentary on the Gospel of Matthew*, by John A. Broadus, iii–xliii. Philadelphia: American Baptist, 1886.

———. "God and the Universe." In *Studies in Ethics and Religion: Or, Discourses, Essays, and Reviews Pertaining to Theism, Inspiration, Christian Ethics, and Education for the Ministry*, 57–70. Boston: Silver, Burdett, 1892.

———. *God With Us; or, the Person and Work of Christ, with an Examination of "The Vicarious Sacrifice" of Dr. Bushnell*. Boston: Gould and Lincoln, 1872.

———. "The Golden Rule." In *Studies in Ethics and Religion: Or, Discourses, Essays, and Reviews Pertaining to Theism, Inspiration, Christian Ethics, and Education for the Ministry*, 232–45. Boston: Silver, Burdett, 1892.

———. "A Good Church History." In *Studies in Ethics and Religion: Or, Discourses, Essays, and Reviews Pertaining to Theism, Inspiration, Christian Ethics, and Education for the Ministry*, 533–60. Boston: Silver, Burdett, 1892.

———. "The Higher Life: Baptism of the Spirit." *Herald & Presbyter*, December 11, 1873. 2.

———. "The Higher Life: Degree of Sanctification Claimed." *Herald & Presbyter*, January 7, 1874. 2.

———. *Historical Address Delivered at the Fiftieth Anniversary of the Newton Theological Institution, June 8, 1875*. Boston: Wright & Potter, 1875.

———. *History, Geography, and Archaeology of the Bible*. Philadelphia: American Baptist Publication Society, 1892.

———. *The Holy Supper: In History and Scripture*. Philadelphia: American Baptist Publication Society, 1880.

———. *How and Why I Should Give*. Philadelphia: American Baptist Publication Society, n.d.

———. "How Can I Give to Foreign Missions?" *Baptist Missionary Magazine* 64 (1877) 34–38.

———. "Imposition of Hands in Ordination." In *Studies in Ethics and Religion: Or, Discourses, Essays, and Reviews Pertaining to Theism, Inspiration, Christian Ethics, and Education for the Ministry*, 429–39. Boston: Silver, Burdett, 1892.

———. *An Inaugural Address, Delivered before the Newton Theological Institution, June 28, 1854*. Boston: J. M. Hewes, 1854.

———. "Infant Baptism an Invention of Men." *The Baptist Quarterly* 3 (1869): 168–92.

———. "Inspiration of the Prophets and Apostles." In *Studies in Ethics and Religion: Or, Discourses, Essays, and Reviews Pertaining to Theism, Inspiration, Christian Ethics, and Education for the Ministry*, 108–81. Boston: Silver, Burdett, 1892.

———. "Inspiration of the Scriptures." In *Studies in Ethics and Religion: Or, Discourses, Essays, and Reviews Pertaining to Theism, Inspiration, Christian Ethics, and Education for the Ministry*, 182–217. Boston: Silver, Burdett, 1892.

———. "The Limitations of State Education and the Consequent Duty of Christians." *New Academy* 1 (1873) 2.

———. "The Lord's Day: Duty and Manner of Keeping It." In *Studies in Ethics and Religion: Or, Discourses, Essays, and Reviews Pertaining to Theism, Inspiration, Christian Ethics, and Education for the Ministry*, 271–320. Boston: Silver, Burdett, 1892.

———. *Manual of Christian Theology*. New York: Silver, Burdett, 1900.

———. *Manual of Systematic Theology and Christian Ethics*. Philadelphia: American Baptist Publication Society, 1877.

———. "The Meaning of Sheol in the Old Testament." *The Old Testament Student* 5 (1885) 49–52.

———. *A Memoir of the Life and Times of the Rev. Isaac Backus, A.M.* Boston: Gould and Lincoln, 1858.

———. *The Miracles of Christ as Attested by the Evangelists*. Boston: Graves and Young, 1864.

———. "Moses Stuart." *The Christian Review* 17 (1852) 288–96.

———. "The New Testament as a Guide to the Interpretation of the Old Testament." *The Old Testament Student* 8 (1889) 207–13.

———. "The New Testament as a Guide to the Interpretation of the Old Testament." In *Studies in Ethics and Religion: Or, Discourses, Essays, and Reviews Pertaining to Theism, Inspiration, Christian Ethics, and Education for the Ministry*, 218–31. Boston: Silver, Burdett, 1892.

———. "Newton from 1875 to 1900." *The Newtonian* 1.2 (1903) 43–48.

———. "Opening Address." In *Proceedings of the Second Annual Baptist Autumnal Conference for the Discussion of Current Questions, at the First Baptist Church, Boston, MA, November 13, 14, 15, 1883*, 3–6. Boston: Boston Missionary Rooms, Tremont Temple, 1883.

———. *Origin and Interpretation of the Bible*. Philadelphia: American Baptist Publication Society, 1892.

———. "Our Knowledge of Infinites." In *Studies in Ethics and Religion: Or, Discourses, Essays, and Reviews Pertaining to Theism, Inspiration, Christian Ethics, and Education for the Ministry*, 1–22. Boston: Silver, Burdett, 1892.

———. *Outlines of Christian Theology*. Boston: G. C. Rand & Avery, 1861.

———. *Outlines of Christian Theology*. Boston: G. C. Rand & Avery, 1866.

———. *Outlines of Christian Theology*. Providence: Providence, 1870.

———. "Patristic Testimonies as to Wine, Especially as Used in the Lord's Supper." *Baptist Quarterly Review* 10 (1888) 78–93.

———. "Post-Graduate Fellowships." In *Studies in Ethics and Religion: Or, Discourses, Essays, and Reviews Pertaining to Theism, Inspiration, Christian Ethics, and Education for the Ministry*, 513–32. Boston: Silver, Burdett, 1892.

———. "Preparation for the Christian Ministry." In *Studies in Ethics and Religion: Or, Discourses, Essays, and Reviews Pertaining to Theism, Inspiration, Christian Ethics, and Education for the Ministry*, 440–75. Boston: Silver, Burdett, 1892.

———. "Present State of the Baptismal Controversy." *The Baptist Quarterly* 9 (1875) 129–48.

———. "Progress of a Century: The Baptists in 1776 and in 1876." *The Baptist Quarterly* 10 (1876) 467–89.

———. "Propitiation and Example." *Herald & Presbyter*, March 7, 1872. 3.

———. "The Relation of God to Nature: A Review." In *Studies in Ethics and Religion: Or, Discourses, Essays, and Reviews Pertaining to Theism, Inspiration, Christian Ethics, and Education for the Ministry*, 23–56. Boston: Silver, Burdett, 1892.

———. "Relation of Monism to Theology." In *Thirteenth Annual Session of the Baptist Congress for the Discussion of Current Questions, Held in the Central Baptist Church, Providence, RI, November 12, 13, and 14, 1895*, 10–21. New York: Baptist Congress, 1896.

———. *Religion and the State: Protection or Alliance? Taxation or Exemption?* Boston: Estes and Lauriat, 1874.

———. "The Religious Basis of Government." *The Baptist Quarterly* 6 (1872) 42–51.

———. *Restatement of Denominational Principles*. Philadelphia: American Baptist Publication Society, 1892.

———. "The Resurrection of the Dead." *The Baptist Quarterly* 1 (1867) 385–99.

———. "The Sacred Writings Described." In *Studies in Ethics and Religion: Or, Discourses, Essays, and Reviews Pertaining to Theism, Inspiration, Christian Ethics, and Education for the Ministry*, 90–107. Boston: Silver, Burdett, 1892.

———. *The Scriptural Law of Divorce*. Boston: Gould and Lincoln, 1866.
———. "The Seat of Authority in Religion." *Watchman*, September 18, 1902. 10–13.
———. "Shekhar and Leaven in Mosaic Offerings." *The Old Testament Student* 6 (1886) 11–16.
———. "Stapfer on the Resurrection of Jesus Christ." *The American Journal of Theology* 4 (1900) 536–54.
———. "The State and Religion." *The Baptist Quarterly* 8 (1874) 65–79.
———. "The State and Religion." In *Studies in Ethics and Religion: Or, Discourses, Essays, and Reviews Pertaining to Theism, Inspiration, Christian Ethics, and Education for the Ministry*, 246–70. Boston: Silver, Burdett, 1892.
———. *The State of the Impenitent Dead*. Boston: Gould and Lincoln, 1859.
———. *State of Men after Death*. Philadelphia: American Baptist Publication Society, 1874.
———. *Studies in Ethics and Religion; or, Discourses, Essays, and Reviews Pertaining to Theism, Inspiration, Christian Ethics, and Education for the Ministry*. Boston: Silver, Burdett, 1892.
———. *Syllabus of Christian Apologetics*. Boston: John Youngjohn, 1900.
———. *Syllabus of Theological Propaedeutics*. New York: Silver, Burdett, n.d.
———. "Tertullian on the Rite of Baptism." *The Baptist Quarterly* 5 (1871) 75–77.
———. "Theories of Inspiration." *Baptist Quarterly Review* 6 (1884) 26–46.
———. *Time of Christ's Second Advent*. Philadelphia: American Baptist Publication Society, 1880.
———. "Time of the Second Advent." *The Baptist Quarterly* 11 (1877) 416–32.
———. "Tischendorf on the Date of the Four Gospels." *The Baptist Quarterly* 1 (1867) 66–80.
———. "The Twenty-Second Psalm." *The Biblical World* 22 (1903) 107–15.
———. "Value of Systematic Theology to Pastors." In *Studies in Ethics and Religion: Or, Discourses, Essays, and Reviews Pertaining to Theism, Inspiration, Christian Ethics, and Education for the Ministry*, 476–96. Boston: Silver, Burdett, 1892.
———. "What Was the 'Fruit of the Vine' Which Jesus Gave His Disciples at the Institution of the Supper?" *Baptist Quarterly Review* 9 (1887) 285–303.
Hovey, Alvah, and Joseph Cook. "Professor Park as Preacher and Teacher." *Bibliotheca Sacra* 63 (1901) 338–59.
Hovey, Alvah, and John Milton Gregory. *Normal Class Manual for Bible Teachers*. Philadelphia: American Baptist Publication Society, 1873.
Hovey, Alvah, and Bradford Pierce. "Prison Chaplaincy." *Zion's Herald*, November 29, 1877. 379.
Hovey, Alvah, et al. "Reforms in Theological Education." *Baptist Quarterly Review* 7 (1885) 407–42.
Hovey, Alvah, et al. "A Symposium: Shall the Analyzed Pentateuch Be Published in the Old Testament Student?" *The Old Testament Student* 7 (1888) 312–19.
Hovey, Alvah, et al. "A 'Symposium' on the 'Gradualness of Revelation.'" *The Old and New Testament Student* 11.3 (1890) 177–85.
Hovey, Alvah, et al, eds. *The New Testament of Our Lord and Savior Jesus Christ: American Bible Union Version*. Philadelphia: American Baptist Publication Society, 1891.

Perthes, Friedrich Matthaeus. *Life of John Chrysostom: Based on the Investigations of Neander, Böhringer, and Others*. Translated by Alvah Hovey and David B. Ford. Boston: J. P. Jewett, 1854.

Planck, Adolf. "Lucian and Christianity, Part 1." Translated by Alvah Hovey. *Bibliotheca Sacra* 10 (1853) 284–305.

———. "Lucian and Christianity, Part 2." Translated by Alvah Hovey. *Bibliotheca Sacra* 10 (1853) 448–75.

Works Cited

Ahlstrom, Sydney E. "The Scottish Philosophy and American Theology." *Church History* 24.3 (1955) 257–72.

———. *Theology in America*. Indianapolis: Bobbs-Merrill, 1967.

———. "Theology in America: A Historical Survey." In *The Shaping of American Religion*, edited by James Ward Smith and A. Leland Jamison, 232–321. Religion in American Life. Princeton, NJ: Princeton University Press, 1961.

Allen, Paul L. *Theological Method: A Guide for the Perplexed*. New York: T&T Clark, 2012.

Allison, William H. "Hovey, Alvah." In vol. 9 of *Dictionary of American Biography*, edited by Dumas Malone, 270. New York: Scribner's, 1932.

Aloisi, John Andrew. "Augustus Hopkins Strong and Ethical Monism as a Means of Reconciling Christian Theology and Modern Thought." PhD diss., Southern Baptist Theological Seminary, 2012.

Archibald, S. H., and W. A. Kinzie, eds. *Minutes of the Vermont Baptist Anniversaries for the Year 1900*. Rutland, VT: Tuttle, 1900.

Armitage, Thomas. *A History of the Baptists: Traced by Their Vital Principles and Practices from the Time of Our Lord and Saviour Jesus Christ to the Year 1886*. New York: Bryan, Taylor, & Co., 1887.

Aubert, Annette G. *The German Roots of Nineteenth-Century American Theology*. New York: Oxford University Press, 2013.

Averill, Lloyd J. *American Theology in the Liberal Tradition*. Philadelphia: Westminster, 1967.

Backman, Milton Vaughn, Jr. "Isaac Backus: A Pioneer Champion of Religious Liberty." PhD diss., University of Pennsylvania, 1959.

Backus, Isaac. *A History of New England with Particular Reference to the Denomination of Christians Called Baptists*. 2nd ed. 2 vols. Newton, MA: Backus Historical Society, 1871.

"Baptist Theology: The Newton Theological Institution and Its Faculty: Considering Questions of Biblical Interpretation: Liberal Ideas Put Professors Hovey and Gould at Variance." *Boston Globe*, July 20, 1882. 4.

Barnes, L. Call. "Newton Men and Missions." In *Historical Addresses: Delivered at the Newton Centennial, June 1925*, 28–41. Newton Centre, MA: Institution Bulletin, 1926.

Barth, Karl. *Protestant Thought in the Nineteenth Century: Its Background and History*. Translated by Brian Cozens and John Bowden. Grand Rapids: Eerdmans, 2002.

Bauder, Kevin T., and Robert Delnay. *One in Hope and Doctrine: Origins of Baptist Fundamentalism 1870–1950*. Schaumburg, IL: Regular Baptist, 2014.

Bayly, C. A. *The Birth of the Modern World, 1780-1914: Global Connections and Comparisons*. Malden, MA: Blackwell, 2004.

Beale, David O. *In Pursuit of Purity: American Fundamentalism Since 1850*. Greenville: Bob Jones University Press, 1986.

Bebbington, David W. *Baptists through the Centuries: A History of a Global People*. Waco, TX: Baylor University Press, 2010.

———. *The Dominance of Evangelicalism: The Age of Spurgeon and Moody*. A History of Evangelicalism: People, Movements and Ideas in the English-Speaking World. Downers Grove, IL: InterVarsity, 2005.

———. "Evangelicalism." In *The Blackwell Companion to Nineteenth-Century Theology*, edited by David Fergusson, 235–50. Malden, MA: Wiley-Blackwell, 2010.

Behney, John Bruce. "Conservatism and Liberalism in the Theology of Late Nineteenth Century American Protestantism: A Comparative Study of the Basic Doctrines of Typical Representatives." PhD diss., Yale University, 1941.

Bendroth, Margaret Lamberts. *A School of the Church: Andover Newton across Two Centuries*. Grand Rapids: Eerdmans, 2008.

Benedict, David. *Fifty Years Among the Baptists*. New York: Sheldon & Company, 1860.

———. *General History of the Baptist Denomination in America, and Other Parts of the World*. 2 vols. Boston: Lincoln & Edmands, 1813.

Berkhof, Hendrikus. *Two Hundred Years of Theology: Report of a Personal Journey*. Grand Rapids: Eerdmans, 1989.

Billingsley, Andrew. *Mighty Like a River: The Black Church and Social Reform*. New York: Oxford University Press, 1999.

Bloch, Ruth H. "Religion and Ideological Change in the American Revolution." In *Religion and American Politics: From the Colonial Period to the 1980s*, edited by Mark A. Noll, 44–61. New York: Oxford University Press, 1990.

Boyle, Daniel Jay. "Isaac Backus and His Ecclesial Thought." PhD diss., Southwestern Baptist Theological Seminary, 2002.

Bozeman, Theodore Dwight. *Protestants in an Age of Science: The Baconian Ideal and Ante-Bellum American Religious Thought*. Chapel Hill: University of North Carolina Press, 1977.

Brachlow, Stephen. "Walter Rauschenbusch." In *Baptist Theologians*, edited by Timothy George and David S. Dockery, 366–83. Nashville: Broadman, 1990.

Brackney, William H. *The Baptists*. Westport, CT: Greenwood, 1988.

———. "Baptists Turn Toward Education: 1764." In *Turning Points in Baptist History: Festschrift in Honor of Harry Leon McBeth*, edited by Michael E. Williams Sr. and Walter B. Shurden, 128–40. Macon, GA: Mercer University Press, 2008.

———. *Congregation and Campus: Baptists in Higher Education*. Macon, GA: Mercer University Press, 2008.

———. "The Development of Baptist Theological Education in Europe and North America: A Representative Overview." *American Baptist Quarterly* 18.2 (1999) 86–93.

———. "The Frontier of Free Exchange of Ideas: The Baptist Congress as a Forum for Baptist Concerns, 1881–1913." *Baptist History and Heritage* 38.3 (2003) 8–27.

———. *A Genetic History of Baptist Thought: With Special Reference to Baptists in Britain and North America*. Macon, GA: Mercer University Press, 2004.

———. *Historical Dictionary of the Baptists*. Lanham, MD: Scarecrow, 1999.

———. "A Turn Toward a Doctrinal Christianity: Baptist Theology, a Work in Progress." In *Turning Points in Baptist History: A Festschrift in Honor of Harry Leon McBeth*, edited by Michael E. Williams Sr. and Walter B. Shurden, 74–90. Macon, GA: Mercer University Press, 2008.

Bradley, James E., and Richard A. Muller. *Church History: An Introduction to Research, Reference Works, and Methods*. Grand Rapids: Eerdmans, 1995.

Breton, Cecil C. "An Inquiry into the Doctrine of the Holy Spirit in the Thought of A. J. Gordon." BD thesis, Gordon Divinity School, 1955.

Briggs, Charles Augustus. *The Authority of Holy Scripture: An Inaugural Address*. New York: Scribner's, 1891.

———. *Biblical Study: Its Principles, Methods, and History*. New York: Scribner's, 1883.

———. *Whither? A Theological Question for the Times*. New York: Scribner's, 1889.

Broadus, John A. *Commentary on the Gospel of Matthew*. American Commentary on the New Testament. Philadelphia: American Baptist, 1886.

Bronson, Walter C. *The History of Brown University 1764–1914*. Providence: Brown University, 1914.

Brown, Jerry Wayne. *The Rise of Biblical Criticism in America, 1800–1870: The New England Scholars*. Middletown, CT: Wesleyan University Press, 1969.

Brown, Stewart J., and Timothy Tackett, eds. *Enlightenment, Awakening and Revolution 1660–1815*. Vol. 7. Cambridge History of Christianity. Cambridge: Cambridge University Press, 2014.

Brown, William Adams. "Review of *Systematic Theology* (vol. 1, 1907 ed.), by Augustus Hopkins Strong." *American Journal of Theology* 12 (1908) 150–55.

———. "The Theology of William Newton Clarke." *Harvard Theological Review* 3.2 (1910) 167–80.

Burnett, Richard E. "Historical Criticism." In *Dictionary for Theological Interpretation of the Bible*, edited by Kevin J. Vanhoozer, 290–93. Grand Rapids: Baker Academic, 2005.

Burrage, Henry S. *History of the Baptists in Maine*. Portland, ME: Marks, 1904.

———. *A History of Baptists in New England*. Philadelphia: American Baptist, 1894.

Bush, L. Russ, and Tom Nettles. *Baptists and the Bible*. Revised and Expanded. Nashville: Broadman & Holman, 1999.

Bushnell, Horace. *Christ in Theology*. Hartford: Brown and Parsons, 1851.

———. *God in Christ*. Hartford: Brown and Parsons, 1849.

———. *The Vicarious Sacrifice: Grounded in Principles of Universal Obligation*. New York: Scribner's, 1871.

Byrne, James M. *Religion and the Enlightenment: From Descartes to Kant*. Louisville: Westminster John Knox, 1997.

Caldwell III, Robert W. *Theologies of the American Revivalists: From Whitefield to Finney*. Downers Grove, IL: IVP Academic, 2017.

Carson, D. A. "Recent Developments in the Doctrine of Scripture." In *Hermeneutics, Authority, and Canon*, edited by D. A. Carson and John D. Woodbridge, 1–48. Eugene, OR: Wipf & Stock, 2005.

Carwardine, Richard J. *Evangelicals and Politics in Antebellum America*. New Haven: Yale University Press, 1993.

———. "Evangelicals, Politics, and the Coming of the American Civil War: A Transatlantic Perspective." In *Evangelicalism: Comparative Studies of Popular*

Protestantism in North America, The British Isles, and Beyond, 1700-1990, edited by Mark A. Noll et al., 198-218. New York: Oxford University Press, 1994.
Cathcart, William. *The Baptist Encyclopedia*. Philadelphia: Louis H. Everts, 1881.
Cauthen, Kenneth. *The Impact of American Religious Liberalism*. 2nd ed. Washington, DC: University Press of America, 1983.
Chadwick, Owen. *The Secularization of the European Mind in the Nineteenth Century*. Cambridge: Cambridge University Press, 1975.
Chase, Irah. "Rev. Irah Chase, D.D.: An Autobiographical Sketch." *Baptist Memorial and Missionary Record* 9 (1850) 70-82.
Christian, Timothy Keith. "The Theology of Augustus Hopkins Strong: The Role of His Key Concepts and the Influence of Modernism as Reflected in the Eighth Edition of His Systematic Theology." DTh diss., University of South Africa, 2007.
Chute, Anthony L. *A Piety Above the Common Standard: Jesse Mercer and the Defense of Evangelistic Calvinism*. Macon, GA: Mercer University Press, 2004.
Chute, Anthony L., et al. *The Baptist Story: From English Sect to Global Movement*. Nashville: Broadman & Holman Academic, 2015.
Clarke, Emily S. *William Newton Clarke: A Biography, with Additional Sketches by His Friends and Colleagues*. New York: Scribner's, 1916.
Clarke, William Newton. *Commentary on the Gospel of Mark*. American Commentary on the New Testament. Philadelphia: American Baptist, 1881.
———. "Dr. Hovey as a Theologian." *Watchman*, September 17, 1903. 12-13.
———. *An Outline of Christian Theology*. New York: Scribner's, 1917.
———. *Sixty Years with the Bible: A Record of Experience*. New York: Scribner's, 1909.
Clipsham, Ernest P. "An Englishman Looks as Rauschenbusch." *Baptist Quarterly* 29.3 (1981) 113-21.
Cochran, Bernard Harvey. "William Newton Clarke: Exponent of the New Theology." PhD diss., Duke University, 1962.
Conforti, Joseph A. *Jonathan Edwards, Religious Tradition and American Culture*. Chapel Hill, NC: University of North Carolina Press, 1995.
———. *Samuel Hopkins and the New Divinity Movement: Calvinism, the Congregational Ministry, and Reform in New England Between the Great Awakenings*. Grand Rapids: Christian University Press, 1981.
Cooley, Daniel W. "The New England Theology and the Atonement: From Jonathan Edwards to Edwards Amasa Park." PhD diss., Trinity Evangelical Divinity School, 2014.
Cragg, Gerald R. *The Church and the Age of Reason, 1648-1789*. The Penguin History of the Church. New York: Penguin, 1970.
Crane, Cephas B. "Dr. Hovey with His Friends." *The Newtonian* 2.3 (1904) 95-101.
———. "The Removal of Professor Gould." *Independent*, October 12, 1882. 2-3.
Crane, Theodore Rawson. "Francis Wayland and Brown University, 1796-1841." PhD diss., Harvard University, 1959.
Creed, J. Bradley. "Baptist Freedom and the Turn Toward Separation of Church and State: 1833." In *Turning Points in Baptist History: A Festschrift in Honor of Harry Leon McBeth*, edited by Michael E. Williams Sr. and Walter B. Shurden, 153-66. Macon, GA: Mercer University Press, 2008.
Crisp, Oliver D., and Douglas A. Sweeney, eds. *After Jonathan Edwards: The Courses of the New England Theology*. New York: Oxford University Press, 2012.

———. "Introduction." In *After Edwards: The Courses of the New England Theology*, edited by Oliver D. Crisp and Douglas A. Sweeney, 1–16. New York: Oxford University Press, 2012.

Crowley, John G. *Primitive Baptists of the Wiregrass South: 1815 to the Present*. Gainesville: University Press of Florida, 1988.

DeBlois, A. K. "Newton Men in Education." In *Historical Addresses: Delivered at the Newton Centennial, June 1925*, 43–63. Newton Centre, MA: Institution Bulletin, 1926.

Dockery, David S. "Looking Back, Looking Ahead." In *Theologians of the Baptist Tradition*, edited by Timothy George and David S. Dockery, 338–60, 406–9. Nashville: Broadman & Holman, 2001.

Dollar, George W. *A History of Fundamentalism in America*. Greenville: Bob Jones University Press, 1973.

Dorrien, Gary. *The Making of American Liberal Theology: Imagining Progressive Religion, 1805–1900*. Louisville: Westminster John Knox, 2001.

Duncan, Pope A. "Crawford Howell Toy (1836–1919)." In *Dictionary of Heresy Trial in American Christianity*, 430–38. Westport, CT: Greenwood, 1997.

———. "Crawford Howell Toy: Heresy at Louisville." In *American Religious Heretics: Formal and Informal Heresy Trials*, edited by George H. Shriver, 56–88. Nashville: Abingdon, 1966.

"Editorial." *Journal and Messenger*, November 1, 1882. 4.

"Editorial Notes." *Independent*, October 5, 1882.

Edwards, Rebecca. *New Spirits: Americans in the Gilded Age. 1865–1905*. New York: Oxford University Press, 2006.

English, John M. "Alvah Hovey, D.D., LL.D." *Bibliotheca Sacra* 56 (1899) 579–83.

———. "Dr. Hovey as a Teacher." *Watchman*, September 17, 1903. 10–11.

———. "Newton Men in the Pastorate." In *Historical Addresses: Delivered at the Newton Centennial, June 1925*, 17–27. Newton Centre, MA: Institution Bulletin, 1926.

Evans, Christopher H. *The Kingdom Is Always but Coming: A Life of Walter Rauschenbusch*. Grand Rapids: Eerdmans, 2004.

———. "Reflections on the Methodist Historical Pie: Re-Engaging the Puzzle of American Methodism." *Methodist Review: A Journal of Wesleyan and Methodist Studies* 7 (2015) 1–20.

———, ed. *Perspectives on the Social Gospel: Papers from the Inaugural Social Gospel Conference at Colgage Rochester Divinity School*. Lewiston, NY: Edwin Mellon, 1999.

Fea, John. *Why Study History?: Reflecting on the Importance of the Past*. Grand Rapids: Baker, 2013.

Fea, John, et al., eds. *Confessing History: Explorations in Christian Faith and the Historian's Vocation*. Notre Dame, IN: University of Notre Dame Press, 2010.

Fiering, Norman. *Jonathan Edwards's Moral Thought and Its British Context*. Chapel Hill: University of North Carolina Press, 1981.

Finke, Roger. "Religious Deregulation: Origins and Consequences." *Journal of Church and State* 32.3 (1990) 609–26.

Finke, Roger, and Rodney Stark. "How the Upstart Sects Won America: 1776–1850." *Journal for the Scientific Study of Religion* 28 (1989) 27–44.

Fitts, Leroy. *A History of Black Baptists*. Nashville: Broadman, 1985.

Foster, Frank Hugh. *A Genetic History of the New England Theology*. New York: Russell & Russell, 1963.

Frei, Hans W. *The Eclipse of Biblical Narrative: A Study in Eighteenth and Nineteenth Century Hermeneutics*. New Haven: Yale University Press, 1974.

Fry, Russell Raymond. "Theological Principles of Isaac Backus and the Move from Congregationalism to Baptist Leadership in New England." PhD diss., Drew University, 1989.

Gardner, Robert G. *A Decade of Debate and Division: Georgia Baptists and the Formation of the Southern Baptist Convention*. Macon, GA: Mercer University Press, 1995.

Garrett, James Leo, Jr. *Baptist Theology: A Four-Century Study*. Macon, GA: Mercer University Press, 2009.

———. "Sources of Authority in Baptist Thought." *Baptist History and Heritage* 13.3 (1978) 41–49.

Gaustad, Edwin Scott. "The Backus-Leland Tradition." *Foundations* 2 (1959) 131–52.

Gaustad, Edwin Scott, and Philip L. Barlow. *New Historical Atlas of Religion in America*. New York: Oxford University Press, 2001.

George, Timothy. *The Theology of the Reformers*. Nashville: Broadman, 1988.

Gibson, Scott M. *A. J. Gordon: American Premillennialist*. Lanham, MD: University Press of America, 2001.

———. "A. J. Gordon and H. Grattan Guinness: A Case Study of Transatlantic Evangelicalism." In *Pilgrim Pathways: Essays in Baptist History in Honor of B. R. White*, edited by William H. Brackney et al., 303–17. Macon, GA: Mercer University Press, 1999.

Giltner, John H. "The Fragmentation of New England Congregationalism and the Founding of Andover Seminary." *Journal of Religious Thought* 20.1 (1964) 27–42.

———. *Moses Stuart: The Father of Biblical Science in America*. Atlanta: Scholars, 1988.

Gloege, Timothy E. W. "A Gilded Age Modernist: Reuben A. Torrey and the Roots of Contemporary Conservative Evangelicalism." In *American Evangelicalism: George Marsden and the State of American Religious History*, edited by Darren Dochuk et al., 199–229. Notre Dame, IN: University of Notre Dame Press, 2014.

———. *Guaranteed Pure: The Moody Bible Institute, Business, and the Making of Modern Evangelicalism*. Chapel Hill: University of North Carolina Press, 2015.

Goen, C. C. *Revivalism and Separatism in New England, 1740–1800: Strict Congregationalists and Separate Baptists in the Great Awakening*. Middletown, CT: Wesleyan University Press, 1987.

Gonzalez, Antonia Lučić. "Balthasar Hubmaier and Early Christian Tradition." PhD diss., Fuller Theological Seminary, 2008.

Gould, Ezra Palmer. *The Biblical Theology of the New Testament*. Edited by Shailer Mathews. New Testament Handbooks. New York: Macmillan, 1900.

———. "A Christocentric Theology." *National Baptist*, October 12, 1882. 644.

———. *Commentary on the New Testament*. Philadelphia: American Baptist, 1887.

———. *A Critical and Exegetical Commentary on the Gospel According to St. Mark*. Edited by Samuel R. Driver. International Critical Commentary on the Holy Scriptures of the Old and New Testaments. Edinburgh: T&T Clark, 1897.

———. "Is God Love?" *National Baptist*, October 5, 1882. 641.

———. "Prof. Gould's Statement." *Independent*, October 12, 1882. 3.

———. "The Supernatural Element in Christianity." *Independent*, October 26, 1882. 8–9.

Green, Steven K. *The Second Disestablishment: Church and State in Nineteenth-Century America*. New York: Oxford University Press, 2010.

Grenz, Stanley J. "Isaac Backus." In *Baptist Theologians*, 102–20. Nashville: Broadman & Holman, 1990.

———. *Isaac Backus—Puritan and Baptist: His Place in History, His Thought, and Their Implications for Modern Baptist Theology*. NABPR Dissertation Series 4. Macon, GA: Mercer University Press, 1983.

Guelzo, Allen C. *Edwards on the Will: A Century of American Theological Debate*. Middletown, CT: Wesleyan University Press, 1989.

Guild, Reuben Aldridge. *History of Brown University with Illustrative Documents*. Providence: Brown University, 1867.

Gundlach, Bradley J. *Process and Providence: The Evolution Question at Princeton, 1845–1929*. Grand Rapids: Eerdmans, 2013.

Hague, William. *Christian Greatness in the Scholar: A Discourse on the Life and Character of Reverend Irah Chase, D.D.*. Boston: Gould and Lincoln, 1866.

Halbrooks, G. Thomas. "Francis Wayland: A Contributor to Baptist Conceptions of Church Order." PhD diss., Emory University, 1971.

Hamburger, Philip. *Separation of Church and State*. Cambridge, MA: Harvard University Press, 2002.

Hampson, Norman. *The Enlightenment: An Evaluation of Its Assumptions, Attitudes, and Values*. New York: Penguin, 1991.

Handy, Robert T. *The Social Gospel in America: 1870–1920: Gladden, Ely, Rauschenbusch*. New York: Oxford University Press, 1966.

———. "The Social Gospel in Historical Perspective." *Andover Newton Quarterly* 9 (1969) 170–80.

———. "Walter Rauschenbusch." In *Twelve Makers of Modern Protestant Thought*, edited by George L. Hunt, 33–39. New York: Association, 1971.

Hart, Nelson Hodges. "The True and the False: The Worlds of an Emerging Evangelical Protestant Fundamentalism in America, 1890–1920." PhD diss., Michigan State University, 1976.

Hatch, Nathan O. *The Democratization of American Christianity*. New Haven, CT: Yale University Press, 1989.

———. "The Democratization of Christianity and the Character of American Politics." In *Religion and American Politics: From the Colonial Period to the 1980s*, edited by Mark A. Noll, 92–120. New York: Oxford University Press, 1990.

———. "The Puzzle of American Methodism." *Church History* 63 (1994) 175–89.

———. *The Sacred Cause of Liberty: Republican Thought and the Millennium in Revolutionary New England*. New Haven: Yale University Press, 1977.

———. "Sola Scripura and Novus Ordo Seclorum." In *The Bible in America*, edited by Nathan O. Hatch and Mark A. Noll, 59–78. New York: Oxford University Press, 1982.

Hauser, Alan J., and Duane F. Watson, eds. *The Enlightenment through the Nineteenth Century*. Vol. 3 of *A History of Biblical Interpretation*. Grand Rapids: Eerdmans, 2017.

Hazard, Paul. *The European Mind: The Critical Years, 1680–1715*. New Haven: Yale University Press, 1953.

Helm, Paul. "Thomas Reid, Common Sense and Calvinism." In *Rationality in the Calvinian Tradition*, edited by Hendrik Hart et al., 71–89. Lanham, MD: University Press of America, 1983.

Helseth, Paul K. *Right Reason and the Princeton Mind: An Unorthodox Proposal*. Phillipsburg, NJ: P & R, 2010.

Henry, Carl F. H. *Personal Idealism and Strong's Theology*. Wheaton, IL: Van Kampen, 1951.

Hoffecker, W. Andrew. *Charles Hodge: The Pride of Princeton*. American Reformed Biographies. Philadelphia: P & R, 2011.

———. *Piety and the Princeton Theologians: Archibald Alexander, Charles Hodge, and Benjamin Warfield*. Phillipsburg, NJ: P & R, 1981.

Holifield, E. Brooks. *The Gentlemen Theologians: American Theology in Southern Culture 1795–1860*. Durham, NC: Duke University Press, 1978.

———. *Theology in America: Christian Thought from the Age of the Puritans to the Civil War*. New Haven: Yale University Press, 2003.

Holmes, Stephen R. *Baptist Theology*. London: T&T Clark, 2010.

Holte, Knut Ragnar. *Die Vermittlungstheologie: Ihre Theologischen Grundbegriffe Kritisch Untersucht*. Translated by Björn Kommer. Uppsala: Almquist & Wiksells, 1965.

Hopkins, Charles Howard. *The Rise of the Social Gospel in American Protestantism, 1865–1915*. New Haven: Yale University Press, 1940.

Horr, George E. "Dr. Hovey and Educational Work." *Watchman*, September 17, 1903. 13–14.

Houghton, George Gerald. "The Contribution of Adoniram Judson Gordon to American Christianity." ThD diss., Dallas Theological Seminary, 1970.

Houghton, Myron James. "An Examination and Evaluation of A. H. Strong's Doctrine of Holy Scripture." ThD diss., Concordia Seminary, 1986.

House, Paul R. "Crawford Howell Toy and the Weight of Hermeneutics." *Southern Baptist Journal of Theology* 3 (1999) 28–39.

The Hovey Book: Describing the English Ancestry and American Descendants of Daniel Hovey of Ipswich, Massachusetts: Compiled and Published under the Auspices of the Daniel Hovey Association, with an Introductory Chapter by the President. Haverhill, MA: Lewis R. Hovey, 1913.

Hovey, George, ed. *Alvah Hovey: His Life and Letters*. Philadelphia: Judson, 1928.

Howard, Thomas Albert. *God and the Atlantic: America, Europe, and the Religious Divide*. New York: Oxford University Press, 2011.

———. *Religion and the Rise of Historicism: W. M. L. de Wette, Jacob Burckhardt, and the Theological Origins of Nineteenth-Century Historical Consciousness*. Cambridge: Cambridge University Press, 2000.

Howe, Claude L., Jr. *The Theology of William Newton Clarke*. New York: Arno, 1980.

———. "William Newton Clarke: Systematic Theologian of Theological Liberalism." *Foundations* 6 (1963) 123–36.

Howe, Daniel Walker. "The Evangelical Movement and Political Culture in the North during the Second Party System." *Journal of American History* 77 (1991) 1216–39.

———. *Making the American Self: Jonathan Edwards to Abraham Lincoln*. Cambridge, MA: Harvard University Press, 1997.

———. *The Political Culture of the American Whigs*. Chicago: University of Chicago Press, 1979.

———. *What Hath God Wrought: The Transformation of America, 1815–1848*. Oxford History of the United States. New York: Oxford University Press, 2009.

Hudson, Winthrop S. "Shifting Patterns of Church Order in the Twentieth Century." *American Baptist Quarterly* 30 (2011) 320–37.

Hurt, Billy Grey. "Crawford Howell Toy: Interpreter of the Old Testament." PhD diss., Southern Baptist Theological Seminary, 1965.

Hutchison, William R., ed. *American Protestant Thought in the Liberal Era*. Lanham, MD: University Press of America, 1968.

———. *The Modernist Impulse in American Protestantism*. Durham, NC: Duke University Press, 1992.

Johnson, E. H., et al. "Missionary Training Schools—Do Baptists Need Them? A Discussion." *Baptist Quarterly Review* 12.45 (1890) 69–100.

Kidd, Thomas S. *God of Liberty: A Religious History of the American Revolution*. New York: Basic, 2010.

———. *The Great Awakening: The Roots of Evangelical Christianity in Colonial America*. New Haven: Yale University Press, 2009.

Kidd, Thomas S., and Barry Hankins. *Baptists in America: A History*. New York: Oxford University Press, 2015.

King, Henry Melville. "Alvah Hovey and Foreign Missions: An Address Delivered at the Memorial Service Held in Honor of Alvah Hovey, DD, LLD, in Tremont Temple, Boston, September 28, 1903." n.d. 1–12.

———. "Alvah Hovey as Theologian and Teacher." *Review & Expositor* 1 (1904) 161–76.

Klager, Andrew P. "'Truth Is Immortal:' Balthasar Hubmaier (c. 1480–1528) and the Church Fathers." PhD diss., University of Glasgow, 2011.

Kuklick, Bruce. *Churchmen and Philosophers: From Jonathan Edwards to John Dewey*. New Haven: Yale University Press, 1985.

Kutilek, Doug. "The Text and Translation of the Bible: Nineteenth Century American Baptist Views." ThM thesis, Central Baptist Theological Seminary, 1998.

Lasch, Christopher. "Religious Contributions to Social Movements: Walter Rauschenbusch, the Social Gospel, and Its Critics." *The Journal of Religious Ethics* 18.1 (1990) 7–25.

Leonard, Bill J. "Baptist Revivals and the Turn Toward Baptist Evangelism: 1755/1770." In *Turning Points in Baptist History: A Festschrift in Honor of Harry Leon McBeth*, edited by Michael E. Williams Sr. and Walter B. Shurden, 91–101. Macon, GA: Mercer University Press, 2008.

———. *Baptist Ways: A History*. Valley Forge, PA: Judson, 2003.

———. *Baptists in America*. Columbia Contemporary American Religious Series. New York: Columbia University Press, 2005.

Lindman, Janet Moore. *Bodies of Belief: Baptist Community in Early America*. Philadelphia: University of Pennsylvania Press, 2008.

Livingston, James C. *Modern Christian Thought: The Enlightenment and the Nineteenth Century*. 2nd ed. Minneapolis: Fortress, 2006.

Livingston, James C., et al. *Modern Christian Thought: The Twentieth Century*. 2nd ed. Minneapolis: Fortress, 2006.

Livingstone, William. "The Princeton Apologetic as Exemplified by the Works of Benjamin B. Warfield and J. Gresham Machen: A Study in American Theology 1880–1930." PhD diss., Yale University, 1948.

Loetscher, Lefferts A. *Facing the Enlightenment and Pietism: Archibald Alexander and the Founding of the Princeton Theological Seminary*. Westport, CT: Greenwood, 1983.
Lord, John King. *A History of Dartmouth College 1815–1909*. Vol. 2. Concord, NH: Rumford, 1913.
Lovejoy, David S. *Religious Enthusiasm in the New World: Heresy to Revolution*. Cambridge, MA: Harvard University Press, 1985.
Mackintosh, Hugh Ross. *Types of Modern Theology: Schleiermacher to Barth*. New York: Scribner's, 1937.
Maring, Norman H. "Baptists and Changing Views of the Bible, 1865–1918, Part I." *Foundations* 1.3 (1958) 52–75.
———. "Baptists and Changing Views of the Bible, 1865–1918, Part II." *Foundations* 1.4 (1958) 30–61.
Marini, Stephen A. *Radical Sects in Revolutionary New England*. Cambridge, MA: Harvard University Press, 1982.
Marsden, George M. "The Collapse of American Evangelical Academia." In *Faith and Rationality: Reason and Belief in God*, edited by Alvin Plantinga and Nicholas Wolterstorff, 219–64. Notre Dame, IN: University of Notre Dame Press, 1983.
———. "Common Sense and the Spiritual Vision of History." In *History and Historical Understanding*, edited by C. T. McIntire and Ronald A. Wells, 55–68. Grand Rapids: Eerdmans, 1984.
———. *The Evangelical Mind and the New School Presbyterian Experience*. New Haven, CT: Yale University Press, 1970.
———. "Everyone One's Own Interpreter? The Bible, Science, and Authority in Mid-Nineteenth-Century America." In *The Bible in America*, edited by Nathan O. Hatch and Mark A. Noll, 79–100. New York: Oxford University Press, 1982.
———. *Fundamentalism and American Culture*. New York: Oxford University Press, 1980.
———. *Fundamentalism and American Culture*. 2nd ed. New York: Oxford University Press, 2006.
———. *Reforming Fundamentalism: Fuller Seminary and the New Evangelicalism*. Grand Rapids: Eerdmans, 1995.
———. "Scotland and Philadelphia: Common Sense Philosophy from Jefferson to Westminster." *Reformed Theological Journal* 29 (1979) 8–12.
Marsden, George M., and John D. Woodbridge. "Christian History Today." Edited by Marshall Shelley. *Christian History* 20.4 (2001) 50–54.
Marty, Martin E. *Protestantism in the United States: Righteous Empire*. 2nd ed. New York: Scribner's, 1986.
Massey, John David. "Solidarity in Sin: An Analysis of the Corporate Conceptions of Sin in the Theologies of Augustus Hopkins Strong and Walter Rauschenbusch." PhD diss., Southwestern Baptist Theological Seminary, 2000.
Maston, Thomas B. "The Ethical and Social Attitudes of Isaac Backus." PhD diss., Yale University, 1939.
———. *Isaac Backus: Pioneer of Religious Liberty*. Rochester: American Baptist Historical Society, 1962.
Mathews, Shailer. *New Faith for Old: An Autobiography*. New York: Macmillan, 1936.
Mathis, James R. *The Making of the Primitive Baptists: A Cultural and Intellectual History of the Anti-Mission Movement, 1800–1840*. New York: Routledge, 2004.

May, Henry F. *The Enlightenment in America*. New York: Oxford University Press, 1976.
McBeth, H. Leon. *The Baptist Heritage*. Nashville: Broadman, 1987.
McCormack, Bruce L. "Introduction: On 'Modernity' as a Theological Concept." In *Mapping Modern Theology: A Thematic and Historical Introduction*, edited by Kelly M. Kapic and Bruce L. McCormack, 1–19. Grand Rapids: Baker, 2012.
McGiffert, Arthur Cushman, Jr. "The Church and Social Change: Theology." *The Journal of Religious Thought* 16 (1958) 3–16.
———. *The Rise of Modern Religious Ideas*. New York: Macmillan, 1922.
———. "Walter Rauschenbusch: Twenty Years After." *Christendom* 3 (1938) 96–109.
McGrath, Alister E. *Reformation Thought: An Introduction*. 2nd ed. Oxford: Blackwell, 1993.
McKibbens, T. R. "Hovey, Alvah (1820–1903)." In *Dictionary of Baptists in America*, edited by Bill J. Leonard, 146–47. Downers Grove, IL: InterVarsity, 1994.
McLaughlin, Brian P. "Philosophy of Mind." In *The Cambridge Dictionary of Philosophy*, edited by Robert Audi, 684–94. 2nd ed. New York: Cambridge University Press, 1999.
McLoughlin, William G. "Introduction." In *The American Evangelicals, 1800–1900*, edited by William G. McLoughlin, 1–27. New York: Harper, 1968.
———. *Isaac Backus and the American Pietistic Tradition*. Library of American Biography. Boston: Little, Brown, 1967.
———. *New England Dissent, 1630–1833: The Baptists and the Separation of Church and State*. 2 vols. Cambridge, MA: Harvard University Press, 1971.
———. *Soul Liberty: The Baptists' Struggle in New England, 1630–1833*. Hanover, NH: University Press of New England, 1991.
Miller, Glenn T. *Piety and Intellect: The Aims and Purposes of Ante-Bellum Theological Education*. Atlanta: Scholars, 1990.
Millet, Joshua. *A History of the Baptists in Maine: Together with Brief Notices of Societies and Institutions, and a Dictionary of the Labors of Each Minister*. Portland, ME: Charles Day & Co., 1845.
Minus, Paul M. *Walter Rauschenbusch: American Reformer*. New York: MacMillan, 1988.
Moore, Leroy, Jr. "The Rise of Religious Liberalism at the Rochester Theological Seminary, 1872–1928." PhD diss., Claremont Graduate School, 1966.
Muller, Richard A. "Biblical Interpretation in the Sixteenth and Seventeenth Centuries." In *Dictionary of Major Biblical Interpreters*, edited by Donald K. McKim, 22–44. Downers Grove, IL: InterVarsity, 2007.
———. "A Note on 'Christocentrism' and the Imprudent Use of Such Terminology." *Westminster Theological Journal* 68 (2006) 253–60.
———. *Prolegomena to Theology*. Vol. 1 of *Post-Reformation Reformed Dogmatics*. Grand Rapids: Baker, 1987.
Nettles, Tom J. *The Baptists*. 3 vols. Fearn: Mentor, 2005–2007.
———. *By His Grace and for His Glory: A Historical, Theological, and Practical Study of the Doctrines of Grace in Baptist Life*. Grand Rapids: Baker, 1986.
Newman, A. H., ed. *A Century of Baptist Achievement*. Philadelphia: American Baptist, 1901.
———. *A History of the Baptist Churches in the United States*. New York: Christian Literature, 1894.

———. "Recent Changes in the Theology of the Baptists." *American Journal of Theology* 10 (1906) 587–609.

"Newton Theological Institute." *American Baptist Magazine* 6 (1826) 128–9.

Newton Theological Institution: A Sketch of Its History, and an Account of the Services at the Dedication of the New Building, September 10, 1866. Boston: Gould and Lincoln, 1866.

Niebuhr, Reinhold. "Walter Rauschenbusch in Historical Perspective." *Religion in Life* 27.4 (1958) 527–36.

Noll, Mark A. *America's God: From Jonathan Edwards to Abraham Lincoln*. New York: Oxford University Press, 2002.

———. "And the Lion Shall Lie Down with the Lamb: The Social Sciences and Religious History." *Fides et Historia* 20.3 (1988) 5–30.

———. "Common Sense Traditions and American Evangelical Thought." *American Quarterly* 37 (1985) 216–38.

———. *In the Beginning Was the Word: The Bible in American Public Life, 1492–1783*. New York: Oxford University Press, 2016.

———. "The Irony of the Enlightenment for Presbyterians in the Early Republic." In *Reckoning with the Past: Historical Essays on American Evangelicalism from the Institute for the Study of American Evangelicals*, edited by D. G. Hart, 131–53. Grand Rapids: Baker, 1995.

———. *The Rise of Evangelicalism: The Age of Edwards, Whitefield and the Wesleys*. A History of Evangelicalism: People, Movements, and Ideas in the English-Speaking World. Downers Grove, IL: InterVarsity, 2003.

Norton, David Fate. "Hume, David." In *The Cambridge Dictionary of Philosophy*, edited by Robert Audi, 398–402. 2nd ed. New York: Cambridge University Press, 1999.

Oberman, Heiko A. *The Dawn of the Reformation: Essays in Late Medieval and Early Reformation Thought*. Grand Rapids: Eerdmans, 1992.

———. *The Harvest of Medieval Theology: Gabriel Biel and Late Medieval Nominalism*. Cambridge, MA: Labyrinth, 1983.

O'Brien, Brandon J. "The Edwardsean Isaac Backus: The Significance of Jonathan Edwards in Backus's Theology, History, and Defense of Religious Liberty." PhD diss., Trinity Evangelical Divinity School, 2013.

Ohtsuka, Noguri. "From Jonathan Edwards to Isaac Backus: Religious Motives for Separation of Church and State." PhD diss., Clark University, 1952.

Osterhammel, Jürgen. *The Transformation of the World: A Global History of the Nineteenth Century*. Translated by Patrick Camiller. Princeton, NJ: Princeton University Press, 2014.

Outram, Dorinda. *The Enlightenment*. 3rd ed. New Approaches to European History. Cambridge: Cambridge University Press, 2013.

Page, Homer. "Francis Wayland: Christian America—Liberal America." PhD diss., University of Missouri-Columbia, 2008.

Patterson, James. *James Robinson Graves: Staking the Boundaries of Baptist Identity*. Nashville: Broadman & Holman, 2012.

Patterson, W. Morgan. "Walter Rauschenbusch: Baptist Exemplar of Social Concern." *Baptist History and Heritage* 7.3 (1972) 129–36.

Pearse, Meic. *The Age of Reason: From the French Revolution to the Wars of Religion (1570–1789)*. Baker History of the Church. Grand Rapids: Baker, 2006.

Phillips, Charles. "Edwards Amasa Park: The Last Edwardsian." In *After Jonathan Edwards: The Courses of the New England Theology*, 151–61, 298–301. New York: Oxford University Press, 2012.

Phillips, Janet M. *Brown University: A Short History*. Providence: Brown University, 2000.

Pierce, Richard Donald, ed. *A General Catalogue of The Newton Theological Institution 1826–1943: With Biographical Sketches of Professors and Students in Andover Theological Seminary 1931–1943*. Newton Centre, MA: Newton Theological Institution, 1943.

Priestley, David Thomas Dettmer. "From Theological Polemic to Nonpolemical Theology: The Absence of Denominational Apology in Systematic Theologies by Nineteenth-Century American Baptists." ThD diss., Lutheran School of Theology at Chicago, 1986.

"Professor Gould." *Boston Globe*, October 15, 1882. 9.

"Professor Gould." *National Baptist*, October 19, 1882. 664.

"Professor Gould." *National Baptist*, November 2, 1882. 693.

Ragosta, John A. *Wellspring of Liberty: How Virginia's Religious Dissenters Helped Win the American Revolution and Secured Religious Liberty*. New York: Oxford University Press, 2010.

Rawlyk, George A. "'A Total Revolution in Religious and Civil Government': The Maritimes, New England, and the Evolving Evangelical Ethos, 1776–1812." In *Evangelicalism: Comparative Studies of Popular Protestantism in North America, The British Isles, and Beyond, 1700–1990*, edited by Mark A. Noll et al., 137–55. New York: Oxford University Press, 1994.

Reardon, Bernard M. G. *Religious Thought in the Nineteenth Century: Illustrated from Writers of the Period*. Cambridge: Cambridge University Press, 1966.

"Removal of Professor Gould from Newton Seminary." *The Independent*, October 12, 1884. 10.

Reventlow, Henning Graf. *The Authority of the Bible and the Rise of the Modern World*. Translated by John Bowden. Minneapolis: Fortress, 1985.

Reymond, Robert L. *Faith's Reasons for Believing*. Fearn, Ross-shire: Mentor, 2008.

Richardson, Kurt A. "Augustus Hopkins Strong." In *Baptist Theologians*, edited by Timothy George and David S. Dockery, 289–306. Nashville: Broadman & Holman, 1990.

Robert, Dana L. "Adoniram Judson Gordon 1836–1895: Educator, Preacher, and Promoter of Missions." In *Mission Legacies: Biographical Studies of Leaders of the Modern Missionary Movement*, edited by Gerald H. Anderson et al., 18–27. Maryknoll, NY: Orbis, 1994.

———. "The Legacy of Adoniram Judson Gordon." *International Bulletin of Missionary Research* 11.4 (1987) 176–81.

Rodgers, Peter R. "Textual Criticism." In *Dictionary for Theological Interpretation of the Bible*, edited by Kevin J. Vanhoozer, 784–87. Grand Rapids: Baker Academic, 2005.

Rogers, Jack B., and Donald K. McKim. *The Authority and Interpretation of the Bible: An Historical Approach*. Eugene, OR: Wipf & Stock, 1999.

Rogers, James. *Richard Furman: Life and Legacy*. Macon, GA: Mercer University Press, 2001.

Rosenberger, Jesse Leonard. *The Making of a University*. Rochester: University of Rochester Press, 1927.

———. *Rochester and Colgate: Historical Backgrounds of the Two Universities*. Chicago: University of Chicago Press, 1925.

Rowe, Henry K. "Newton Theological Institution Historical Address." In *Historical Addresses: Delivered at the Newton Centennial, June 1925*, 3–16. Newton Centre, MA: Institution Bulletin, 1926.

Russell, C. Allyn. "Adoniram Judson Gordon: Nineteenth-Century Fundamentalist." *American Baptist Quarterly* 4.1 (1985) 61–89.

Samson, George Whitefield. *The Divine Law as to Wines: Established by the Testimony of Sages, Physicians, and Legislators against the Use of Fermented and Intoxicating Wines: Conformed by Their Provision of Unfermented Wines to Be Used for Medicinal and Sacramental Purposes*. New York: National Temperance Society, 1880.

Sandeen, Ernest R. "The Princeton Theology: One Source of Biblical Literalism in American Protestantism." *Church History* 31.3 (1962) 307–21.

———. *The Roots of Fundamentalism: British and American Millenarianism, 1800–1930*. Chicago: University of Chicago Press, 1970.

———. "Towards a Historical Interpretation of the Origins of Fundamentalism." *Church History* 36 (1967) 66–83.

Satta, Ronald F. *The Sacred Text: Biblical Authority in Nineteenth-Century America*. Princeton Theological Monograph Series. Eugene, OR: Pickwick, 2007.

Saxon, David L. "Fundamentalist Bibliology 1870–1890: An Analysis of the Early Fundamentalist Views of Inspiration, Bible Translations, and Bible Criticism from the Writings of James H. Brookes, A. J. Gordon, and A. T. Pierson." PhD diss., Bob Jones University, 1998.

Schott, E. "Vermittlungstheologie." In vol. 6 of *Die Religion in Geschichte Und Gegenwart: Handwörterbuch Für Theologie Und Religionswissenschaft*, edited by Kurt Galling, 1362–64. Tübingen: Mohr Siebeck, 1962.

Sharpe, Dores Robinson. *Walter Rauschenbusch*. New York: MacMillan, 1942.

Sheppard, Gerald T., and Anthony C. Thiselton. "Biblical Interpretation in the Eighteenth and Nineteenth Centuries." In *Dictionary of Major Biblical Interpreters*, edited by Donald K. McKim, 45–66. Downers Grove, IL: IVP Academic, 2007.

Sherouse, Craig A. "Toward a Twentieth-Century Baptist Identity in North America: Insights from the Baptist Congresses, 1881–1913." *Baptist History and Heritage* 47.3 (2012) 76–90.

Short, Kenneth R. M. "Baptist Training for the Ministry: The Francis Wayland-Barnas Sears Debate of 1853." *Foundations* 11 (1968) 227–34.

Shrader, Matthew C. "New England Baptist Alvah Hovey: A Later Chapter in Baptist Edwardsianism." *Jonathan Edwards Studies* 10.1 (2020) 48–64.

Singer, Anna. *Walter Rauschenbusch and His Contribution to Social Christianity*. Eugene, OR: Wipf & Stock, 2007.

Smith, James Ward. "Religion and Science in American Philosophy." In vol. 1 of *The Shaping of American Religion*, edited by James Ward Smith and A. Leland Jamison, 402–42. Religion in American Life. Princeton, NJ: Princeton University Press, 1961.

Smyth, Newman. "Orthodox Rationalism." *Princeton Review* 58 (1882) 294–312.

Stewart, John William. "The Tethered Theology: Biblical Criticism, Common Sense Philosophy, and the Princeton Theologians, 1812–1860." PhD diss., University of Michigan, 1990.

Stiver, Dan R. "Method." In *Dictionary for Theological Interpretation of the Bible*, edited by Kevin J. Vanhoozer, 510–12. Grand Rapids: Baker, 2005.

Storr, Richard J. *Harper's University: The Beginnings. A History of the University of Chicago*. Chicago: University of Chicago Press, 1966.

Straub, Jeffrey Paul. *The Making of a Battle Royal: The Rise of Liberalism in Northern Baptist Life, 1870–1920*. Monographs in Baptist History. Eugene, OR: Pickwick, 2018.

Strong, Augustus Hopkins. *Christ in Creation; and, Ethical Monism*. Philadelphia: Roger Williams, 1899.

———. *Miscellanies*. Philadelphia: Griffith and Rowland, 1912.

———. *Systematic Theology: A Compendium and Commonplace Book Designed for the Use of Theological Students*. Rochester: E. R. Andrews, 1886.

———. *Systematic Theology: A Compendium and Commonplace Book Designed for the Use of Theological Students*. 2nd ed. New York: A. C. Armstrong and Son, 1889.

———. *Systematic Theology: A Compendium and Commonplace Book Designed for the Use of Theological Students*. 3rd ed. New York: A. C. Armstrong and Son, 1890.

———. *Systematic Theology: A Compendium and Commonplace Book Designed for the Use of Theological Students*. 4th ed. New York: A. C. Armstrong and Son, 1893.

———. *Systematic Theology: A Compendium and Commonplace Book Designed for the Use of Theological Students*. 5th ed. New York: A. C. Armstrong and Son, 1896.

———. *Systematic Theology: A Compendium and Commonplace Book Designed for the Use of Theological Students*. 6th ed. New York: A. C. Armstrong and Son, 1899.

———. *Systematic Theology: A Compendium and Commonplace Book Designed for the Use of Theological Students*. 7th ed. New York: A. C. Armstrong and Son, 1902.

———. *Systematic Theology: A Compendium and Commonplace Book Designed for the Use of Theological Students*. 8th ed. Philadelphia: Judson, 1907.

———. *Union With Christ: A Chapter of Systematic Theology*. Philadelphia: American Baptist, 1913.

———. *What Shall I Believe? A Primer of Christian Theology*. New York: Fleming H. Revell, 1922.

Stuart, Moses. "Are the Same Principles of Interpretation to Be Applied to the Scriptures as to Other Books?" *The Biblical Repository* 2 (1832) 124–37.

Sweeney, Douglas A. "Edwards and His Mantle: The Historiography of the New England Theology." *The New England Quarterly* 71 (1998) 97–119.

———. *Nathaniel Taylor, New Haven Theology, and the Legacy of Jonathan Edwards*. New York: Oxford University Press, 2002.

Sweeney, Douglas A., and Allen C. Guelzo. *The New England Theology: From Jonathan Edwards to Edwards Amasa Park*. Grand Rapids: Baker, 2006.

Sweet, William Warren. "The Rise of Theological Schools in America." *Church History* 6.3 (1937) 260–73.

Szasz, Ferenc Morton. *The Divided Mind of Protestant America, 1880–1930*. Tuscaloosa: University of Alabama Press, 1982.

Tait, Jennifer L. Woodruff. *The Poisoned Chalice: Eucharistic Grape Juice and Common-Sense Realism in Victorian Methodism*. Tuscaloosa: University of Alabama Press, 2011.

Thielicke, Helmut. *Modern Faith and Thought*. Grand Rapids: Eerdmans, 1990.
Thiselton, Anthony C. *Hermeneutics: An Introduction*. Grand Rapids: Eerdmans, 2009.
Thornbury, Gregory A. "Augustus Hopkins Strong." In *Theologians of the Baptist Tradition*, edited by Timothy George and David S. Dockery, 139–62. Nashville: Broadman & Holman, 2001.
———. "The Legacy of Natural Theology in the Northern Baptist Theological Tradition, 1827–1918." PhD diss., Southern Baptist Theological Seminary, 2001.
Torbet, Robert G. *History of the Baptists*. 3rd ed. Philadelphia: Judson, 1973.
Toulouse, Mark G., and James O. Duke. "General Introduction." In *Makers of Christian Theology in America*, 13–19. Nashville: Abingdon, 1997.
Toy, Crawford Howell. *The Claims of Biblical Interpretation on Baptists*. New York: Lange and Hillman, 1869.
Treier, Daniel J. "Scripture and Hermeneutics." In *Mapping Modern Theology: A Thematic and Historical Introduction*, edited by Kelly M. Kapic and Bruce L. McCormack, 67–96. Grand Rapids: Baker, 2012.
Trueman, Carl R. *Histories and Fallacies: Problems Faced in the Writing of History*. Wheaton: Crossway, 2010.
Tull, James E. *High-Church Baptists in the South: The Origin, Nature and Influence of Landmarkism*. Macon, GA: Mercer University Press, 2000.
———. *Shapers of Baptist Thought*. Macon, GA: Mercer University Press, 1984.
Vander Stelt, John. *Philosophy and Scripture: A Study of Old Princeton and Westminster Theology*. Marlton, NJ: Mack, 1978.
Van Kley, Dale K. *The Religious Origins of the French Revolution: From Calvin to the Civil Constitution, 1560–1791*. New Haven: Yale University Press, 1996.
Van Pelt, Peter S. "An Examination of the Concept of the Atonement in Selected Northern Baptist Theologians: William Newton Clarke, Augustus Hopkins Strong, and Shailer Mathews." ThD diss., Mid-America Baptist Theological Seminary, 1994.
Vedder, Henry C. "Editorial Department: The New Missionary Training Schools." *Baptist Quarterly Review* 12 (1890) 101–8.
———. *A Short History of the Baptists*. Valley Forge, PA: Judson, 1907.
Vidler, Alec R. *The Church in an Age of Revolution: 1789 to the Present Day*. The Penguin History of the Church. New York: Penguin, 1990.
Warfield, Benjamin Breckinridge. "Review of *Systematic Theology* (5th ed., 1896), by Augustus Hopkins Strong." *Presbyterian and Reformed Review* 8 (1897) 356–58.
Wacker, Grant. *Augustus H. Strong and the Dilemma of Historical Consciousness*. Macon, GA: Mercer University Press, 1985.
———. *Augustus H. Strong and the Dilemma of Historical Consciousness*. Waco, TX: Baylor University Press, 2018.
Weber, Timothy P. "The Two-Edged Sword: The Fundamentalist Use of the Bible." In *The Bible in America*, edited by Nathan O. Hatch and Mark A. Noll, 101–20. New York: Oxford University Press, 1982.
Welch, Claude. "Nineteenth Century: An Overview." In *The Oxford Companion to Christian Thought*, edited by Adrian Hastings et al., 481–86. New York: Oxford University Press, 2000.
———. *Protestant Thought in the Nineteenth Century*. 2 vols. New Haven: Yale University Press, 1972, 1985.

Wells, David F. "The Debate over the Atonement in Nineteenth-Century America, Part 1: American Society as Seen from the Nineteenth-Century Pulpit." *Bibliotheca Sacra* 144 (1987) 123–43.

———. "The Debate over the Atonement in Nineteenth-Century America, Part 2: The Shaping of the Nineteenth-Century Debate over the Atonement." *Bibliotheca Sacra* 144 (1987) 243–53.

———. "The Debate over the Atonement in Nineteenth-Century America, Part 3: The Collision of Views on the Atonement." *Bibliotheca Sacra* 144 (1987) 363–76.

———. "The Debate over the Atonement in Nineteenth-Century America, Part 4: Aftermath and Hindsight of the Atonement Debate." *Bibliotheca Sacra* 145 (1988) 3–14.

Weston, Henry G. "Dr. Hovey as an Author." *Watchman*, September 17, 1903. 11–12.

White, Ronald C., Jr., et al. *The Social Gospel: Religion and Reform in Changing America*. Philadelphia: Temple University Press, 1976.

Whittemore, George H., ed. *Memorials of Horatio Balch Hackett*. Rochester: E. R. Andrews, 1876.

Wiard, Jennifer. "The Gospel of Efficiency: Billy Sunday's Revival Bureaucracy and Evangelicalism in the Progressive Era." *Church History* 85 (2016): 587–616.

Williams, Daniel Day. *The Andover Liberals: A Study in American Theology*. New York: Octagon, 1970.

Williams, George Huntston. *The Radical Reformation*. 3rd ed. Kirksville, MO: Sixteenth Century Journal, 1992.

Wills, Gregory A. *Democratic Religion: Freedom, Authority, and Church Discipline in the Baptist South, 1785–1900*. New York: Oxford University Press, 1997.

———. *Southern Baptist Theological Seminary, 1859–2009*. New York: Oxford University Press, 2009.

Wilson, Lon Ervin. "Adoniram Judson Gordon: The Pastor's Ideal." ThM thesis, Northern Baptist Theological Seminary, 1951.

Wolffe, John. *The Expansion of Evangelicalism: The Age of Wilberforce, More, Chalmers, and Finney*. A History of Evangelicalism: People, Movements and Ideas in the English-Speaking World. Downers Grove, IL: InterVarsity, 2007.

Wolterstorff, Nicholas. "Locke, John." In *The Cambridge Dictionary of Philosophy*, edited by Robert Audi, 506–9. 2nd ed. New York: Cambridge University Press, 1999.

Woodbridge, John D. *Biblical Authority: A Critique of the Rogers/McKim Proposal*. Grand Rapids: Zondervan, 1982.

———. "Is Biblical Inerrancy a Fundamentalist Doctrine?" *Bibliotheca Sacra* 142 (1985) 292–305.

———. "Sola Scriptura: Original Intent, Historical Development, and Import for Christian Living." *Presbyterion* 44.1 (2018) 4–24.

Woodbridge, John D., and Randall H. Balmer. "The Princetonians and Biblical Authority: An Assessment of the Ernest Sandeen Proposal." In *Scripture and Truth*, edited by D. A. Carson and John D. Woodbridge, 251–79, 396–410. Grand Rapids: Baker, 1992.

Woodbridge, John D., and Frank A. James III. *From Pre-Reformation to the Present Day: The Rise and Growth of the Church in Its Cultural, Intellectual, and Political Context*. Vol. 2 of *Church History*. Grand Rapids: Zondervan, 2013.

Zaspel, Fred G. *The Theology of B. B. Warfield: A Systematic Summary*. Wheaton: Crossway, 2010.

Index

Abbot, Lyman, 192
Acadia University, 161n121, 189n83
Ahlstrom, Sydney, 2, 89
Aloisi, John, 183n56, 185n66, 195
American Commentary on the
    Old and New Testaments, 7,
    47, 116, 135, 145–48, 153–54,
    155, 157–59, 208
American Protestantism
    antebellum, 4, 8–9, 84–94, 200
    contrasted to European,
        9, 84–86, 93–94
    and democratization, 8
    and disestablishment,
        2, 22–23, 93–94
    and Edwardsianism, 35–36
    and orthodox rationalism, 9–10
    postbellum, 9–11, 46–
        49, 84–94, 200–202
    and reasonableness,
        9, 10–11, 15–16
    and theological meth-
        od, 84–94, 200–202
American Revolution, the, 22, 52
Andover Newton Theo-
    logical School, xi
Andover Theological Seminary, 5, 18,
    26, 28, 29, 34–40, 189, 202
Angus, Joseph, 33n76
Anselm, 123
Armitage, Thomas, 12
Aubigne, Merle d', 42
Augustine, 101, 123, 179
Aquinas, Thomas, 179

Backus, Isaac, 3, 46, 174, 201
Bacon, Francis, 88
Baconianism, 10, 88–94, 201
Baldwin, Thomas, 72
Baptist(s)
    British, 53
    and disestablishment, 22n22, 93–94
    and education, 4, 28–29, 33n73,
        50, 51–59, 70, 76
    epistemology and theological
        method, 92–94, 126–28, 132, 201
    Freewill, 55, 58
    and the Great Awakening, 22n21
    Landmark, 55
    nineteenth century, 2, 14–16, 22–
        23, 47–49, 90–94, 145–62, 170–
        99, 180–99, 200–202, 206, 207–9
    Northern, ix, 2–3, 11–13, 24,
        31n63, 54–57, 155, 177,
        181n47, 201, 206–9
    Southern, 2, 54–56, 146, 208
    Swedish, 55
Baptist Congress (Baptist
    Autumnal Conference),
    127, 162–64, 194–95
Baptist Union Theological Seminary
    (Morgan Park), 4n14
Barth, Karl, 109
Bates College, 58
Bauder, Kevin, 13
Bauer, Ferdinand Christian,
    133n2, 134, 139, 140
Beale, David, 13
Bebbington, David, 89
Bendroth, Margaret, 31, 42

Benedict, David, 51–52
Berkeley, George, 180n45
Bible, the
    scientific study of, 34
biblical criticism, 4, 9, 15,
    47–50, 87, 107n100, 112–
    13, 118–19, 133–69
biblical rationalism, 10, 87–94
biblicist theological reasoning,
    31, 33, 49, 202
Boston Missionary and
    Training School, 58
Bosworth, George, 151
Bowdoin College, 26
Bozeman, Theodore Dwight, 88
Brackney, William,
    and Baptist education, 53–59, 200–201
    and Baptist theology, 92n36
    and Newton's importance, 6
    and Hovey, 14,
        165n142, 168–69, 208n12
Bradley, F. H., 180n45
Brandon Literary and Scientific Institution, 5, 21
Broadus, John, 7, 47, 62, 146–48, 208
Brown University, 4, 23n29, 39, 46,
    54, 56, 154n93, 161n121
Brown, William Adams, 185n65
Bullen, George, 151, 154n93
Bunyan, John, 72
Burrage, Henry, 7, 161n121
Bushnell, Horace, 47, 85n4, 172–74

Calvin, John, 73, 109
Cambridge University, 53, 76
Cappadocians, the, 73
Cathcart, William, 12
Chadwick, Owen, 85n4
Chase, Irah, 5, 29–31, 34, 36, 57, 67
Chicago, the University of,
    56, 161n121, 192
Clarke, William Newton, 7, 48,
    62, 155–62, 207–8
Clement of Alexandria, 179
Conant, Thomas, 161n121
conservative theology, 9, 10n36,
    11–14, 18, 43, 47, 50, 83,
    86–94, 99n66, 129, 132–34, 145,
    152–54, 159, 168–69, 181, 183,
    185, 201, 204, 207–9
Colby College (Waterville College),
    23n29, 55n18, 161n121
Colgate University (Madison), 4n14,
    46, 55n18, 57, 155, 161n121
Cornell University, 189n83, 192
Crane, Cephas, 148, 151
Crozer Theological Seminary, 4n14, 46
Cyprian of Carthage, 73, 179

Dalhousie College, 189n83
Dartmouth College, 5, 18, 22–29, 49,
    54, 161n121, 202
Darwinism. *See* evolution
democratization, 8, 15, 94, 201–9
Denison College, 55n18
Delitzsch, Franz, 6, 42–43, 134
Delnay, Robert, 13
Descartes, Rene, 180n45
disestablishment, 293
Dockery, David, 4
Dodge, Ebenezer, 155
Dollar, George, 13
Dorner, Isaac, 6, 42–44, 109, 134

Ebrard, Johannes Heinrich August, 140
Edwards, Jonathan, 35, 40, 73
Edwardsianism, 35–36, 38
Eichhorn, Johann Gottfried, 133n2
English, John M., 151
Enlightenment, the, 84, 85n4, 207
ethical monism, 48, 163, 180–99
Exercisers, 35
evolution (Darwinism), 87, 105

Faunce, William H. P., 161n121
Fichte, Immanuel Hermann, 182
Finke, Roger, 93
First African Baptist Church,
    Richmond, VA, 25n39
Fletcher, Robert, 161n121
Fosdick, Harry Emerson, 208
Foster, John, 75
Franklin College, 55n18
French Revolution, the, 84n3
Fuller, Andrew, 72

Fundamentalism,
  Fundamentalist-Modernist
    controversy, 13
  fundamentalistic, 10, 87
Furman University, 55n18

Gabler, Johann Philipp, 133n2
Garrett, James Leo, 154n92,
  169n160, 187n72, 208n12
Gerhart, Emmanuel, 109
Gesenius, Wilhelm, 31, 33
Godet, Frédéric Louis, 140
Gordon, Adoniram Judson, 3, 12, 39,
  58, 151, 154n93, 208n12
Gould, Ezra Palmer, 7, 148–55,
  156–57, 159–60, 162
Great Awakening, the, 22, 51n1

Hackett, Horatio, 5, 33–34, 36, 116,
  148–59, 150, 156
Hague, William, 30
Hamilton, William, 99
Hankins, Barry, 51n2
Harper, William Rainey, 56, 161n121
Hartranft, C. D., 161n121
Harvard Biblical Club, 46
Harvard University, 53, 148, 192
Hatch, Nathan, xi, 8, 94, 201, 206
Hartford Theological
  Seminary, 161n121
Hazard, Paul, 84n3
Hegel, Georg W. F., 182
Helm, Paul, 90–91
Hengstenberg, Ernst,
  6, 33, 42–43, 134
Henry, Carl F. H., 185n65, 185n66
Hobbes, Thomas, 180n45
Hodge, Charles, 87
Holifield, E. Brooks, 9, 90n25,
  98n57, 201, 206n9
Hopkins, Samuel, 38
Hopkinsianism, 38
Horr, George, 161n121
Hovey, Abigail, 19
Hovey, Alfred, 19–20
Hovey, Alvah, 4
  and abolition, 23–25
  and Andover Theological
    Seminary, 34–40
  and anthropology, 128–29
  and atonement theories, 39,
    172–74, 188–89, 198–99
  and Augustus Hopkins Strong, 48,
    61, 161n121, 180–99
  and authority, 13, 14–16, 49–50,
    81–82, 106–16, 131–32, 145,
    168–69, 171–72, 174, 177,
    179, 198–99, 202–9
  and Baptist life, 49–
    50, 162–99, 207–9
  and Barnas Sears, 32–33, 67
  and Bible wine, 177–79
  and biblical criticism, 15, 38,
    47–50, 107n100, 112–13,
    118–19, 133–69, 204
  and biblical interpretation, 15,
    34, 37–38, 62–63, 97, 103–4,
    106–20, 125–26, 171–74, 177,
    179, 198–99, 202–4
  and bibliology, 106–16, 132, 162–69
  biography of, 5
  and Brown University,
    6, 39, 46, 154n93
  children of, 41n115
  and Christology, 106–16, 135–38
  and church history, 67–68, 179, 199
  and Colgate Universi-
    ty (Madison), 46
  commentary work of, 7
  conversion of, 20–21
  and Crawford Howell Toy,
    146–48, 154, 162
  and Crozer Theologi-
    cal Seminary, 46
  and Dartmouth College, 22–29,
    49, 161n121, 202
  and divorce, 170–72
  and (theological) educa-
    tion, 15, 28–29, 33n73,
    44–45, 50, 59–82, 203
  early life of, 18–22
  and Edwards Amasa
    Park, 38–40, 49
  and epistemology, 15, 39,
    63–65, 68, 70–71, 74–75,
    78–81, 95, 97–102, 123, 128–32,
    136, 190n86, 206–9

Hovey, Alvah *(continued)*
  and eschatology, 80n124, 129
  and evolution, 105
  and European education, 6, 41–45, 50, 134–35, 203
  and Ezra Palmer Gould, 148–55, 159–60, 162
  and government, 174–77
  honorary degrees of, 6
  and Horace Bushnell, 47, 172–74
  and Horatio Hackett, 33–34, 116
  importance of, xi, 6–8, 12–14, 207–9
  and inerrancy/infallibility, 15, 112–16, 120, 138–45, 165, 167–69, 204, 206
  and inspiration, 15, 110–16, 120, 138–45, 165–69, 204, 206
  and Irah Chase, 31, 67
  and Isaac Dorner, 42–44, 134
  and John Broadus, 47, 62, 147, 208
  and languages, 29, 45, 67, 117, 178–79
  and liberalism, 48, 208–9
  marriage of, 41n115
  and miracles, 135–38, 141n30, 164
  and Moses Stuart, 37–38, 49, 116, 202
  and Nathan Lord, 24–29
  and natural revelation, 104–6
  and Newton Theological Institute, 6, 7–8, 12, 29–34, 41, 46, 50, 61, 148–55, 159, 195–96, 202
  and Princeton, 105n93
  professional activity of, 6n23, 45–47, 148
  and reasonableness, 15, 63–65, 74–75, 78–81, 98–102, 128–36, 202–9
  publications of, 7n25, 46–47, 59–62, 106n99, 121–22, 208, 211–16
  and Richmond College and Denison University, 6
  and sanctification, 71, 81, 100–101, 130–31, 204
  and science, 97, 114, 142–43, 168
  siblings of, 19n10

  systematic theology of, 7n24, 102n82, 161
  and theism, 95–98, 99, 101–2, 104–6, 135–38, 180–99, 205
  and theological method, 27–28, 32–33, 39–40, 44, 49–50, 67, 71, 83–132, 202–4, 206
  and theological prolegomena, 94–103
  and theological science, 26–27, 34, 74–75, 95, 98–100, 132, 206
  and tradition, 15, 67–68, 96, 120–28, 191–92, 198–99, 202–3, 205–6
  and William Newton Clark, 47–48, 62, 155–62
Hovey, Augusta (Rice), 41
Hovey, George, 13, 17, 20, 21, 24, 41n115, 46, 135n7, 152, 155, 178
Howard, Thomas Albert, 9n31, 85n4
Howe, Daniel Walker, 89n22
Hudson, Winthrop, 14
Hume, David, 47, 86, 87n14, 135
Huss, John, 73

Irenaeus, 73, 109, 179

James, William, 192
Jerome, 179

Kalamazoo College, 55n18
Kant, Immanuel, 86, 182
Kerfoot, F. H., 161n121
Kidd, Thomas, 51n2
Kierstead, E. M., 161n121
Knox, John, 73

Ladd, George T., 192
Lange, Johann Peter, 6, 42, 134
Lasher, George, 152
Leland, John, 3
liberalism. *See* theological liberalism
Lincoln, Abraham, 25n38
Lincoln, Heman, 151
Literary and Theological (L & T) Schools, 55–56
Livingston, James, 1
Locke, John, 87n14
London Confession of Faith, 128

Lord, Nathan, 24–26, 34
Lotze, Rudolf Herman, 95–96, 190–92
Luthardt, Christoph Ernst, 140
Luther, Martin, 73
Lyons, D. G., 46, 148

Madison University and Theological Seminary. *See* Colgate University (Madison)
Manly, Basil, 47n132
Manual Labor Schools, 55
Marsden, George, 92
Maring, Norman, 5, 13, 14, 34, 169
Mathews, Shailer, 46
McBeth, Leon, 52
McCosh, James, 99
McGrath, Alister, 121
McLaughlin, William, 2n5, 93
McTaggart, John M. E., 180n45
Melanchthon, Phillip, 73
Meyer, Heinrich, 140
Michaelis, Johann David, 133n2
Miller, Glenn, 54n11
missionary and pastoral training school, 58
Moody Bible Institute, 58
Moore, Halsey, 177
Morgan Park Theological Seminary. *See* Baptist Union Theological Seminary
modernistic theology, 9n33, 10, 12–13, 87, 143, 183n56, 198, 207
Muller, Richard, 109
Mullins, E. Y., 48n135

Neander, Johann August Wilhelm, 18, 33, 140
New Divinity, 35, 38
New England theology, 28, 35–36
New England Theology, the, 35–36, 39–40, 49–50, 202–3
New Gloucester Baptist Church, 6, 41
New Hampshire Confession of Faith, 92n36, 124n175, 128
New Haven Theology, 35
New Light Stir, 19, 51
New School, the, 35, 186n70, 187
New Theology, the, 9n33, 208
Newman, Albert H., 12

Newman, John Henry, 87
Newton Theological Institute, xi, 4, 12, 18, 21, 29–34, 34, 55n18, 57, 148–55, 159, 202
Noll, Mark, 2, 8, 90, 92
Northern Baptist(s), 2
    seminaries, 3
    postbellum theology of, 11–14
Noyes, Daniel J., 25
Nyack Missionary Training College, 58

Oberman, Heiko, 120–21, 128
Old School, the, 35, 186n70, 187
Origen, 179
orthodox rationalism, 9–10, 15, 87n13, 92, 99–100, 201, 205
Osterhammel, Jürgen, 85n4
Oxford University, 53, 76

Park, Edwards Amasa, 5, 18, 38–40, 49
Parkhurst, C. H., 192
Pascal, Blaise, 73
Paulus, Heinrich Eberhard Gottlob, 133n2, 136
Pepper, George D. B., 161n121
Philadelphia Confession of Faith, 124n175, 128
Phillips, Charles, 38
Pidge, J. B. Gough, 33n72
Polycarp, 73
Pressensé, Edmond de, 140
Priestley, David, 12
Princeton theologians, 10, 35, 89, 90n26, 105n93
Princeton University and Theological Seminary, 31, 54
progressive theology, 9n33

Ranke, Leopold von, 6, 42
Rauschenbusch, Walter, 3, 12, 194, 201, 207–8
Reardon, Bernard, 86
Reid, Thomas, 90
Renaissance, the, 84n3
Richmond College, 55n18
Ritschl, Albrecht, 6, 42–43
Robinson, Ezekiel Gilman, 92n36

Rochester University and Theological Seminary, 4n14, 56, 57–58, 61–62, 161n121, 181
Rockefeller, John D., 56
Rödiger, Emil, 134
Rothe, Richard, 134
Ryland, Robert, 25n39

Samson, George Whitefield, 177
Satta, Ronald, 90n26
Schaff, Phillip, 140
Schelling, Friedrich William Joseph von, 182
Schleiermacher, Friedrich Daniel Ernst, 18
Schurman, Jacob, 95–96, 189–92
Scottish Common Sense Realism, 8, 10–11, 87–94, 99, 201
Sears, Barnas, 5, 31–33, 57–58, 67
Second Great Awakening, the, 51n2
secularization, 85n4
Semler, Johann Salomo, 133n2
Shurtleff College, 55n18
Socrates, 187
Southern Baptist Theological Seminary, 4n14, 62, 146, 161n121
Southern Baptists, 2
Spinoza, Baruch, 47, 133n2, 136, 180n45
Spurgeon, Charles, 6, 42
Stearns, Oakman S., 154n93
Straub, Jeffrey, 13, 155
Strauss, David Friedrich, 47, 133, 134, 136, 139, `40
Strong, Augustus Hopkins, 3, 12, 31, 48, 61, 92, 96, 161n121, 180–99, 201, 207
Stuart, Moses, 29, 36–38, 49, 116, 202
Sweeney, Douglas, 35, 38

Tasters, 35
Taylor, Nathaniel William, 36, 38
Tertullian, 73, 179
theological liberalism, 4–5, 9, 12–14, 38, 43n122, 46, 48, 90n26, 146, 155–57, 162, 169, 185n65, 201, 208–9

theological method, 84–94, 208
Thetford Academy, 20
Thirty Years War, 84n3
Thirty-Nine Articles, 127
Tholuck, Friedrich August, 6, 31–32, 33, 33n76, 42
Thomas, Cornelius A., 21
Thomasius, Gottfried, 6, 42, 109, 134
Thornbury, Gregory, 12, 186n70
Torbet, Robert, 52
Toronto Baptist College, 62, 155
Toy, Crawford Howell, 7, 46, 146–48, 154, 162
Tuck, Amos, 25n38

Ullmann, Karl Christian, 140

Van Pelt, Peter Stephen, 187n72
Vermittlungstheologie, 43
Vidler, Alec, 1

Wacker, Grant, 92, 207n11
Wake Forest College, 55n18
Warfield, Benjamin Breckinridge, 185n65
Waterville College. *See* Colby College
Wayland, Francis, 3, 57–58, 201
Welch, Claude, 43n122, 84–85, 87
Wellesley College, 6n23, 161n121
Wesley, John, 73
Westcott, B. F., 33n76
Westminster Confession of Faith, 127
Westminster Shorter Catechism, 25–26
Weston, Henry, 208
Whitefield, George, 73
Whitman, B. L., 161n121
Williams, George Huntston, 121
Wills, Gregory, 146
wine, Bible, 177–79
Wolffe, John, 93
Wood, Nathan, 208n12
Wycliffe, John, 73

Yale University, 36, 53, 54, 181, 192

Zöckler, Otto, 87
Zwingli, Huldrych, 73

www.ingramcontent.com/pod-product-compliance
Lightning Source LLC
Chambersburg PA
CBHW050850230426
43667CB00012B/2231